DAVID

A Man of Passion & Destiny

Publications by Charles R. Swindoll

BOOKS

Active Spirituality
The Bride
Come Before Winter
Compassion: Showing We Care in a Careless World
Dear Graduate
Dropping Your Guard
Encourage Me
The Finishing Touch
Flying Closer to the Flame
For Those Who Hurt
The Grace Awakening
Growing Deep in the Christian Life
Growing Strong in the Seasons of Life
Growing Wise in Family Life
Hand Me Another Brick
Home: Where Life Makes Up Its Mind
Hope Again
Improving Your Serve
Intimacy with the Almighty
Killing Giants, Pulling Thorns

Laugh Again
Leadership: Influence That Inspires
Living Above the Level of Mediocrity
Living Beyond the Daily Grind, Books I and II
The Living Insights Study Bible—General Editor
Living on the Ragged Edge
Man to Man
Paw Paw Chuck's Big Ideas in the Bible
The Quest for Character
Recovery: When Healing Takes Time
Sanctity of Life
Simple Faith
Starting Over
Strengthening Your Grip
Stress Fractures
Strike the Original Match
The Strong Family
Three Steps Forward, Two Steps Back
Victory: A Winning Game Plan for Life
You and Your Child

MINIBOOKS

Abraham: A Model of Pioneer Faith
David: A Model of Pioneer Courage
Esther: A Model of Pioneer Independence

Moses: A Model of Pioneer Vision
Nehemiah: A Model of Pioneer Determination

BOOKLETS

Anger
Attitudes
Commitment
Dealing with Defiance
Demonism
Destiny
Divorce
Eternal Security
Forgiving and Forgetting
Fun Is Contagious
God's Will
Hope
Impossibilities
Integrity
Intimacy with the Almighty
Leisure
The Lonely Whine of the Top Dog

Make Your Dream Come True
Making the Weak Family Strong
Moral Purity
Our Mediator
Peace . . . in Spite of Panic
Portrait of a Father
The Power of a Promise
Prayer
Reflections from the Heart—A Prayer Journal
Seeking the Shepherd's Heart—A Prayer Journal
Sensuality
Stress
This is No Time for Wimps
Tongues
When Your Comfort Zone Gets the Squeeze
Woman

GREAT LIVES FROM GOD'S WORD

A Man of Passion & Destiny

DAVID

Profiles in Character from

CHARLES R. SWINDOLL

WORD PUBLISHING
Dallas·London·Vancouver·Melbourne

All Scripture quotations in this book, except those noted otherwise, are from the New American Standard Bible © 1960, 1962, 1963, 1971, 1973, 1975, and 1977 by the Lockman Foundation, and are used by permission.

Other Scripture quotations are from the following sources:

The *New International Version* of the Bible (NIV), copyright © 1983 by the International Bible Society. Used by permission of Zondervan Bible Publishers.

The Living Bible (LB), copyright © 1971 by Tyndale House Publishers, Wheaton, Ill. Used by permission.

The Modern Language Bible, The Berkeley Version in Modern English. Copyright © 1945, 1959, 1969, by Zondervan Publishing House. Used by permission.

The *King James Version* of the Bible (KJV).

Portions of chapters 7 and 13 were adapted from material that originally appeared in *Growing Strong in the Seasons of Life*, by Charles Swindoll, copyright © 1983 by Charles R. Swindoll, published by Multnomah Press, Portland, Oregon, and are used by permission.

ISBN: 0-8499-1382-9

Printed and bound in the United States of America

DEDICATION

It is with much delight
that I dedicate this volume
to the four men in our family:

My sons, Curt Swindoll and Chuck Swindoll
My sons-in-law, Byron Nelson and Mark Dane

May each of you, like David,
become "a man after God's own heart."
May your lives, like his,
be marked by
humility, dependability, and integrity.

CONTENTS

Contents

INTRODUCTION

David: A Man of Passion & Destiny

Our world is desperately in need of models worth following. Authentic heroes. People of integrity, whose lives inspire us to do better, to climb higher, to stand taller. This has always been true. Maybe that explains why biographies of great men and women have fascinated me throughout my life. I can still remember the first Bible I owned because of the colorful pictures of various characters interspersed through its pages. I spent many a Sunday morning, stting beside my parents in church, fighting boredom by leafing through that Bible, staring at those strong-hearted ancients. Each one loomed larger than life as I relived each drama, imagining the sounds, entering into the action-packed scenes portrayed on the pages.

- There was Noah, surrounded by every animal in the zoo, riding out the storm.
- There was Jacob, wet with sweat, wrestling with an angel who had a pair of huge, mysterious wings.
- There was Joseph with his coat of many colors, looking at the angry faces of his brothers.
- Next was Moses, leading the Hebrews across the dry bottom of the Red Sea as the waters were miraculously pushed aside.
- Then came one of my all-time favorites, Samson with bulging muscles, arms outstretched between two marble columns.

- Esther, with her glistening queen's crown, was pictured in an opulent setting as she knelt before the king, pouring out her heart on behalf of her people.
- Amidst a treacherous sea, Jonah was being swallowed by a giant fish.
- Mary was pouring ointment on Jesus' feet.
- Peter, with the reflection of a fire flickering off his face, stood in the shadows as a rooster was crowing in the distance.
- Paul, under a laserlike light from heaven, was blinded as he stood beside his mount on the road to Damascus.

There were others, all intriguing . . . all igniting one's imagination to take over and live the scene yet again.

My love for biographies has intensified as time has passed. While building my library over more than forty years, I have taken special delight in collecting and digesting great biographical works, most of them no longer in print. I still find delight in reentering those scenes from antiquity. My soul is stirred and my heart inspired as those saints of old, people "of whom the world was not worthy" (Heb. 11:38) play out their lives, make their mistakes, accomplish incredible feats, and finally pass on into glory. What encouragement, what enrichment!

The words of the Russian poet, Boris Pasternak, come to mind, "It is not revolutions and upheavals that clear the road to new and better days, but someone's soul inspired and ablaze."[1] Because that's true, I have remained a serious student of the great lives woven through the Scriptures. For more than thirty years in the pastorate, I found the lives of those inspiring men and women to be rich sources of sermon material. Again and again I found that people were ministered to in deep and meaningful ways whenever I spoke on the characters of the Bible.

Interestingly, each time we would broadcast my biographical pulpit messages on our radio program, *Insight for Living*, the interest among our listening audience was invariably heightened. People appreciate hearing about those who have gone on before us . . . leaving us models to exemplify, teaching us lessons about life. In fact, no series we have aired over the radio since 1977 has received a greater response from our listening audience than my studies on the life of David.

Realizing the inspirational value of biblical biographies, for years I have wanted to write a series of books based on the lives of various men and women who appear on the sacred page. My desire has been to provide a set of volumes that would acquaint readers with each individual, helping them see how relevant and realistic those lives are . . . and how closely they track the situations and struggles of our own times. I am delighted to see this long-awaited desire become a reality.

It is with profound feelings of gratitude that I express my thanks to several of my friends at Word Books for their vision and commitment to this multivolume project: Byron Williamson, Kip Jordon, David Moberg, and Joey Paul . . . true friends, long-term friends. And it is also appropriate that I state how greatly I appreciate the hard work of two very faithful ladies: Judith Markham, for her splendid editorial assistance, and Helen Peters for her tireless efforts in preparing my manuscript with such personal care and excellent attention to detail. Thank you, ladies, for your outstanding work. You have no peers!

Back in the late 1930s, Carl Sandburg finished a four-volume master-piece, *Abraham Lincoln: The War Years*. It is among my most treasured volumes and has afforded me hours of reading pleasure. As the author sought for an appropriate title of the seventy-fifth chapter, covering the events immediately following Lincoln's assassination, he settled on a quaint line from an old woodsman's proverb, "A tree is best measured when it's down."[2]

In Sandburg's opinion, not until a life is "down" can we adequately measure its length of significance, its breadth of impact, its depth of character.

What is true of a once great president named Lincoln is equally true of a once great king named David. The only one in all of Scripture to be called "a man after God's own heart," this single individual is mentioned more than any other Old Testament character in the pages of the New Testament. Poet, musician, courageous warrior, and national statesman, David distinguished himself as one of God's greatest men. In battle, he modeled invincible confidence. In decisions, he judged with wisdom and equity. In loneliness, he wrote with transparent vulnerability and quiet trust. In friendship, he was loyal to the end. Whether a humble shepherd boy or an obscure musician before King Saul, he remained faithful and trustworthy. Even in his promotion to the highest position in the land, David modeled integrity and humility. What a man of God!

But, as we shall see, he (like us) was anything but perfect. Having earned the public's trust and respect, he forfeits it all in a brief season of sensual pleasure. Then, as the consequences kick in, we discover another side of the man's makeup—lustfulness as a husband, weakness as a father, and partiality as a leader. It's all there, written for all to learn, preserved for all to remember. A great man, though far from perfect, nevertheless lived a life with strengths worth emulating. Since our world is desperately in need of models worth following, here is one deserving of our time and attention: David, a man of passion and destiny.

CHUCK SWINDOLL
Dallas, Texas

CHAPTER ONE

God's Heart, God's Man, God's Ways

On the surface, there seemed to be nothing about David that would have impressed God. Nothing caused Him to say, "Wow! That's my man!" David didn't look much different from any of the other Jewish boys his age. Samuel simply said, "He was ruddy, with beautiful eyes and a handsome appearance." That's the only physical description we have of young David. So we know he was handsome, had beautiful eyes, and had a healthy complexion. He may have had red hair or, more likely, he was reddened or bronzed from the hours he spent out in the sun and the wind. David's outward appearance didn't seem to set him apart in any way.

He was nothing more than a shepherd, and a very young one at that, living in the little village of Bethlehem. Yet God said, in effect, "You have what I'm looking for, young man. You are the future king of Israel."

If we had been living in the farmhouse next door to David's family on the Judean hillside, we might not even have known the name of Jesse's youngest son. After all, his own father didn't even think of including him until Samuel asked, "Are these all your sons?" Then Jesse rubbed his beard and said, "Oh, yeah, there's my youngest. Almost forgot about him. He's out in the field tending the sheep."

"Go and fetch him," Samuel said.

And suddenly, this young nobody, a boy even his own father forgot about, became somebody.

But before we get to David the king of Israel, we need to go back about forty years and get a sense of background and history, so we can appreciate the world in which he lived.

G. Frederick Owen, in his book *Abraham to the Middle-East Crisis,* describes those ancient times perfectly in one sentence: "The people were on a long drift from God."[3] That was the world into which David was born.

Eli, the high priest, and his wicked sons were gone. His God-chosen successor, Samuel, the last of the judges, was an old man. The people had heard all the stories about the days when Israel was a great nation and about the years when Samuel was at the zenith of his career, when he subdued the Philistines and judged the land wisely and well. But most of them knew nothing of that personally.

They knew only that Samuel was an aged man and that he had appointed his sons to judge Israel. And what a mistake that was! Look at what the Bible says about them:

> And it came about when Samuel was old that he appointed his sons judges over Israel. . . . His sons, however, did not walk in his ways, but turned aside after dishonest gain and took bribes and perverted justice.
>
> 1 Samuel 8:1–3

So the people were disillusioned, and they wanted something done about it. What they really wanted was a king.

Actually, Samuel's wayward sons weren't the only reason for their demand. The elders of Israel held a summit meeting at Ramah—a place in the hill country about five miles north of Jerusalem—and they said, "Samuel, there are three reasons we want a king. First, you are old. Second, your sons don't walk in your ways. And third, we want to be like the other nations. So appoint a king to judge us like all the nations" (1 Sam. 8:5).

SAUL: THE PEOPLE'S CHOICE

People have always wanted to be like everybody else, to do the popular thing, and these folks were no exception.

"We're tired of worshiping an invisible God. Everybody says, 'Where's your king?' And we have to say, 'Oh, he's in the heavens.' We want a leader here on earth, Samuel. We want to be like all the other nations. Look at the Philistines, and the Moabites and the Jebusites and all the other nations. They've all got kings. We want to be like all of them!"

They didn't say, "We want to wait on God to provide what we need." This broke Samuel's heart, and so he went to God in prayer about it.

> And the LORD said to Samuel, "Listen to the voice of the people in regard to all that they say to you, for they have not rejected you, they have rejected Me from being king over them. . . . Now then, listen to their voice; however, you shall solemnly warn them and tell them of the procedure of the king who will reign over them."
>
> 1 Samuel 8:7–8

So God let them have exactly what they wanted. Did He ever! The man they chose, Saul, was tall, dark, and handsome. That's how people choose kings. They go for someone who looks good. "Wow, he'll be a good image for Israel. Saul's our guy." So Saul came on the scene and swept them off their feet. He had a measure of humility to begin with, and he seemed able to rally people around a cause. He had enough moxie to get an army together, and before long the Israelites thought, "He's the man for the job."

But guess what? Even though Saul was forty years old when he started to rule, before long he became thin-skinned, hot-tempered, and given to seasons of depression, even thoughts of murder. So much for the man who was the people's choice.

David was born about ten years after Saul became king. Talk about being born into volatile times! The people of Israel were on a long drift from God, and now, to make matters worse, they were becoming disillusioned with the leader they had chosen. But what do you do when your king doesn't walk with God? What do you do when you've gotten your own way and it's all wrong? It's the most disillusioning, insecure feeling in the world, yet you can't put your finger on what's wrong.

But graciously, God does not abandon His people. Through Samuel, He intervenes.

DAVID: THE LORD'S CHOICE

> And Samuel said to Saul, "You have acted foolishly; you have not kept the commandment of the LORD your God, which He commanded you, for now the LORD would have established your kingdom over Israel forever.
>
> "But now your kingdom shall not endure. The LORD has

3

sought out for Himself *a man after His own heart*, and the
LORD has appointed him as ruler over His people, because you
have not kept what the LORD commanded you."

1 Samuel 13:13–14 (emphasis added)

Look at that little three-letter word in verse 14: *man.* God had sought
out a man. Only a man . . . but what a man he was!

Would it surprise you to learn that more has been written about David
than about any other biblical character? Abraham has some fourteen chapters dedicated to his life, and so does Joseph. Jacob has eleven. Elijah has
ten. But do you have any idea how many are dedicated to David? Sixty-
six, if my counting is correct, and that does not include some fifty-nine
references to his life in the New Testament.

When you realize how much is said about David in the Scriptures,
coupled with the fact that on two occasions he is specifically called "a man
after God's own heart," you could get the feeling that he was some sort
of super phenomenal person. Some superhero.

But I don't want you to get the wrong idea about why God chose
David—or why He chooses anyone, for that matter. So before we begin
to look at the fascinating life of this man, we need to set the record straight.

Why does God choose people? Or perhaps the question should be:
What kind of people does God choose and use? To determine that, we
need to look first at a New Testament passage, in 1 Corinthians 1. The
context here has to do with the way different people viewed the apostle
Paul. Some readers of Paul's letter were Jewish, and they were looking for
a miracle, for a sign that proved this man was of God. Some of his readers
were Greeks, and they were looking only at surface impressions. One's
inner life meant little to them. The Greeks of that day were influenced by
brains, brawn, and/or beauty.

In light of this, then, Paul's whole thrust in the first chapter of his first
letter to the believers at Corinth was, "I'm not coming to you with bril-
liance or human wisdom, and I'm certainly not coming to you with any
kind of impressionable physique. Instead, I come in the power of God.
And there's a good reason for that." Note carefully how Paul put it:

> For consider your calling, brethren, that there were not many
> wise according to the flesh, not many mighty, not many noble;
> but God has chosen the foolish things of the world to shame
> the wise, and God has chosen the weak things of the world to
> shame the things which are strong, and the base things of the

world and the despised, God has chosen, the things that are not, that He might nullify the things that are, that no man should boast before God.

1 Corinthians 1:26–29

I especially like the way the New Berkeley Version translates the last two verses of that passage: "God also has chosen the world's insignificant and despised people and nobodies in order to bring to nothing those who amount to something, so that nobody may boast in the presence of God" (vv. 28–29).

Paul says, "Look around, Corinthians. You won't find many impressive people here." Why? So that no one can boast before God. That's a principle we tend to forget, because many of us are still a lot like the Greeks. When we look for people to admire, when we choose our role models, our heroes, we are often swayed or impressed by things that are cause for boasting. We want the beautiful people, the brilliant people, the "successful" people. We want the best and the brightest. We are terribly enamored of the surface. The superficial impresses us much more than we'd like to admit. We even elect a president because he looks good on television!

But God says, "That's not the way I make my choices. I choose the nobodies and turn them into somebodies."

And that, in a nutshell, is the story of the life of David.

THREE PRIORITIES FOR GOD-APPOINTED SERVANT LEADERS

When God scans the earth for potential leaders, He is not on a search for angels in the flesh. He is certainly not looking for perfect people, since there are none. He is searching for men and women like you and me, mere people made up of flesh. But He is also looking for certain qualities in those people, the same qualities He found in David.

The first quality God saw in David was *spirituality*. "The LORD has sought out . . . a man after His own heart." What does it mean to be a person after God's own heart? Seems to me, it means that you are a person whose life is in harmony with the Lord. What is important to Him is important to you. What burdens Him burdens you. When He says, "Go to the right," you go to the right. When He says, "Stop that in your life," you stop it. When He says, "This is wrong and I want you to change," you come to terms with it because you have a heart for God. That's bottom-line biblical Christianity.

When you are deeply spiritual, you have a heart that is sensitive to the things of God. A parallel verse in 2 Chronicles confirms this:

> For the eyes of the LORD move to and fro throughout the earth that He may strongly support those whose heart is *completely* His. . . .
>
> 2 Chronicles 16:9 (emphasis added)

What is God looking for? He is looking for men and women whose hearts are completely His—*completely*. That means there are no locked closets. Nothing's been swept under the rugs. That means that when you do wrong, you admit it and immediately come to terms with it. You're grieved over wrong. You're concerned about those things that displease Him. You long to please Him in your actions. You care about the motivations behind your actions. That's true spirituality, and that's the first quality David had.

The second quality God saw in David was *humility*.

> Now the LORD said to Samuel, "How long will you grieve over Saul, since I have rejected him from being king over Israel? Fill your horn with oil, and go; I will send you to Jesse the Bethlehemite, for I have selected a king for Myself among his sons."
>
> 1 Samuel 16:1

The Lord had gone to the home of Jesse in spirit form. Jesse didn't know God was there. Nobody did. God was on a secret surveillance mission in that home, and he spotted Jesse's youngest son and said, in effect, "That's My man!"

Why? Because the Lord saw in David a heart that was completely His. The boy was faithfully keeping his father's sheep. God saw humility: He saw a servant's heart. If you want further confirmation of this, go to the Psalms.

> He also chose David His servant,
> And took him from the sheepfolds.
> Psalm 78:70

"I have found David My servant;
With My holy oil I have anointed him. . . ."

Psalm 89:20

It's as if God says, "I don't care about all that slick public image business. Show me a person who has the character, and I'll give him all the image he needs. I don't require some certain temperament, I don't care if he has a lot of charisma, I don't care about size, I don't care about an impressive track record. I care about character! First, is the person deeply authentic in his or her spiritual walk or is he faking it? And second, is he or she a servant?"

When you have a servant's heart, you're humble. You do as you're told. You don't rebel. You respect those in charge. You serve faithfully and quietly.

That's David. God looked at David, out in the fields in the foothills surrounding Bethlehem, keeping his father's sheep, faithfully doing his father's bidding, and God passed His approval on the lad.

It should also be noted that a servant doesn't care who gets the glory. Remember that. A servant has one great goal, and that is to make the person he serves look better, to make that person even more successful. A servant does not want the person he serves to fail. A servant doesn't care who gets the glory, just so the job gets done.

So while David's brothers were off in the army making rank and fighting big, impressive battles, David was all alone keeping the sheep. He possessed a servant's heart.

The third quality David had was *integrity.*

From the care of the ewes with suckling lambs He brought him,
To shepherd Jacob His people,
And Israel His inheritance.
So he shepherded them according to the integrity of his heart,
And guided them with his skillful hands.

Psalm 78:71–72

Circle the word *integrity.* That is so significant! God is not looking for magnificent specimens of humanity. He's looking for deeply spiritual, genuinely humble, honest-to-the-core servants who have integrity.

Listen to some of the synonyms for this Hebrew word *thamam,* translated "integrity": "complete, whole, innocent, having simplicity of life,

7

wholesome, sound, unimpaired." Isn't that beautiful? Integrity is what you are when nobody's looking. It means being bone-deep honest.

Today, we live in a world that says, in many ways, "If you just make a good impression, that's all that matters." But you will never be a man or woman of God if that's your philosophy. Never. You cannot fake it with the Almighty. He is not impressed with externals. He always focuses on the inward qualities . . . those things that take time and discipline to cultivate.

GOD'S METHOD OF TRAINING HIS SERVANTS

In this regard, it is enlightening to look at how God trained David for a leadership role. His training ground was lonely, obscure, monotonous, and real. Let me describe each of these four disciplines.

First, God trained David in *solitude*. He needed to learn life's major lessons all alone before he could be trusted with responsibilities and rewards before the public. As the late biographer, F. B. Meyer, writes,

> But Nature was his nurse, his companion, his teacher. Bethlehem is situated six miles to the south of Jerusalem, by the main road leading to Hebron. Its site is two thousand feet above the level of the Mediterranean, on the northeast slope of a long gray ridge, with a deep valley on either side; these unite at some little distance to the east, and run down toward the Dead Sea. On the gentle slopes of the hills the fig, olive, and vine grow luxuriantly; and in the valleys are the rich cornfields, where Ruth once gleaned, and which gave the place its name, the House of Bread. The moorlands around Bethlehem, forming the greater part of the Judaean plateau, do not, however, present features of soft beauty; but are wild, gaunt, strong—character-breeding. There shepherds have always led and watched their flocks; and there David first imbibed that knowledge of natural scenery and of pastoral pursuits which colored all his after life and poetry, as the contents of the vat the dyer's hand.
> Such were the schools and schoolmasters of his youth. . . .[4]

Solitude has nurturing qualities all its own. Anyone who must have superficial sounds to survive lacks depth. If you can't stand to be alone with yourself, you have deep, unresolved conflicts in your inner life. Solitude has a way of helping us address those issues.

When was the last time you got all alone with nature and soaked it in—so alone that the sound of silence seemed deafening? That's where David lived. That's where he first learned to "king it." For many nights he sat alone under the stars. He felt the blustery winds of autumn and the cold rains of winter. He learned to endure the burning rays of summer's sun. Solitude was one of the teachers God used as He trained young David for the throne.

Second, David grew up in *obscurity*. That's another way God trains His best personnel—in obscurity. Men and women of God, servant-leaders in the making, are first unknown, unseen, unappreciated, and unapplauded. In the relentless demands of obscurity, character is built. Strange as it may seem, those who first accept the silence of obscurity are best qualified to handle the applause of popularity.

Which leads us to the third training ground, *monotony*. That's being faithful in the menial, insignificant, routine, regular, unexciting, uneventful, daily tasks of life. Life without a break . . . without the wine and roses. Just dull, plain L-I-F-E.

Actually, it's a lot like flying. I have a friend who's been a commercial pilot for over thirty years. He says, "Flying is nothing more than hours and hours of monotony, punctuated by a few seconds of sheer panic."

That describes one of God's favorite methods of training, although perhaps without the panic. Just constant, unchanging, endless hours of tired monotony as you learn to be a man or woman of God . . . with nobody else around, when nobody else notices, when nobody else even cares. That's how we learn to "king it."

That brings us to the fourth training ground: *reality*. Up until now you might have the feeling that despite the solitude, obscurity, and monotony, David was just sitting out on some hilltop in a mystic haze, composing a great piece of music, or relaxing in the pastures of Judea and having a great time training those sheep to sit on their hind legs. That's not true.

Think ahead with me to 1 Samuel 17. Here is David, standing by Saul, as a giant lumbers across the distant landscape.

Remember Saul? Great big tall guy? Scared to death, knees knocking, inside his tent, hiding from Goliath. And here's little David, saying, "Hey, let's go whip the giant."

Saul says, "Who are you?"

"I'm David."

Saul says, "Where have you been?"

"I've been with my father's sheep."

Then Saul says, "You can't fight this Philistine. You're just a kid."

And David responds without hesitation:

> "Your servant was tending his father's sheep [that's solitude, obscurity, monotony]. When a lion or a bear came and took a lamb from the flock [that's reality], I went out after him and attacked him, and rescued it from his mouth; and when he rose up against me, I seized him by his beard and struck him and killed him."
>
> 1 Samuel 17:34–35

Where did David get such courage? He had learned it all alone before God. What kind of man is this David? He's a man of reality. He's a man who remained responsible when nobody was looking.

"So this guy, Goliath," says David, "I'm not worried about him." And you know what happens after that. (I can hardly wait to get to that chapter. It's one of my favorites.)

Goliath was no big deal. Why? Because David had been killing lions and bears while nobody was around. He'd been facing reality long before he squared off against Goliath.

Somehow we've gotten the idea that "getting alone with God" is unrealistic, that it's not the real world. But getting alone with God doesn't mean you sit in some closet and think about infinity. No, it means you get alone and discover how to be more responsible and diligent in *all* the areas of your life, whether that means fighting lions or bears or simply following orders.

That's why I have a problem with the kind of "deeper life" teaching that says you stand back and God does everything for you. I'll be honest with you, I've never had God fix a flat tire for me. Or change a baby's diaper . . . or confront some giant in my life. Neither did David. He rolled up his sleeves and he fought for those sheep. It was in such scenes of reality that David learned to "king it."

A COUPLE OF LASTING LESSONS

David may have lived many centuries ago, but the things we can learn from him are as current as this morning's sunrise. Two stand out in my mind as we draw this chapter to a close.

First, *it's in the little things and in the lonely places that we prove ourselves capable of the big things.* If you want to be a person with a large vision, you must cultivate the habit of doing the little things well. That's when God puts iron in your bones! The way you fill out those detailed reports, the way you take care of those daily assignments, the way you complete the tasks of home or dormitory or work or school is just a reflection of whether you personally are learning to "king it." The test of my calling is not how well I do before the public on Sunday; it's how carefully I cover the bases Monday through Saturday when there's nobody to check up on me, when nobody is looking.

Second, *when God develops our inner qualities, He's never in a hurry.* Alan Redpath, the late pastor of Moody Memorial Church, put it this way: "The conversion of a soul is the miracle of a moment, the manufacture of a saint is the task of a lifetime."[5] When God develops character, He works on it throughout a lifetime. He's never in a hurry.

It is in the schoolroom of solitude and obscurity that we learn to become men and women of God. It is from the schoolmasters of monotony and reality that we learn to "king it." That's how we become—like David—men and women after God's own heart.

CHAPTER TWO

A Nobody, Nobody Noticed

King Saul was a real piece of work.

After he became king of Israel, his actions and decisions soon revealed to the people that he was a selfish, angry, hateful, mean-spirited man. Eventually something snapped in his mind, and during the later years of his rule, he lost touch with reality, thus proving himself unqualified for the job.

Not long after Saul began his reign, Samuel caught him in three serious acts of disobedience: first Saul made a terrible decision (1 Sam. 13); then he made a rash vow against his own son (1 Sam. 14); and finally, he openly disobeyed God (1 Sam. 15). When Samuel pointed his finger at the king, Saul at first tried to rationalize what he had done, then finally admitted, "I am guilty." But even then, he qualified his confession.

> Then Saul said to Samuel, "I have sinned; I have indeed transgressed the command of the LORD and your words, *because I feared the people and listened to their voice.* Now therefore, please pardon my sin and return with me, that I may worship the LORD."
>
> 1 Samuel 15:24–25 (emphasis added)

You can see here that Saul was greatly concerned about his image. He didn't want the people to know that he had sinned. So he said, "Samuel, why don't you come with me, and nobody will know that I've disobeyed.

You just return and let's worship together like we've always done." His greatest concern was his image.

Samuel didn't buy it . . . not for a minute. His reply was a straight-from-the-shoulder jab that Saul would never forget:

> But Samuel said to Saul, "I will not return with you; for you have rejected the word of the LORD, and the LORD has rejected you from being king over Israel."
>
> And as Samuel turned to go, Saul seized the edge of his robe, and it tore.
>
> So Samuel said to him, "The LORD has torn the kingdom of Israel from you today, and has given it to your neighbor who is better than you.
>
> "And also the Glory of Israel will not lie or change His mind; for He is not a man that He should change His mind."
>
> Then he [Saul] said, "I have sinned; but please honor me now before the elders of my people and before Israel, and go back with me, that I may worship the LORD your God."
>
> 1 Samuel 15:26–30

Saul, the great rationalizer, again pleaded, "Look, Samuel, you've caught me in the act, and I've confessed it privately. Now why don't you come on back with me and we'll go right on as if nothing happened."

But Samuel, being a man of integrity, saw through the whole thing. Clearly, Saul had failed God. So Samuel said to the king, "I won't humiliate you before the people. I'll go back and go through the ritual of this sacrificial act of worship, but, Saul, that's the last day I want to see you."

> And Samuel did not see Saul again until the day of his death; for Samuel grieved over Saul. . . .
>
> 1 Samuel 15:35

If you check your geography, you'll see that Samuel went home in one direction and Saul went home in another . . . and they never met again until the day of Saul's death.

The tragic story of Saul is that he never, ever fully repented of his sin. Saul's greatest concern was his image, how he looked before the people. Even after Samuel gave him a break, Saul took advantage of it and continued in that same vein until the day he took his own life.

That's jumping ahead a bit, though. Because it is at about this point that Samuel panics. Samuel has reached the end of his rope. The people have elected Saul king, but he's no longer qualified. What are they to do? Israel is surrounded by enemies, and they need someone to carry the scepter. But who? Samuel didn't know and couldn't imagine. The people didn't know either. No one knew . . . except God.

MAN PANICS . . . GOD PROVIDES

What Samuel didn't realize—what we often don't realize—is that behind the scenes, before He ever flung the stars into space, God had today in mind. He had this very week in mind. In fact, He had you in mind. And He knew exactly what He was going to do. God is never at a loss to know what He's going to do in our situations. He knows perfectly well what is best for us. Our problem is, *we* don't know. And we say to Him, "Lord, if You just tell me, then I'll be in great shape. Just reveal it to me. Explain Your plan to me, and I'll count on You." But that's not faith. Faith is counting on Him when we do *not* know what tomorrow holds.

When a man or a woman of God fails, nothing of God fails. When a man or woman of God changes, nothing of God changes. When someone dies, nothing of God dies. When our lives are altered by the unexpected, nothing of God is altered or unexpected. It was the prophet Isaiah who wrote: "Before they call, I will answer; and while they are yet speaking, I will hear" (Isa. 65:24).

"Before you even utter a word," God promises, "I'm involved in answering. In fact, while you're speaking, I'm involved in bringing to pass the very thing I have planned from the get go."

God knows *exactly* what He's going to do, and nothing can restrain His bringing it to pass.

That's the beautiful part of this story. Look at how the Lord reveals Himself to Samuel. He says,

> "How long will you grieve over Saul, since I have rejected him from being king over Israel? Fill your horn with oil, and go; I will send you to Jesse the Bethlehemite, for I have selected a king for Myself among his sons."
>
> 1 Samuel 16:1

God always knows what He's doing. So He says to Samuel, "You go to Bethlehem, and there you will find the man I have already chosen."

This is the first Samuel has heard that God had already zeroed in on a man to replace Saul.

I think it's so exciting how this plan of God unfolds. God says, "I've selected a king for Myself. The people haven't chosen this man. He's *My* man."

> But Samuel said, "How can I go? When Saul hears of it, he will kill me."
>
> 1 Samuel 16:2

Does this sound familiar? God says, "Go," and we say, "Right." Then before we're off our knees, we're saying, "Now wait, Lord, how can I pull that off?"

What was Samuel's problem? He was panic-stricken. He was just plain scared. Where were Samuel's eyes? Well, they certainly weren't on the Lord. They were riveted on Saul.

From a human viewpoint, of course, Samuel was right. King Saul was murderous. But God was completely aware of the situation. After all, Saul was the one God was going to use to shape David's life in the in-between years, between the sheep and the throne, so He knew Saul very well.

By the way, do you have a Saul in your life? Is there somebody who irritates and rubs and files and scrapes and bothers you? God knows all about it. That person is all part of His plan, strange as that may seem.

The Lord doesn't answer Samuel's remark about Saul. Instead, He says,

> "Take a heifer with you, and say, 'I have come to sacrifice to the Lord.' And you shall invite Jesse to the sacrifice, and I will show you what you shall do; and you shall anoint for Me the one whom I designate to you."
>
> 1 Samuel 16:2–3

Follow the Leader! That's what He's saying. You don't have to be smart to be obedient. You don't have to be clever. All you have to do is obey. We think we have to sort of outwit God on the horizontal. But God says, "I know your situation. I'm telling you exactly what you ought to do, so go do it. Take a heifer, go to Jesse, offer the sacrifice, and look around. I'll tell you the man I've chosen for the job." Isn't that simple?

Meanwhile, behind the scenes, there's David. And he doesn't know *anything* about what Samuel and God are talking about over there on the other side of the country. What's David doing? He's keeping the sheep. That's his job.

With poetic eloquence, F. B. Meyer expresses David's situation this way:

> No angel trumpet heralded it; no faces looked out of heaven; the sun arose that morning according to his wont over the purple walls of the hills of Moab, making the cloud curtains saffron and gold. With the first glimmer of light the boy was on his way to lead his flock to pasture-lands heavy with dew. As the morning hours sped onwards, many duties would engross his watchful soul—strengthening the weak, healing that which was sick, binding up that which was broken, and seeking that which was lost; or the music of his song may have filled the listening air.[6]

That was David. For him, it was just like any other morning. Little did he know that his life would never be the same again—or that, beginning that very day, he was destined for the throne of Israel.

God has some extremely exciting things in mind for His children. For some it may happen tomorrow. For some it may happen next month or next year or five years down the road. We don't know when. For some . . . it could happen today. But the beautiful thing about this adventure called faith is that we can count on Him never to lead us astray. He knows exactly where He's taking us. Our job is to obey, to live in close fellowship with God as we walk our earthly path. In the process of that simple arrangement, God engages us in His eternal plan.

> So Samuel did what the LORD said.
>
> 1 Samuel 16:4

Now you're talking, Samuel! What a model! That's what we have to do! He did just what God said. He got a heifer, and he went to the home of Jesse in Bethlehem, full of expectation.

MAN CHOOSES . . . GOD CORRECTS

And the elders of the city came trembling to meet him and said,

"Do you come in peace?"

1 Samuel 16:4

There was real fear stretching across the land at that time. You can see it reflected in the elders' immediate reaction. There were problems in the Oval Office, which made the people in the countryside uneasy. So when a prophet came to visit, they said, "What's Samuel doing here?" "Why is he coming to Bethlehem?" "What's wrong?" "What's happening?"

They don't know why Samuel is there, so they're fearful. "Do you come in peace?"

And he [Samuel] said, "In peace; I have come to sacrifice to the LORD. Consecrate yourselves and come with me to the sacrifice." He also consecrated Jesse and his sons, and invited them to the sacrifice.

1 Samuel 16:5

I don't know exactly what this ancient act of consecration included. Perhaps the sacrifice of a lamb or some other animal. Perhaps it involved some kind of liturgical washing to cleanse themselves. Maybe it required spending a period of time in prayer. But whatever it was, there was some sort of preparation before the anointing, and it appears that Jesse and his sons went through this ritual to prepare themselves for what God was going to say.

So here they are in the room, and they don't have a clue what's going to happen. Even Samuel doesn't know which man God is going to choose. They're standing around, looking at Samuel. And he's looking at them.

Then it came about when they entered, that he looked at Eliab and thought, "Surely the LORD's anointed is before Him."

1 Samuel 16:6

Hey, that must be the one, Samuel thought. He didn't say it out loud, but that's what he was thinking. Why? Because Eliab looked like the type you'd normally choose for a king. No doubt he was tall and impressive. Certainly he was a man of battle, because he's the one who is fighting with Saul and the troops against Goliath in the next chapter.

What Samuel did not see was the character of Eliab. He didn't see, as we will in that seventeenth chapter, that Eliab was critical and negative and looked down on his younger brother. Samuel was enamored of the externals, like most of us are.

But Exhibit A was not God's man, and neither were Exhibits B and C.

> Then Jesse called Abinadab, and made him pass before Samuel. And he said, "Neither has the LORD chosen this one."
>
> 1 Samuel 16:8

Here's Abinadab, the second oldest, who probably looked as impressive as Eliab. Jesse had eight sons and two daughters, and Abinadab is always listed as the second son. But God told Samuel, "That's not the man." We're not told why; we're just told he's not the one. For some reason, Abinadab wasn't king material either.

Next came Exhibit C.

> Next Jesse made Shammah pass by. And he [Samuel] said, "Neither has the LORD chosen this one."
>
> 1 Samuel 16:9

Then, suddenly, in the midst of this parade of possibles, we find God's principle of choice. Read the following very carefully.

> The LORD said to Samuel, "Do not look at his appearance or at the height of his stature, because I have rejected him; for God sees not as man sees, for man looks at the outward appearance [literally, the Hebrew says, "man looks at the face"], but the LORD looks at the heart."
>
> 1 Samuel 16:7

If I could change one thing about my focus or vision, that would be the thing I'd change: I would like to see people not by face but by heart. But only God can do that. So we have to look to Him to give us, with our limited focus, that kind of discernment, because we don't have it in ourselves.

That's why God says, "Samuel, here's the principle of choice. And that's why I've repeatedly said no." He saw Eliab, Abinadab, Shammah, and Jesse's other sons as they really were. He saw their hearts.

Remember, God had said, "I've already chosen my man; I will designate him." And way back in chapter 13, God said, "I'm looking for a man after My heart. I'm searching for that person." He knew exactly who that man was.

It's highly significant to me that Jesse didn't even have his youngest son in the room. It's remarkable, isn't it, how Jesse reveals two very common mistakes parents make. Number one, he didn't have an equal appreciation for all of his children. And number two, he failed to cultivate a mutual self-respect among them. Jesse saw his youngest as nothing more than the one who tended the sheep.

MAN FORGETS . . . GOD REMEMBERS

And Samuel said to Jesse, "Are these all the children?" And he said, "There remains yet the youngest, and behold, he is tending the sheep." Then Samuel said to Jesse, "Send and bring him; for we will not sit down until he comes here."

1 Samuel 16:11

You see, Samuel, with God's help, now has the proper perspective. Nothing would hinder his pursuing the one God had chosen! "What does it matter what he does? What does it matter how old he is? Go get him!"

Oh, for the ability to see beyond the obvious. To see beyond the bad track record. To see beyond someone's age or size or the level of intelligence. To see worth and value down deep inside. That's the kind of vision that Samuel, with God's help, finally demonstrates at this point.

Ah, this beautiful moment. Remember, David's out with the sheep. He doesn't know what's going on back home. He's faithfully keeping the sheep, when suddenly someone runs across the fields and calls to him, "Hey, David, they want you back at the house."

So he [Jesse] sent and brought him [David] in. . . . And the LORD said, "Arise, anoint him; for this is he."

Then Samuel took the horn of oil and anointed him in the midst of his brothers. . . .

1 Samuel 16:12–13

Here's David, just a teenager. He walks into the house, still smelling like sheep, and all of a sudden an old man hobbles over and pours oil on his head. It drips down his hair and drops on his neck. Josephus the historian says that "Samuel the aged whispered in his ear the meaning of the symbol, 'You will be the next king.'"

What did David do? What *do* you do in a situation like that? I mean, it doesn't come along every other day, you know. God's ways are so marvelous, aren't they? At the most surprising moment, the most magnificent things happen. "You're going to be the next king." What did he do? Well, I'm happy to report, he did not go down to the nearest department store and try on crowns. He didn't order a new set of business cards, telling the printer, "Change it from shepherd to king-elect." Didn't have a badge saying, "I'm the new man." Didn't shine up a chariot and race through the streets of Bethlehem, yelling, "I'm God's choice . . . you're looking at Saul's replacement!"

What did he do? Well, look down at verses 17 through 19. We'll look at these verses again later, but for now just let me show you what David did after he was elected king, because it tells us a lot about why God chose him.

> So Saul said to his servants, "Provide for me now a man who
> can play well, and bring him to me."
>
> 1 Samuel 16:17

Saul is depressed. So he says, "Bring me a musician who can make me feel better."

> Then one of the young men answered and said, "Behold, I
> have seen a son of Jesse the Bethlehemite who is a skillful mu-
> sician, a mighty man of valor, a warrior, one prudent in speech,
> and a handsome man; and the LORD is with him."
> So Saul sent messengers to Jesse, and said, "Send me your
> son David who is with the flock."
>
> 1 Samuel 16:18–19

Don't miss those last three words. He went right back to the sheep . . . even after being anointed king.

Then in the next chapter, where there's a battle going on in the valley of Elah between Israel and the Philistine's giant, Goliath, we see David again.

> And David was the youngest. Now the three oldest followed
> Saul, but David went back and forth from Saul to tend his
> father's flock at Bethlehem.
>
> 1 Samuel 17:14–15

Hey, David is the king's musician now! What's he doing still tending his father's flock? Well, when you have a heart like David's, that's what you do. That was his job and he was faithful to do it. It made no difference that Samuel had anointed him with oil. He didn't bronze that horn and hang it up in his tent. He didn't expect special treatment from others. No, he just went back to the sheep. And when the king said, "Come on over here and play for me," David went over and played a little. And when he got through, he thought, *Hey, I gotta get back with my sheep; that's my job.*

David was sensitive enough to hear the whisper of God's voice, "You will be the next king." But as soon as the big moment was over and they turned out the lights, he was humbly back with his sheep. People had to actually pull him from the sheep to get him to do anything that was related to the limelight. In fact, I think that's one of the reasons he was a man after God's heart. He was always approachable, always believable, always authentic . . . and always faithful in the little things.

GOD SPEAKS . . . WE RESPOND

Three timeless lessons ring through my head as I look at these significant scenes in David's life.

First, *God's solutions are often strange and simple, so be open.* We try to make God complex and complicated. He isn't. Amid all the complications with Saul and the throne, God simply said to Samuel, "Go where I tell you to go. I've got a simple answer. A new man. You just follow Me and I'll show you." Don't make the carrying out of God's will complicated. It isn't. Stay open to His strange yet simple solutions.

Second, *God's promotions are usually sudden and surprising, so be ready.* At the time you least expect it, it'll come. Just like His Son's return from heaven. Suddenly and surprisingly He will split the clouds and be with us. Just when we expect Him the least He'll be there, like a thief in the night. And that's the way His promotions are. He watches you as you faithfully carry out your tasks and He says to you, "I know what I'm doing. In a sudden and surprising moment, you be ready. I know where you are, and I know how to find you. You just stay ready as you carry out your job."

Finally, *God's selections are always sovereign and sure, so be sensitive.* That applies to choosing a mate as well as losing a mate. It applies to our being moved from one place to another, even though we thought we'd remain there ten more years. It also applies to those God appoints to fill the shoes of another. How easy to second-guess God's selections! How necessary, when tempted to do that, to remind ourselves that His selections are sovereign and sure.

God is looking at your town, your city, your neighborhood, and He's looking for His people to whom He can say, "You are Mine. I want to use you there. Because you proved yourself faithful there." The only difference is our geography. Our calling is to be faithful in the demanding tasks, whether that is our education, our marriage, our occupation, or just the daily grind of life. That's the kind of men and women God wants to use.

The year 1809 was a very good year. Of course those who were alive that year didn't know that. Only history tells the story. Those who were living in 1809 were focused on Napoleon who was marching across Austria like a fire across a Kansas wheat field. As hamlets, villages, and cities fell into his grip, people began to wonder if all the world would someday fall into his hands.

During that same period of time, thousands of babies were born in Britain and in America. But who cared about babies and bottles and cribs and cradles while Napoleon was doing his thing in Austria.

Well, someone should have cared, because in 1809 William Gladstone was born in Liverpool. Alfred Tennyson began his life in Lincolnshire. Oliver Wendell Holmes cried out for the first time in Cambridge, Massachusetts. A few miles away in Boston, Edgar Allan Poe began his brief and tragic sojourn on earth. That same year, Charles Robert Darwin and Robert Charles Winthrop wore their first diapers. And in a little log cabin in Hardin County, Kentucky, an illiterate laborer and his wife named their newborn son Abraham Lincoln.

The lives of these statesmen, writers, and thinkers would mark the genesis of an era. But nobody cared about those nobodies while Napoleon was moving through Austria. The strange thing is, today only history buffs could name one battle that Napoleon fought in Austria. But there is not a life of a person alive today that has not been touched in some way by the lives of those men I've just named. Nobodies, nobody noticed.

If you and I had been Jews living in the year 1020 B.C., the same could have been said of us. All of our attention would have been focused upon a man named Saul, the first king of Israel. He was the focal point of the Jewish world at that time. He was taking the country by storm. Meanwhile, a "nobody" was keeping the sheep for his father on the Judean hillsides near the hamlet of Bethlehem. A little boy named David whom nobody noticed . . . except God.

CHAPTER THREE

Soft Music for a Hard Heart

Whatever our individual taste might be, there's something about music that soothes and ministers to us. It must go all the way back to the first genealogical record where we read that Jubal "was the father of all those who play the lyre and the pipe" (Gen. 4:21). A little later we find a whole book of songs, 150 of them, right in the middle of the Bible, as if God were saying, "Sing them often and learn them well, these are My psalms." More than half of them were written by David . . . some of them may have been written in the very context we're going to look at in this chapter of David's life—in the threatening presence of a madman named Saul.

After Samuel anoints David with oil, indicating that God has chosen him as the next king of Israel, to succeed Saul, we read some disquieting things about Saul.

> Now the Spirit of the LORD departed from Saul, and an evil spirit from the LORD terrorized him.
> Saul's servants then said to him, "Behold now, an evil spirit from God is terrorizing you."
>
> 1 Samuel 16:14–15

Before we talk about the misery of this malady that Saul wrestled with, I think it's important that we notice that the Spirit of the Lord departed *from* Saul before an evil spirit came.

Christians read those words about "an evil spirit from God" and they fear that could happen today. I've heard evangelists use that as a tool to shock Christians. "You continue to walk in the flesh," they say, "and God will lift His Spirit from you and you won't have God's presence within you as you once had." Then they'll quote this verse or the one in Judges 16 where Samson is in Delilah's lap, and it says, "He knew not that the Lord had departed from him." Or the one in Psalm 51:11 that says, "Take not Thy Holy Spirit from me." That's a fearful thought, that God could lift His Spirit from us and we'd be lost, having once been saved.

So let's go on record right now with a good dose of theology. Before the Holy Spirit came at Pentecost (Acts 2), the Spirit of God never permanently rested on any believer except David and John the Baptizer. Those are the only two. It was not uncommon for the Spirit of God to come for a temporary period of strengthening or insight or whatever was the need of the moment and then to depart, only to return again for another surge of the need of the moment, then to depart, once again.

However, at Pentecost and from that time all the way through our present era, when the Spirit of God comes into the believing sinner at salvation, He never leaves. He comes and baptizes us into the body of Christ. That happens at salvation. We remain sealed by the Spirit from that time on. We're never exhorted to *be* baptized by the Spirit. We *are* baptized into the body of Christ, placed there by the Spirit, sealed until the day of redemption (Eph. 4:30). That's the day we die. So He's there, and He never leaves. Furthermore, our bodies are the temple of the Holy Spirit in which the Spirit of God dwells. He permanently resides within us and will never, ever depart. So, rest easy, Christian friend.

SAUL'S STRANGE MALADY

But this is centuries before Pentecost, so we should not be surprised to read that in this moment of severity in the life of Saul, the Spirit of God departed from him and there was a vacuum created, into which God sent an evil spirit to terrorize him.

I don't know why. (No one knows why.) What seems most probable is that God was disgusted with Saul. It was as if He were saying, "I will punish you for presuming on your office as a king and walking against My will. You have not taken Me seriously. You will learn to do that, Saul. I'm jealous for My name." So He departed from Saul and permitted an evil spirit to terrorize him.

The Hebrew word here is *baath,* which means "to fall upon, to startle, to overwhelm." In his misery, Job uses it to curse the day of his birth. "Let the blackness of the day terrify [same word—*baath*] it [the day of his birth]" (Job 3:5). In essence he says, "Let the blackness of my days overwhelm the day of my birth." Or, as we might put it, "Oh, that I'd never been born."

Keil and Delitzsch, two reputable Old Testament scholars, say this about the evil spirit that came upon Saul.

> The *"evil spirit from Jehovah"* which came into Saul in the place of the Spirit of Jehovah, was not merely an inward feeling of depression at the rejection announced to him, which grew into melancholy, and occasionally broke out in passing fits of insanity, but a higher evil power, which took possession of him, and not only deprived him of his peace of mind, but stirred up the feelings, ideas, imagination, and thoughts of his soul to such an extent that at times it drove him even into madness. The demon is called *"an evil spirit* (coming) *from Jehovah"* because Jehovah had sent it as a punishment. . . . [7]

That was Saul's malady, and it was so visible to those around him that even his servant realized he needed help and boldly suggested:

> "Let . . . your servants . . . seek a man who is a skillful player on the harp; and it shall come about when the evil spirit from God is on you, that he shall play the harp with his hand, and you will be well."
>
> So Saul said to his servants, "Provide for me now a man who can play well, and bring him to me."
>
> 1 Samuel 16:16–17

Earliest archaeological records, carvings, and inscriptions show us that the ancients believed music soothed passions, healed mental diseases, and even held in check riots and tumults. It is interesting how God uses this belief to provide the missing link needed to connect David to Saul and the throne. Someone happens to hear that Saul is depressed and is looking for someone to provide him with soothing music, and he knows a fellow who knows David, and he says, "I know a guy who can do that." God never runs out of creative ways to carry out His sovereign plan.

> "[He is] a son of Jesse the Bethlehemite who is a skillful mu-
> sician, a mighty man of valor, a warrior, one prudent in speech,
> and a handsome man; and the LORD is with him."
>
> 1 Samuel 16:18

Now that's not a bad resume, is it? He's a skilled musician; he's a man of valor; he's a warrior; he has control of his tongue; he's handsome; and the Lord is with him.

One important thing this says to me is that you should never discount anything in your past. God can pick it up and use it in the most incredible ways. You never know when something that happened years ago will open a door of opportunity into the future.

That's precisely what happened to David. There he was, plucking away on his harp, out in the fields of Judea. He'd never even met Saul, yet he's ultimately to be Saul's replacement. Get that! So God works out a way to bring them together—music! Soon David receives a message that says, "Saul wants to see you." It's incredible how it all falls together. I never cease to be amazed at how perfectly God weaves His will together without our help!

> So Saul sent messengers to Jesse, and said, "Send me your son
> David who's with the flock."
>
> And Jesse took a donkey loaded with bread and a jug of
> wine and a young goat, and sent them to Saul by David his
> son.
>
> 1 Samuel 16:19–20

Even though Samuel had anointed David earlier, Jesse let him go back with the sheep. And now a runner comes from the king, saying, "Saul wants to see your youngest son." So Jesse releases David, but first he loads him down with gifts for the king. Now David trudges along with a donkey loaded with bread and a jug of wine and a goat, and his stringed instrument slung over his shoulder!

DAVID'S UNIQUE ABILITY

David didn't know it, but he was getting ready to enter boot camp on the road to becoming a king. That's the way God's program works. You may think some skill you learned or used years ago is lost, or that you've wasted all your time doing such and such, but don't you believe it. God can draw what may seem to be a most insignificant part of your past and put you in exactly the right place to use that particular gift or skill.

That's the way it was with David. He never once said to Saul, "I'm gonna take your place, pal." Never once did he pull rank on Saul. He was never jealous or envious of the king's position. He wasn't presumptuous. He'd been anointed, but he let the Lord open all the doors. Remember, David was a man after God's heart.

He "came to Saul and attended him." When David walked into the king's presence, Saul had no idea who he was, this young man standing in front of him with a musical instrument slung over his shoulder. Saul's successor was standing in front of him, and the king never knew it. David certainly didn't mention it. He came for one purpose—to minister to the king in his depression.

> David came to Saul and attended him, and Saul loved him greatly; and he became his armor bearer.
>
> 1 Samuel 16:21

Why did Saul love David? Because . . .

> it came about whenever the evil spirit from God came to Saul, David would take the harp and play it with his hand; and Saul would be refreshed and be well, and the evil spirit would depart from him.
>
> 1 Samuel 16:23

Isn't that beautiful? There was Saul on his cot, or pacing his bedchamber, writhing in the madness of his depression, and in the corner sits David playing his harp and perhaps singing one of his psalms. Who knows, maybe they sang together after a while. Maybe he taught Saul some of his songs. We're not told. But somehow, through David's presence, mixed with his soothing music, Saul began to love that young man because he brought him relief. Through David's unique ability, deliverance from depression became a reality.

King Saul then says, "Let David now stand before me; for he has found favor in my sight" (1 Sam. 16:22).

What a statement. First the young shepherd was invited to the king's private tent; then he won the heart of the king. And now the king says to the father, "Let your son stay. Ah, he's effective. He's got it together."

MUSIC'S EFFECTIVE MINISTRY

David's music was effective. It refreshed Saul: "David would take the harp and play it with his hand; and Saul would be refreshed" (1 Sam. 16:23). The Berkeley Version says, "It eased Saul." The Hebrew word translated "refreshed" and "eased" is *ravach,* which means "to be wide, to be spacious, to give space so as to bring relief." Moffatt translates it, "He played for Saul till Saul breathed freely."

God had His hand on this young man whose music not only would fill the heart of a depressed king overwhelmed by blackness, but also would someday fill His written Word. Thus, David, with his primitive stringed instrument, walked bravely into that dark place where Saul was living.

Saul was willing to try anything. "Provide a man," he says. "I don't care who it is. Bring him to me."

Somehow David's music unleashed the caged feelings inside this tormented man and then soothed the savage beast within. By the time David left him, Saul was relieved. The evil presence had departed.

God used the gift of music to put David into the very presence of the king's chamber. And the king not only found relief from his torment, he found love in his heart for the young shepherd boy whose music touched his soul.

Martin Luther believed that the Reformation was not complete until the saints of God had two things in their possession: a Bible in their own tongue, and a hymnal, which they called a Psalter. He believed they needed the Book that could lead them to a deeper understanding of their faith and a companion volume that would help them express with joy and delight the depths of that faith.

I don't think there can be genuine worship without those two elements blending together: the declaration of the doctrines that deepen our roots in biblical truth, and then the expression of our faith in melody as it flows from our lips and our voices in song.

Long before there was man or the voice of mankind on the earth, there was music. Did you realize that? Job tells us "the morning stars sang together." Now that either means that the stars had voices then or the angelic host had voices and sang unto God. I rather believe it was the latter. I think the angels of heaven surrounded the throne and sang praises to the Creator. It must have been some kind of harmony.

Also, if I understand the scene in Revelation correctly, when we gather around the throne in the future, our best expression will be in song. We will sing unto Him, "Worthy is the Lamb that was slain." Since there was singing before the earth was formed and there will be singing after the earth is gone, then it stands to reason there should be a lot of singing while we are on the earth, doesn't it?

But we really don't give praises to Him in song except at church. Stop and think: how often have you sung this past month just on your own? I mean, really sung your praise unto God. Our voices frequently are involved in the reading of Scripture, but we are seldom involved in singing Scripture to our God. How easy to forget that's all part of the development of our worship of God.

The longer I continue my walk with Him, the more I appreciate the importance of music in ministry. I think Martin Luther was exactly right when he wrote these words, "Next to the Word of God, music deserves the highest praise." God seems to have cast His vote in favor of music, too. In His Book, the longest of all the sixty-six books is the one dedicated to the hymns of the Hebrews.

In the preface of his book *The Treasury of David,* the great Charles Haddon Spurgeon wrote, "The delightful study of the Psalms has yielded me boundless profit and ever-growing pleasure."[8] He later calls the Psalms the "peerless book."

But if you like shallow lyrics and easy-to-hum-along-with ditties, then you're not going to enjoy the Psalms. The Psalms are for folks who have decided that music is an art that requires the discipline of keen thinking and a heart that is right before God. It is music for the mature. It is not a superficial statement. There are a few, of course, that are very popular: Psalms 1, 23, 91, 100, and parts of 119. But for the most part, only the mature spend lengthy times in the Psalms.

As a matter of fact, I have observed that those who are on their way to spiritual maturity spend hours in the Psalms for times of refreshment, times of recovery, times in which emotions seem to be getting out of line. Always, they come back to the Psalms.

No wonder G. Campbell Morgan said,

> The Book of Psalms . . . is the book in which the emotions of the human soul find expression. Whatever your mood, and I suppose you have changing moods as well as I do . . . I can find you a Psalm that will help to express it. Are you glad? I can find you a Psalm that you can sing. Are you sad? I can find you a Psalm that will suit that occasion.
>
> The psalms range over the whole gamut of human emotions. . . . They were all written for us in the consciousness of

and in the sense of the presence of God. . . . In every one of these Psalms, from the first to the last, whatever the particular tone, whether major or minor, the singer is conscious of God. That gives peculiar character to the Book of Psalms.[9]

My own devotional time with God seems to reach its highest point at those times when I sing my praise to Him.

The Spirit-filled saint is a song-filled saint. And your melody is broadcast right into heaven—live—where God's antenna is always receptive, where the soothing strains of your song are always appreciated.

Never mind how beautiful or how pitiful you may sound. Sing loud enough to drown out those defeating thoughts that normally clamor for attention. Release yourself from that cage of introspective reluctance. SING OUT! SING OUT! You're not auditioning for the church choir; you're making melody with your heart to the Lord your God! If you listen closely when you're through, you may hear the hosts of heaven answering back for joy.

Soft music for a hard heart, that's what David provided for Saul. That's the soul music that Christ the Savior provides, and that's the place we all must begin. He died for us. He rose from the dead to give us the desire and the power to live a positive, fulfilling life free of the cage of human depression and despair. He is our shepherd, and we are his sheep, needing the music of his voice. We can rejoice and exult in God together.

CHAPTER FOUR

David and the Dwarf

The most famous battle described in the Old Testament was not fought between two armies, but between two people. It was the battle in the Valley of Elah between David and Goliath.

But before we look at that fearsome duel, I want to look again at something that occurred prior to that battle, when the Lord said to Samuel,

> "Do not look at his appearance or at the height of his stature, because I have rejected him; for God sees not as man sees, for man looks at the outward appearance, but the Lord looks at the heart."
>
> 1 Samuel 16:7

Literally, God said, "for man looks at the face, but the Lord looks at the heart."

We, being human, are subject to that very problem. We are impressed with, or not impressed with, individuals because we judge on the basis of surface appearance. We look at the externals and we form opinions that are usually erroneous.

If God's statement ever applied, it applied in the story of this battle. Goliath had all the things that would normally impress and intimidate. In this instance, however, David had been given the ability to see as God always sees, and he was neither impressed nor intimidated. Because no matter how big the giant might be, God is greater. And no matter how powerful he might be, God is all-powerful.

Now, with that in mind, let's take a look at the battleground.

> Now the Philistines gathered their armies for battle; and they were gathered at Socoh which belongs to Judah, and they camped between Socoh and Azekah, in Ephes-dammim.
>
> And Saul and the men of Israel were gathered, and camped in the valley of Elah, and drew up in battle array to encounter the Philistines.
>
> And the Philistines stood on the mountain on one side while Israel stood on the mountain on the other side, with the valley between them.
>
> 1 Samuel 17:1–3

The Valley of Elah was not a narrow ravine, but more like a vast canyon. The ancient site was probably about a mile wide, and toward the mouth of the canyon it opened up even wider. At the bottom of the canyon or ravine between the slopes was the streambed where David found the stones for his sling. To one side there was a great slope a half mile or more in size. Opposite was another vast slope of another half mile, stretching a full mile across. Bivouacked on one slope was the army of Israel and on the other, the army of the Philistines.

This was the setting. Now let's consider the major characters in our drama. First there was Goliath, whose size and appearance were so impressive that the writer describes him in exacting detail.

GOLIATH: FRONT AND CENTER

> Then a champion came out from the armies of the Philistines named Goliath, from Gath, whose height was six cubits and a span.
>
> 1 Samuel 17:4

We don't understand precisely what that description means at face value, because we don't measure things by a cubit or a span. We measure them by feet and inches. So let's put it into our lingo. Goliath was somewhere near 9' 9" tall . . . an enormous man. The NBA would love him! And if you add to his height the length of his arms when he would lift them up over his head, you can imagine what an imposing creature he must have been.

But it wasn't just his size.

> And he had a bronze helmet on his head, and he was clothed with scale armor which weighed five thousand shekels of bronze.
>
> He also had bronze greaves on his legs and a bronze javelin slung between his shoulders.
>
> And the shaft of his spear was like a weaver's beam, and the head of his spear weighed six hundred shekels of iron; his shield-carrier also walked before him.
>
> 1 Samuel 17:5–7

He was wearing what we would call a coat of mail. The Philistines garbed themselves for battle with a heavy canvaslike undergarment interlaced with overlapping ringlets of bronze. This coat of mail went from shoulder to knee, covering and protecting against the enemy's weapons. Body armor of such material and size weighed five thousand shekels of bronze—in our terms, it weighed between 175 and 200 pounds. That was the armor alone—just the coat of mail. But Goliath also wore a bronze helmet, and bronze leggings (greaves) to protect his shins, and he carried a bronze javelin or spear slung between his shoulders. The head of his spear alone weighed six hundred shekels of iron, or about 20 to 25 pounds.

The written account also says that he had a "shield-carrier" who walked before him. The Hebrew word here is one that refers to the largest shield used in battle, the size of a full-grown man. It was obviously designed to protect his body from the arrows of the enemy. So in addition to his body armor, Goliath had this fellow running in front of him, carrying a man-size shield as double protection.

Pause a moment and allow your mind to picture such an imposing sight. Imagine how frightening it would be to take on a giant of this size protected by this amount of armor. Clearly, the odds are stacked against *anyone* foolish enough to face him in battle.

Notice what this gigantic warrior did.

> He stood and shouted to the ranks of Israel, and said to them, "Why do you come out to draw up in battle array? Am I not the Philistine and you servants of Saul? Choose a man for yourselves and let him come down to me.

"If he is able to fight with me and kill me, then we will
become your servants; but if I prevail against him and kill him,
then you shall become our servants and serve us."

1 Samuel 17:8–9

What Goliath did was suggest a tactic commonly used in the Eastern
world, and that is, a representative battle, a one-on-one fight. He would
represent the Philistine army, and whoever Israel chose would represent
the Israelite army. Whoever won, his army won. And whoever lost, his
whole army lost.

"There's no reason for your entire army to be involved in this. Just
send a fighter and I'll take him on. I am the champion. I am the greatest."

Goliath didn't issue this challenge one time and then leave. No. His
challenge went on for *forty days* (17:16). Every morning and every evening
for well over a month, he marched out there, flaunting his size and his
strength, daring someone to take him on.

How applicable to any "giant" we encounter! That's the way with the
giants of fear and worry, for example. They don't come just once; they
come morning and evening, day after day, relentlessly trying to intimidate.
They come in the form of a person, or a pressure, or a worry. Some fear
that hammers on your heart every morning and every night, day in and
day out, yelling across the ravine in your own personal valley. Few things
are more persistent and intimidating than our fears and our worries . . .
especially when we face them in our own strength.

ENTER DAVID . . . THE REAL "GIANT"

Meanwhile, about ten or fifteen miles away, up in the Judean mountains
in the little hamlet of Bethlehem, a teenager named David was keeping his
father's sheep. He was too young to be fighting in the army. In fact, at
that point, David probably knew very little about what was happening
between the Israelites and the Philistines. He may have never even heard
of Goliath. All he knew was that his three oldest brothers were off fighting
in Saul's army.

David's father, however, was very concerned about his three eldest sons.
Jesse was getting old and probably unable to make the trip through the
mountains himself. So he called his youngest son and said, "David, I want
you to run an errand for me."

"Take now for your brothers an ephah of this roasted grain and these ten loaves, and run to the camp to your brothers.

"Bring also these ten cuts of cheese to the commander of their thousand, and look into the welfare of your brothers, and bring back news of them."

1 Samuel 17:17–18

David wasn't going there to fight. He was just sent by his father to bring his brothers some refreshments, make sure they were all right, and let them know that Dad was concerned about them.

The sun rose that morning just like any other morning for both David and Goliath. That's the way it often is in life. No warning. But the truth is, that forty-first morning of Goliath's challenge would be the last day of his life, and the first day of David's heroic life. Nobody announced it. No angel blasted a horn from heaven saying, "Goliath, today you're history" or "David, this is your day."

That morning, David arose early and, after leaving his flock of sheep with another shepherd, did exactly what his father had told him to do. "And he came to the circle of the camp while the army was going out in battle array shouting the war cry" (17:20).

I'm trying to imagine what must have been going through David's mind as he came over the top of the last rise and saw that army spread out below him. I wonder if he stood and stared with his mouth open as he sized up the scene. I wonder what went through his mind. It must have been exciting and frightening all at the same time for this young man who had spent years out on the lonely hillside with only the sheep and the other shepherds for company.

Then, as he gets to the edge of the Israelite camp, he sees the troops heading out for battle and hears the war cry. You can tell he's excited. He wants to watch—to see what's going to happen. Any kid would.

Then David left his baggage in the care of the baggage keeper, and ran to the battle line and entered in order to greet his brothers.

As he was talking with them, behold, the champion, the Philistine from Gath named Goliath, was coming up from the army of the Philistines, and he spoke these same words [the ones he's been yelling for the past forty days]; and David heard them.

1 Samuel 17:22–23

Picture the moment. David is standing there talking to his three brothers, when all of a sudden he hears this loud cry from across the ravine. And suddenly everyone around him is rushing to the rear and climbing in their tents—"when all the men of Israel saw the man, they fled from him and were greatly afraid" (17:24).

Remember, David has never seen this giant from Gath or heard his challenge. Suddenly he's standing there alone as everyone around him runs for cover! At least that's the way I read it.

He looks across the battlefield, and he sees this giant of a guy, encased in armor, shouting out threats and defiance and cursing the God of Israel. And that made David livid!

No one talks that way about the God of Israel, he thought. *So why is everybody running away?*

Remember now, this is the forty-first day the Israelites have encountered Goliath . . . but this is the first time it's happened to David.

Isn't it interesting how hindsight gives a lot of insight? Have you ever faced a Goliath, and then three days later you look back and say, "Man, I wish I'd done such and such"? That's hindsight perspective . . . and it's usually infallible! When you look back you always know a better way, but at the time it happens you sort of shoot from the hip. Unless you're a David.

David had the character to see the present as though seeing with hindsight, and he wasn't impressed. Nor was he intimidated. What a wise young man. Look at what he does.

> Then David spoke to the men who were standing by him, saying, "What will be done for the man who kills this Philistine, and takes away the reproach from Israel? For who is this uncircumcised Philistine, that he should taunt the armies of the living God?"
>
> And the people answered him in accord with this word, saying, "Thus it will be done for the man who kills him."
>
> 1 Samuel 17:26–27

Now, Saul had devised an incentive plan for killing the giant. The problem was, he was actually the one man in the camp of Israel who was qualified to fight Goliath. Remember, he stood head and shoulders above everybody else—and, he was the leader of the people. But Saul was a coward, because he was not walking with God. So he had worked out a plan that, hopefully, would get somebody else out in the battle. He promised the man who killed Goliath a reward of great riches, he promised him his daughter's hand in marriage, and he promised to exempt his father's house from paying taxes. Well, I'm not sure the daughter was much of a reward (you'll see when we meet her later!), but a bride, great riches, and a perpetual tax exemption plan don't sound too bad! But not even that was enough to prompt a volunteer.

The guys standing around David told him about this incentive plan—all sorts of external motivations.

By the way, I want you to notice something about Goliath's position on this particular day. When Goliath first issued his challenge, "He stood and shouted to the ranks of Israel, and said to them . . . 'Choose a man for yourselves and let him come down to me' " (17:8). But look at what is said the day David arrives: " 'Have you seen this man who is *coming up?* ' " (17:25, emphasis added).

That's right. Goliath has now crossed the ravine at the base of the valley and is coming up Israel's side. You see, if you tolerate a Goliath, he'll take over your territory. He'll move into your camp. He'll take your thoughts that normally ought to be on God, and he'll put them on himself. That's why you can't afford to tolerate giants; you kill them.

The next thing that happens to David is what I call the "older brother" syndrome. It's what Christians often go through during a time of standing by faith: they get flak, and often it comes from members of their own family.

> Now Eliab his oldest brother heard when he spoke to the men; and Eliab's anger burned against David and he said, "Why have you come down? And with whom have you left those few sheep in the wilderness? I know your insolence and the wickedness of your heart; for you have come down in order to see the battle."
>
> 1 Samuel 17:28

Don't forget who Eliab really is. He's the son of Jesse who first walked into the house and Samuel thought, *That's the king!* Remember? That was when God put His hand on Samuel's shoulder and said, "No, no, that's not the one." And a little later on Eliab was standing there when the horn of oil was emptied on the head of David, and the older brother saw the younger brother chosen to be the king. The younger gets blessed above the older. Usually, it's hard for the older brother to handle that. It certainly was in this instance.

Eliab remembered that this was his little brother who had been anointed by the great priest and prophet Samuel, and now he got his strokes in. He said to David, "Why have you *really* come?" (Berkeley Version) In other words, he attacks David's motive. "Look, David, why have you *really* showed up here?"

Then he asks the second question, which was designed to humiliate David. "Hey, David, where did you leave that handful of sheep?" Just sort of twisting the knife. And then he gets downright ugly. "I know your insolence and the wickedness of your heart. You just came here for the excitement. You just wanted to see the battle."

Isn't it interesting how we can so easily and readily see our own guilt in somebody else's life? Who really had the insolent wicked heart? Eliab, the older brother. "I know where you're coming from," he said. "You've come down in order to see the battle." There's also a possibility that the Hebrew text implies, "You have come down *to be seen* in the battle."

Now, at this point, the average person would have rolled up his sleeves and used all his energy to punch his brother's lights out, rather than dealing with Goliath. Instead, David just ignores him, as if to say, "Hey, all I did was ask a question. Now, let's go on to the important thing. That giant out there." And he just turns away.

David knew who to fight and who to leave alone. We need to choose our battles wisely. If you don't watch it, all of your battles will be fought among fellow members of the family of God. Meanwhile, the real enemy of our souls roams around our territory winning victory after victory.

The scene suddenly changes from Eliab and David to Saul and David. When Saul heard about the questions David was asking and the comments he was making, Saul sent for him. Now, keep in mind that King Saul is the guy who doesn't want to fight, but he won't admit it.

> And David said to Saul, "Let no man's heart fail on account of him; your servant will go and fight with this Philistine."
> Then Saul said to David, "You are not able to go against this Philistine to fight with him; for you are but a youth while he has been a warrior from his youth."
>
> 1 Samuel 17:32–33

Man is impressed with the externals; he doesn't see the heart. God is different. He doesn't judge by appearance or intelligence. King Saul hadn't learned that, however, so he looked at David and said, "You don't have the size for it. You're just a kid. Look over there at that giant!"

As I picture it, David was blinking and thinking, *What giant? The only giant in my life is God. That's a dwarf over there, Saul. God is not impressed with the externals; He looks on the heart. God is omnipotent! And if He's on my side, omnipotence can't lose.*

David then describes to Saul how in the past God proved Himself faithful when David slew a bear and a lion. "The LORD who delivered me from the paw of the lion and from the paw of the bear, He will deliver me from the hand of this Philistine" (17:37).

So often, when facing our own giants, we forget what we ought to remember and we remember what we ought to forget. We remember our defeats and we forget the victories. Most of us can recite the failures of our lives in vivid detail, but we're hard-pressed to name the specific, re-markable victories God has pulled off in our past.

Not so with David! He says, "You know why I can fight Goliath, Saul? Because the same God who gave me power over a lion and a bear will give me power over Goliath. It is God who will empower me . . . so just let me at him."

Well, that let Saul off the hook, so he says, "Go, and may the Lord be with you." Isn't it remarkable how people can use spiritual clichés to cover up their empty lives? They know all the right words to use . . . all the pious-sounding sayings. Saul sure did.

Then Saul said, "Now wait a minute, David. We have to fix you up for battle." Imagine it! You can't tell me the Bible doesn't have humor, because it says that "Saul clothed David with his garments." Here's Saul, a 52 long, and David is a 36 regular. And so Saul drags in all this heavy armor and then says, "Put this on, David." He hands David his sword, but it's so big he can't even hold the thing. He drops his oversize helmet onto his head—clunk! He wraps his coat of mail around the young man. And David says, "Saul, I can't fight with this stuff. I can't even walk in it, and I sure haven't tested it myself in battle." So David dropped Saul's sword and slid out of the armor.

What works for one person will not necessarily work for someone else. We're always trying to put our armor on someone else or put someone else's armor on ourselves—but that's not the way to do battle. It was a great breakthrough in my own life when I finally discovered that I could be me and God would use me. I couldn't operate well, wearing another's armor. God provides unique techniques for unique people.

So here's David, stripped down to his own simple garments, and armed with his own simple shepherd weapons—his sling and his staff—ready to do battle. Then comes that crucial moment:

And he took his stick in his hand and chose for himself five smooth stones from the brook, and put them in the shepherd's bag which he had, even in his pouch, and his sling was in his hand; and he approached the Philistine.

1 Samuel 17:40

The beautiful thing about this story is that it's a perfect example of how God operates. He magnifies HIS name when we are weak. We don't have to be eloquent or strong or handsome. We don't have to be beautiful or brilliant or have all the answers to be blessed of God. He honors our faith. All He asks is that we trust Him, that we stand before Him in integrity and faith, and He'll win the battle. God is just waiting for His moment, waiting for us to trust Him so He can empower us to battle our giants.

Remember, Goliath is still a giant . . . still an imposing presence. David had all the odds against him. There wasn't a guy in the Philistine camp—or probably the Israelite camp either—who would have bet on David. But David didn't need their backing. He needed God—none other. After picking up the stones, he approaches the gigantic Philistine warrior. The shepherd boy made the giant smile. What a joke!

Then the Philistine came on and approached David, with the shield-bearer in front of him.

When the Philistine looked and saw David, he disdained him; for he was but a youth. . . .

And the Philistine said to David, "Am I a dog, that you come to me with sticks?" And the Philistine cursed David by his gods.

The Philistine also said to David, "Come to me, and I will give your flesh to the birds of the sky and the beasts of the field."

Then David said to the Philistine, "You come to me with a sword, a spear, and a javelin, but I come to you in the name of the LORD of hosts, the God of the armies of Israel, whom you have taunted.

"This day the LORD will deliver you up into my hands, and I will strike you down and remove your head from you. And I will give the dead bodies of the army of the Philistines this day to the birds of the sky and the wild beasts of the earth, that all the earth may know that there is a God in Israel."

1 Samuel 17:41–46

EXIT GOLIATH . . . "THE DWARF"

Just imagine it! David stood before this massive creature unintimidated!

Intimidation. That's our MAJOR battle when we face giants. When they intimidate us, we get tongue-tied. Our thoughts get confused. We forget how to pray. We focus on the odds against us. We forget whom we represent, and we stand there with our knees knocking. I wonder what God must think, when all the while He has promised us, "My power is available. There's no one on this earth greater. *You trust Me.*"

But David's eyes weren't on the giant. Intimidation played no part in his life. What a man! His eyes were fixed on God. With invincible confidence in his God, David responded, "that all this assembly may know the LORD does not deliver by sword or by spear; for the battle is the LORD's" (17:47). There it is. That's the secret of David's life. "The battle is the LORD's."

Are you trying to do your own battle? Trying to fight it your way? Trying to outsmart the enemy, outfox him? You can't. But God can. And He's saying to you, "You do it My way and I'll honor you. You do it your way and you're doomed to fail. The battle is Mine."

David lived by a very simple principle: *nothing to prove, nothing to lose.* He didn't try to impress anybody in the army of Israel. He didn't try to impress his brothers. He didn't even try to impress God. He just ran to meet Goliath.

> And David put his hand into his bag and took from it a stone and slung it, and struck the Philistine on his forehead. And the stone sank into his forehead, so that he fell on his face to the ground.
>
> Thus David prevailed over the Philistine with a sling and a stone, and he struck the Philistine and killed him; but there was no sword in David's hand.
>
> 1 Samuel 17:49–50

All David had was a sling and a stone against a giant wearing two hundred pounds of armor. It may seem silly, but that's the way God operates. In the final analysis, there was a whoosh, whoosh, whoosh—one stone flew through the air and that's all there was to it. Goliath fell like a sack full of rocks. Got any more giants?

The Philistines didn't wait around after that. When they saw that their champion was dead, they split the scene. Then David took the Philistine's head to Jerusalem. David had to use Goliath's own sword to cut off his head, but notice what he did with Goliath's weapons afterward. "He put his weapons in his tent." He drags that huge spear and that heavy sword into his own tent, back on the Judean hillside, as a reminder of what God has done. They stood there like silent trophies . . . alongside the lion's skull and bear's paw.

I wonder if perhaps David kept those trophies for the rest of his life. Who knows? Maybe after he became king he had a weapon room with a trophy case where he kept the memories of God's past victories in his life.

Out of this battle, the real truth emerged, evident to the troops on both sides of the Valley of Elah: Goliath was the dwarf and David was the giant.

GIANT LESSONS WORTH REMEMBERING

Winning victories is extremely significant. Remember them! Where do you keep your memories? Do you quickly pass over the victories? Break that habit! God doesn't waste victories. When He pulls something off that only He can do, He says to us, "Now don't you forget that." In Old Testament times, God had His people pile up huge stacks of stones as reminders of His winning various victories on their behalf. Those "stones of remembrance" were to remain for all to see . . . and remember.

Four lessons emerge from this significant battle between David and Goliath. Read them slowly. Remember them well.

1. *Facing giants is an intimidating experience.* We can look back at David's bravery and victory with the perfect hindsight and the safe distance of two thousand years. But humanly speaking, imagine what it must have felt like to face the intimidating presence of that brute, even with the eyes of faith. Yet David said, "My God is greater than he."

2. *Doing battle is a lonely experience.* No one else can fight for you. Your Goliath is *your* Goliath. Someone else might say, "Ah, don't worry about that." But to you, it's a Goliath. And nobody else can battle him for you, not even a coun-

selor or a pastor, not even a parent or a friend. It's lonely, but it enables you to grow up. It's on the lonely battlefield that you learn to trust God.

3. *Trusting God is a stabilizing experience.* David brought down Goliath with the first stone. His aim was true and didn't miss the mark. We can't know for sure, but from every indication he didn't have the jitters when he went into battle. He was stabilized by his trust in God. If you try to tackle the giant in the flesh, you cannot get it done. You'll lose. But when you have spent sufficient time on your knees, it's remarkable how stable you can be.

4. *Winning victories is a memorable experience.* We're to remember the victories of our past. We're to pass on our lion-and-bear stories . . . our own Goliath victories.

I don't know what your intimidating giant is today. It may relate to your job, your roommate, or your school. Maybe it is a person, a lawsuit, unemployment, a disaster . . . maybe even your own partner in life. Perhaps it is some fear that is lurking around the corner, sucking your energy and draining your faith. God is saying to you right now, "All I ask of you is five smooth stones and a sling of faith. I'll take it from there. You don't have to wear somebody else's armor. You just trust Me. And I'll strip you down to nothing but faith, and then I'll accomplish a victory where I'll get the glory. But as for you . . . *you trust Me.*"

Perhaps you don't know what lies across the valley. Maybe you can't get a handle on what that giant is; but it's there, haunting you. That uncertainty alone is a giant. But look at that worry in comparison to the Lord God Himself, and say, by faith, "The battle is Yours, Lord. It is Your battle. I lean on You. I give You all my weapons, all my skills, and I stand before You, trusting You."

It is God's love for us that causes Him to bring us to an end of our own strength. He sees our need to trust Him, and His love is so great that He will not let us live another day without turning over our arms to Him, our fears, our worries, even our confusion, so that nothing becomes more significant to us than our Father.

Never, ever forget it: The battle is the Lord's!

CHAPTER FIVE

Aftermath of a Giant-Killing

When was the last time you thanked the Lord for not showing you the future? I'm convinced that one of the best things God does for us is to keep us from knowing what will happen beyond today. Just think of all the stuff you didn't have to worry about just because you never knew it was coming your way!

It's true, God never changes . . . but we certainly do. The places we live change. People change. Even friends change. Jobs change.

Or how about your home? Things change there, too. Children are conceived unexpectedly. Many parents are brokenhearted because their older children are not walking with God. Others are sorrowing because death has taken a parent or a son or daughter. Our health changes. Or how about tests in life? Just think of what has happened in the past five years. Aren't you glad God didn't tell you about all of those things *five years ago?* Aren't you glad He didn't give you your life ahead of time, on credit? Instead, we just take life one day at a time. That's the way He dispenses life. Because He never changes and He knows what will work together for good. You and I don't. We sort of ricochet from one moment to the next, trying to put together what life is all about. And we often don't have the time or wisdom to figure it out.

God is good not to show us tomorrow. That's what makes the Bible so relevant. The same was true back in ancient times while His Word was being lived out and recorded.

How gracious of God to give David one day at a time. I wonder how many people think that David, after he killed the giant, within a matter of just a few days took the throne and became the youngest king in the history of Israel? Well, in case you were one who thought that, you need to know it didn't happen that way. As a matter of fact, the aftermath of the giant-killing led David into one of the deepest, longest, and darkest valleys of his entire life. This young man who had proved himself faithful among the sheep and on the battlefield went from the highest pinnacle of popularity to the lowest depression of despair. God was good not to tell David all that was coming his way.

REVIEW: A GIANT SLAIN

As we saw in the previous chapter, David had just accomplished an incredible thing, a remarkable achievement. A young man, not yet twenty years old, who had never worn the uniform of the Israeli army, never once suited up for battle, never once known what it was to carry a sword, had run out onto the battlefield, faced a giant almost ten feet tall, and killed him with one throw of his sling.

As a result, David gained instant popularity. He became a national hero. The people began to sing his praises. Saul made good on his promise to enrich the man who killed Goliath. David became a permanent part of the king's court. David became an overnight celebrity. Very few people could take all that in stride, but David did. He knew how to live with success without having it affect him. It's a rare person who can do that . . . especially if he is young and has never lived his life before the public.

RELATIONSHIPS: FOUR DIFFERENT EXPERIENCES

At this point, David's life unfolds into four different relationships: a relationship of submission with Saul; a relationship of affection with Saul's son, Jonathan; a relationship of elevation or exaltation with the people of Israel; and a relationship of opposition with Saul that lasted year after year after year.

God's hand was on David. Ultimately, the Lord was going to use him as the greatest king in the history of Israel, but in order to do that, He had to break him and hone him and sharpen him, which included crushing him. David was about to enter the crucible of pain. Thankfully, he had no idea how excruciating the pain would be.

The first thing that happened was that Saul would not let David return to his sheep.

> And Saul took him that day and did not let him return to his
> father's house. . . . So David went wherever Saul sent him. . . .
>
> 1 Samuel 18:2, 5

Here is the champion of champions, the slayer of the giant, and he went wherever Saul sent him. He was in loyal submission to his king. He served as sort of an intern incognito—a king in the making (without Saul's realizing it). And what happened? He prospered. Four times in the same chapter it says David prospered, or that he behaved himself wisely. What a man. He simply did what God led him to do. He submitted to authority, and God lifted him up above his peers.

Meanwhile, standing in the shadows as David stood before the king was another young man, Jonathan, the son of King Saul. Apparently these two young men had not met until this moment, but immediately their lives were knitted together.

> It came about when he [David] had finished speaking to Saul,
> that the soul of Jonathan was knit to the soul of David, and
> Jonathan loved him as himself.
>
> Then Jonathan made a covenant with David because he
> loved him as himself.
>
> 1 Samuel 18:1, 3

God knew that David needed an intimate friend to walk with him through the valley that was ahead of him. Intimate friends are rare in life. Often we have only one, occasionally two . . . usually not more than three in our entire lives. There's something about an intimate friend that causes your souls to be knit together. It's what we call a kindred spirit.

Intimate friendship has four characteristics, and we find all of them in this story.

First, *an intimate friend is willing to sacrifice.* You don't have to beg a close friend for a favor, which was certainly the case with Jonathan.

> And Jonathan stripped himself of the robe that was on him
> and gave it to David, with his armor, including his sword and
> his bow and his belt.
>
> 1 Samuel 18:4

He wanted to give David something that belonged to him and was meaningful to him. Friends do that. They're never stingy with their possessions. Later, Jonathan says to David, "Whatever you say, I will do for you" (20:4). That's the word of an intimate friend. You can hardly impose on an intimate friend. He doesn't keep score. An intimate friend is there to assist whenever and in whatever way is needed. Unselfishness prevails.

Second, *an intimate friend is a loyal defense before others.* He's not a fair-weather friend. He won't talk against you when you're not around. It says, "Jonathan spoke well of David to Saul his father" (19:4). That was very significant, because Saul was not only the king and Jonathan's father, but also, by that time, Saul had determined to be David's enemy. Yet Jonathan stood up to his father and said, "Dad, you're wrong about David." In fact, he not only defended his friend, he also rebuked his father for his attitude toward David.

> Jonathan . . . said to him [Saul], "Do not let the king sin against his servant David, since he has not sinned against you, and since his deeds have been very beneficial to you.
>
> "For he took his life in his hand and struck the Philistine, and the LORD brought about a great deliverance for all Israel; you saw it and rejoiced. Why then will you sin against innocent blood, by putting David to death without a cause?"
>
> 1 Samuel 19:4–5

What a friend Jonathan was! No pettiness, no envy, no jealousy. After all, Jonathan, as Saul's son, might have been the heir apparent. He might have wanted the praise of the people, yet here was this kid from the hills of Bethlehem, garnering all of it. Still, Jonathan stood in defense of his friend against his own father, who was ready to take David's life. This is what we might call bottom-line theology. This is putting shoe leather to your belief, to your faith. He stood in his defense because he was his friend.

Third, *intimate friends give each other complete freedom to be themselves.* When you've got a friend this close, this knitted to your own soul, you don't have to explain why you do what you do. You just do it.

> David rose from the south side and fell on his face to the ground, and bowed three times. And they kissed each other and wept together, but David more.
>
> 1 Samuel 20:41

When your heart is broken, you can bleed all over a friend like this and he will understand. He won't confront you in your misery or share with you three verses, then tell you to straighten up.

When a good friend is hurting, let him hurt. If a good friend feels like weeping, let him weep. If a good friend needs to complain, listen. An intimate friend doesn't bale; he's right there with you. You can be yourself, no matter what that self looks like.

And finally, *an intimate friend is a constant source of encouragement.*

> Now David became aware that Saul had come out to seek his life while David was in the wilderness of Ziph at Horesh.
> And Jonathan, Saul's son, arose and went to David at Horesh, and encouraged him in God.
>
> 1 Samuel 23:15–16

Think of that. There was a hit man after David, and his name was Saul (Jonathan's father!). David was out in the wilderness, and at any moment, behind any bush or rock or hill, Saul and his men might have been waiting to strike him down. The murderous hatred of Saul haunted David's life.

And what does the son of this hit man do? He encourages his friend. Wow! That's the kind of friend to have. He sees David at the lowest moment of his life, frightened, beleaguered, stumbling through the wilderness, and he brings him encouragement. "I understand how that feels. You have every right to have those feelings. There'll be a brighter day some day, but right now I'm here with you, no matter what."

Someone has said, "Loneliness is the most desperate of all English words." Even Jesus surrounded Himself with friends.

I think it is shameful that some have tarnished this beautiful story by trying to claim that the friendship between David and Jonathan provides a biblical basis for homosexuality. It was a true, deep friendship that transcended the circumstances in which both men found themselves. It was a wholesome, God-honoring relationship that God used in the lives of both men—and even in the future lives of their families.

As the plot thickens, we come to the third relationship in David's life: the relationship of elevation or exaltation with the people of Israel.

> So David went out wherever Saul sent him, and prospered; and Saul set him over the men of war. And it was pleasing in the sight of all the people and also in the sight of Saul's servants.
>
> 1 Samuel 18:5

David had never served in the army, let alone been in any official role of leadership. But now he commanded the troops, and he did it so well that even the king's servants were impressed.

Despite his youth and inexperience, David knew how to conduct himself with everyone. The servants liked him. The troops followed him. And even Saul, when he was not in the grip of his evil spirit, respected him.

> When David returned from killing the Philistine, . . . the women came out of all the cities of Israel, singing and dancing, to meet King Saul, with tambourines, with joy and with musical instruments.
>
> And the women sang as they played, and said,
> "Saul has slain his thousands,
> And David his ten thousands."
>
> 1 Samuel 18:6–7

They were singing and dancing in the streets, welcoming and honoring this young man who had defended the name of their God. If there is a single statement that best describes David at this time in his life, it would be this one:

> And David was prospering in all his ways for the LORD was with him.
>
> 1 Samuel 18:14

As I mentioned earlier, it says he "prospered" four times in this chapter. That interested me, so I looked up the Hebrew word *sakal* from which "prospered" is derived. I discovered two insightful things about that term. Proverbs 10:19 reveals the first: "When there are many words, transgression is unavoidable, but he who restrains his lips is wise *[sakal]*."

A person who is wise (who *prospers*), knows how to keep his mouth shut. He can keep confidences when people say, "Look, don't share that." That's another characteristic of a good friend, by the way. A good friend can be trusted with the details of your life; he keeps his mouth closed.

Furthermore, when he opens his mouth, he opens it with discretion. That's a sign of a *sakal* person. That was David.

And, the second insight, is in Proverbs 21:11: "When the scoffer is punished, the naive becomes wise; but when the wise is instructed *[sakal]*, he receives knowledge."

The *sakal* person is *teachable*. That's the kind of man David was. He was wise because he guarded his lips, and he kept a teachable spirit. No matter how fast the promotion or how high the exaltation may be, we are never to lose our teachability. We never reach a level where we are above criticism or we no longer need the input of others. And, frankly, there are times when our best lessons can be learned from our enemies.

That leads us to David's fourth relationship, which was one of opposition with Saul. Keep in mind that David had done nothing to deserve the treatment Saul gave him. He was a *sakal* man. His motives were right, his actions were right, his leadership was right, but Saul's jealousy got in the way.

> Then Saul became very angry, for this saying [the praises the women were singing about David] displeased him; and he said, "They have ascribed to David ten thousands, but to me they have ascribed thousands. Now what more can he have but the kingdom?"
>
> And Saul looked at David with suspicion from that day on.
>
> 1 Samuel 18:8–9

First Samuel 18:8 says that "Saul became very angry." The Hebrew word translated "angry" is vivid. *Charah* means "to burn within." We would say Saul did a slow burn.

"For this saying *displeased* him." The Hebrew word here means "inner turmoil." His stomach turned. As Saul did a slow burn, his stomach sort of gripped him.

Then, as fear and worry intensified, Saul became paranoid. "What more can he have now but the kingdom?" His self-talk lost control. "Hey, I've got a problem on my hands. I got a giant-killer who's gonna become a king-killer. What am I gonna do about that?" He's afraid of his own shadow.

That's Saul. Within a matter of minutes, he "looked at David with suspicion from that day on." When imagination is fueled by jealously, suspicion takes over . . . and at that point, dangerous things occur.

David has done nothing to deserve that kind of treatment! He has served God, killed a giant, submitted himself to his superior, and behaved properly. In fact, verse 15 says, "When Saul saw that he was prospering greatly, he dreaded him."

Why? Because Saul saw that God was on David's side, and he realized that he, himself, didn't have that kind of power. It was more than he could handle.

The Bible is so practical, isn't it? Jealousy is a deadly sin, and the suspicion of Saul shackled him in its prison. Because he operated in that tight radius of fear, worry, and paranoia, Saul's great goal in life became twisted. Instead of leading Israel onto bigger and better things, he focused on making David's life miserable. And, as we shall see in the next several chapters, Saul's madness causes him to lose sight of all wholesome and responsible objectives, as David, the object of his jealousy, lives like a fugitive . . . for years. How gracious of God not to reveal to David the pain of those tragic years! With that, we leave him, for now, and glean at least three relevant applications for today.

RELEVANCE: OUR LIVES TODAY

First, *not knowing the future forces us to take one day at a time.* That's the sum and substance of the life of faith. As Jesus taught: "Each day has enough trouble of its own" (Matt. 6:34).

Second, *having an intimate friend helps us face whatever comes our way.* If you don't have a friend, ask God to give you one—someone you can relate to and who will be a source of encouragement and support.

Third, *being positive and wise is the best reaction to an enemy.* When you see your enemy coming, don't roll up your mental sleeves, deciding which jab you will throw. Remember how David handled Saul. David just kept prospering—just kept behaving himself wisely. And when the heat rose, he fled the scene. He refused to fight back or get even.

So if you are rubbing shoulders with a jealous individual, whether it be a roommate, a boss, a friend, or even a mate, remember the model of David.

Living for Christ is the most exciting adventure in the world. But it's hard. G. K. Chesterfield said, "The Christian ideal has not been tried and found wanting; it has been found difficult and left untried."[10] It's a lot easier to punch your enemy's lights out . . . to devise ways to fight back, to get even, because that satisfies your flesh. It's a lot easier to keep than to give, because that comes naturally. It's a lot easier to work up your own suspicion, and when he's not looking, whomp, get in your stroke. But that's not God's way . . . and that's not best.

It boils down to this: Walking in victory is the difference between what pleases us and what pleases God. Like David, we need to stand fast, to do what is right without tiring of it. Plain and simple, that's what pleases God. And in the final analysis, that's why we're left on earth, isn't it?

CHAPTER SIX

Every Crutch Removed

I n the last chapter, we saw how angry and suspicious King Saul became when he heard the people singing David's praises and saw how the young hero prospered. Saul could no longer contain himself.

The writer H. G. Wells says of one of his strange characters, Mr. Polly, "He was not so much a human being as a civil war."[11] I think that is a perfect description of Saul. He became a living civil war, miserable, possessed of an evil spirit, mentally breaking, a suspicious, angry, jealous man. As a result, he struck out against the most trusted and trustworthy servant in his camp—David.

> An evil spirit from God came mightily upon Saul, and he raved in the midst of the house, while David was playing the harp with his hand, as usual; and a spear was in Saul's hand.
>
> And Saul hurled the spear for he thought, "I will pin David to the wall."
>
> 1 Samuel 18:10–11

Stop and picture that volatile scene in your mind. Imagine the mounting pressure. Chances are, you've never had anyone threaten your life, let alone hurl a spear in hopes of killing you. But here's David, doing what he can to lighten the king's dark spirits, when all of a sudden, *whoosh*, a sharp-pointed spear flies right past his head. Suddenly reality strikes. "Man, this guy is nuts! He's out of his head."

Yet the next verse says that "Saul was afraid of David" (18:12). Isn't that intriguing? The very people who are out to get us are often the ones who are afraid of us. That was certainly the case with Saul and David.

> And David was prospering in all his ways for the LORD was with him.
> When Saul saw that he was prospering greatly, he dreaded him.
>
> 1 Samuel 18:14–15

Now, please remember, David had done nothing wrong. He had been a model of humility, dependability, and integrity. He had done right . . . but everything was now backfiring. God begins to pull the crutches from beneath David, one by one. It must have been a terrifying experience for the young man, especially since he had done nothing to deserve such treatment.

> When there was war again, David went out and fought with the Philistines, and defeated them with great slaughter, so that they fled before him.
>
> 1 Samuel 19:8

Obviously, David is now an officer in Saul's army, possibly commanding a battalion or a division of men. In that role of leadership, he went out, battled the Philistines, and defeated them.

> Now there was an evil spirit from the LORD on Saul as he was sitting in his house with his spear in his hand, and David was playing the harp with his hand.
> And Saul tried to pin David to the wall with the spear, but he slipped away out of Saul's presence, so that he struck the spear into the wall. And David fled and escaped that night.
>
> 1 Samuel 19:9–10

THE REMOVAL OF FIVE SIGNIFICANT CRUTCHES

Let's understand, this is now the second time Saul has attacked David with a spear. Mark the words, "David fled and escaped," because you will hear them again and again during this segment of David's life. It becomes a pattern, a means of survival.

The first thing David lost was *the crutch of a good position*. He had been brought into the army, he had proven himself a faithful—even heroic—soldier, and now it's all gone in the flash of a spear. Never again will he serve in Saul's army.

The next crutch God removes is *David's wife*. We haven't talked about her yet, so let's go back a bit in the chronology of David's life. Remember, Saul had promised the man who slew Goliath that he would have his daughter as a wife. But Saul's motives were not pure.

> Now Michal, Saul's daughter, loved David. When they told Saul, the thing was agreeable to him.
>
> And Saul thought, "I will give her to him that she may become a snare to him, and that the hand of the Philistines may be against him."
>
> 1 Samuel 18:20-21

Saul deceitfully used his daughter as a pawn, asking that David pay a dowry for her that required him to kill a hundred Philistines, perhaps secretly hoping that David would be killed instead. David managed to deliver what Saul asked without being killed, which made Saul even more afraid of him, and more desirous of killing him.

After David fled from Saul, he went home to his wife.

> Then Saul sent messengers to David's house to watch him, in order to put him to death in the morning. But Michal, David's wife, told him, saying, "If you do not save your life tonight, tomorrow you will be put to death."
>
> So Michal let David down through a window, and he went out and fled and escaped.
>
> 1 Samuel 19:11–12

David is a fugitive, running to get away from Saul, and Michal deceives her father, so that David can escape. What goes around, comes around.

Now dad faces daughter and says, "What's this all about? Why have you deceived me and let my enemy escape?"

"I had to," she lies. "He threatened to kill me if I didn't help him" (19:17, LB).

In essence, David's wife deliberately walked away from him. Never again will they live in harmony. And her lie doesn't help David; it only deepens Saul's anger against him. Thus, God has removed another crutch—David's wife.

Now David is running through the hills, trying to find some secure place to lean. As we might expect, he goes to Samuel, the man who had anointed him with oil as the chosen one to succeed Saul.

> Now David fled and escaped and came to Samuel at Ramah, and told him all that Saul had done to him. And he and Samuel went and stayed in Naioth.
>
> 1 Samuel 19:18

In an archaeological dig at Naioth some time ago, the archaeologists found ancient remains of what we would call condominiums, houses built back to back, side to side, top to bottom—a mazelike arrangement. No wonder Samuel said, "Let's go to Naioth. That's the kind of place where they can't find us."

So David and Samuel went there together, but no sooner had they gotten there, than someone informed Saul that "David is at Naioth in Ramah." So once again, David was on the move. He "fled from Naioth in Ramah, and came to Jonathan" (19:18–20:1). In the process, *he lost Samuel* as a crutch to lean on.

Gradually, David was losing all his support, everything he might have leaned on: his position in the king's court and in the army, his wife, and now Samuel. David's emotional stability is slowly eroding. The once calm, confident young warrior is feeling the squeeze. We see this clearly in his initial encounter with the next person he seeks out—his closest friend, Jonathan.

David cries out to Jonathan, "Why is your father trying to kill me? What have I done wrong? What sin have I committed? Why is he doing this, Jonathan?"

"This can't be, my friend!" says Jonathan. "You are not going to die. My father does nothing, great or small, without telling me about it. So why would he hide something like this from me? It just can't be!"

> Yet David vowed again, saying, "Your father knows well that I have found favor in your sight, and he has said, 'Do not let Jonathan know this, lest he be grieved.' But truly as the LORD

lives and as your soul lives, *there is hardly a step between me and death.*"

1 Samuel 20:3 (emphasis added)

What a statement! Death was dogging his steps. Ever live like that? A hair's breadth away from death? Some war veterans could identify with that. There was a man in my former congregation who faced that kind of experience during World War II in Italy; his hair turned white virtually overnight in one of those horrendous battles. Makes you wonder if perhaps David began to turn gray young in life.

The truth, of course, was that Saul hated David and wanted him dead. In a poignant exchange, David and Jonathan come to that moment of truth and what it will require.

And Jonathan said to David, "Go in safety, inasmuch as we have sworn to each other in the name of the LORD, saying, 'The LORD will be between me and you, and between my descendants and your descendants forever." Then he rose and departed, while Jonathan went into the city.

1 Samuel 20:42

After working out how Jonathan could signal to David if his life truly was hanging by a thin thread, the two parted company. The story told in 1 Samuel 20 is a very dramatic one. Rather than my attempting to retell it here, I suggest you set this book aside and read the account directly from the Scriptures. The scenes are vividly portrayed and well worth your reading it on your own. Ultimately, Jonathan went in one direction and David went in another.

What a moment that was for David! God had taken away his position, his wife, and Samuel. Now, he loses *his closest friend, Jonathan.*

Then comes the final blow: *David loses self-respect.* That's the last crutch. In fact, it is the lowest tide of a person's life.

Then David arose and fled that day from Saul, and went to Achish king of Gath.

1 Samuel 21:10

Gath? Could it really be Gath? That was where Goliath, the champion of the Philistines, had lived. Gath was the headquarters, the Washington

D.C., the Oval Office of the Philistines. And, of all people, here was David at Gath, of all places, looking for the king!

Was he conspicuous? Without doubt. Here was the man who had killed their champion, walking deliberately into enemy headquarters. As you would expect, David was recognized immediately.

> But the servants of Achish said to him, "Is this not David the king of the land? Did they not sing of this one as they danced, saying, 'Saul has slain his thousands, and David his ten thousands'?"
>
> 1 Samuel 21:11

"This is David of all people. What's he doing here?" Well, David wasn't stupid. You didn't have to hit him over the head. But you won't believe what he did next. Read the following very carefully . . . imagine the scene.

> And David took these words to heart, and greatly feared Achish king of Gath.
>
> So he disguised his sanity before them, and acted insanely in their hands, and scribbled on the doors of the gate, and let his saliva run down into his beard.
>
> 1 Samuel 21:12–13

Oh, man! That's David! That's our champion! Foaming at the mouth, scratching on the gate, looking like a madman as the foam dribbles into his beard. David had hit rock bottom.

I'll tell you, when every one of your crutches is removed, things begin to erode. As the erosion continues, you begin to think differently. And then you begin to replace those thoughts with strange thoughts. And then you begin to lose sight of the truth. And then *you hit bottom.*

Again, never let it be said that the Scriptures lack humor. In the midst of all this tragedy, God offers us a touch of comedy.

> Then Achish said to his servants, "Behold, you see the man behaving as a madman. Why do you bring him to me?
>
> "Do I lack madmen, that you have brought this one to act the madman in my presence? Shall this one come into my house?"
>
> 1 Samuel 21:14–15

"I've got enough nuts in this court already," screams Achish, "don't bring me another one!"

"Get rid of him," is what it implies. David couldn't even find relief in the enemy's camp. Even they tossed him out!

David had a position and he lost it. He had a wife and he lost her. He had a wise counselor, and he lost him. He had a friend, and he lost him. He had self-respect, and he lost it. Not unlike Job, it hit him with such back-to-back force, his head must have spun for hours.

There might be centuries between us and David, but this man and his experiences are more relevant than ever in our times. One of those is the very familiar experience of leaning on others, other people and other things, rather than leaning on the Lord. David knew what it meant to have the crutches stripped away, and so do we.

As children, we lean on our parents. In school, we lean on our teachers, our peers, and even on education itself. As we head toward some ideal or goal, we lean on our hope for the future. When we reach adulthood, we lean on our job or profession, our mate or our financial security. We may lean on an older friend who is like an adult parent to us. All these things can become crutches and can have bad effects in our lives. Three come to mind.

THREE WARNINGS TO ALL WHO PREFER CRUTCHES

First, *crutches become substitutes for God.* Deuteronomy 33:27 says, "The eternal God is a dwelling place, and underneath are the everlasting arms." Only God is to be our strength; in the final analysis, we are to lean only on his everlasting arms.

Isaiah 41:10 says, "Do not fear, for I am with you; do not anxiously look about you, for I am your God. I will strengthen you, surely I will help you, surely I will uphold you with My righteous right hand."

I will hold you up, God says. But as long as you lean on someone else, you can't lean on Me. As long as you lean on some other thing, you won't lean on Me. They become substitutes for Me, so that you are not being upheld by My hand.

Second, *crutches keep our focus horizontal.* When you lean on another person or another thing, your focus is sideways, not vertical. You find yourself constantly looking to that other person, or relying on that thing, that nice, secure bank account that's in the vault. Those things keep our focus horizontal. Human crutches paralyze the walk of faith.

Third, *crutches offer only temporary relief.* I sound like an ad for headache medicine, don't I? But that's actually what we do. We turn to some remedy that will soothe us or comfort us or dull our pain. People take billions of tablets and capsules each year to find a tranquilizing experience in order to endure the storms of life.

Now, I'm not against taking medicine or accepting help when it's necessary. I'm saying when we fall back on those as a regular habit rather than on the Lord, that's when the problem intensifies.

God doesn't give temporary relief. He offers a permanent solution.

Aside from the Bible, there are few books that I have found more helpful or that I have read more often than *The Pursuit of God,* by A. W. Tozer. The finest chapter (in my opinion) is titled "The Blessedness of Possessing Nothing," which is another way of saying, "The Blessedness of Losing All Crutches."

Tozer writes:

> Before the Lord God made man upon the earth He first pre-pared for him by creating a world of useful and pleasant things for his sustenance and delight. In the Genesis account of the creation these are called simply "things." They were made for man's uses, but they were meant always to be external to the man and subservient to him. In the deep heart of the man was a shrine where none but God was worthy to come. Within him was God; without, a thousand gifts which God had showered upon him.
>
> But sin has introduced complications and has made those very gifts of God a potential source of ruin to the soul.
>
> Our woes began when God was forced out of His central shrine and "things" were allowed to enter. Within the human heart "things" have taken over. Men have now by nature no peace within their hearts, for God is crowned there no longer, but there in the moral dusk, stubborn and aggressive usurpers fight among themselves for first place on the throne.
>
> This is not a mere metaphor, but an accurate analysis of our real spiritual trouble. There is within the human heart a tough fibrous root of fallen life whose nature is to possess, always to possess. It covets "things" with a deep and fierce passion. The pronouns "my" and "mine" look innocent enough in print, but their constant and universal use is signif-icant. They express the real nature of the old Adamic man better than a thousand volumes of theology could do. They are

verbal symptoms of our deep disease. The roots of our hearts have grown down into *things*, and we dare not pull up one rootlet lest we die. Things have become necessary to us, a development never originally intended. God's gifts now take the place of God, and the whole course of nature is upset by the monstrous substitution. . . .

There can be no doubt that this possessive clinging to things is one of the most harmful habits in the life. Because it is so natural, it is rarely recognized for the evil that it is; but its outworkings are tragic. . . .

. . . The ancient curse will not go out painlessly; the tough old miser within us will not lie down and die obedient to our command. He must be torn out of our heart like a plant from the soil; he must be extracted in agony and blood like a tooth from the jaw. He must be expelled from our soul by violence as Christ expelled the money changers from the temple. And we shall need to steel ourselves against his piteous begging, and to recognize it as springing out of self-pity, one of the most reprehensible sins of the human heart.[12]

Some of you who read these pages are in the process of having every crutch removed from your life. This creates enormous pain and instability when support we had counted on is torn from us.

For some, it is represented by a broken romance. The man or woman you felt was God's choice has now vanished, and it hurts deeply.

Some of you have witnessed or are witnessing the demise of your marriage. The last possible thing on earth you thought would ever happen is happening.

For some, it has been the death of a dream. Everything you hoped and planned for has gone up in smoke.

Now, you have a choice. You can look around for some other something or someone to lean on—or you can lean on God, and God ALONE.

The prayer Tozer uses to close that chapter is appropriate here:

Father, I want to know Thee, but my coward heart fears to give up its toys. I cannot part with them without inward bleeding, and I do not try to hide from Thee the terror of the parting. I come trembling, but I do come.

Please root from my heart all those things which I have cher-

ished so long and which have become a very part of my living self, so that Thou mayest enter and dwell there without a rival. Then shalt Thou make the place of Thy feet glorious. Then shall my heart have no need of the sun to shine in it, for Thyself wilt be the light of it, and there shall be no night there.

In Jesus' name, Amen.[13]

That's what a man can say when his wife comes home and sighs, "Honey, I've got the doctor's report, and there is a strong chance of a malignancy." That's what a parent can experience when the word comes back, "It's leukemia," or "It's multiple sclerosis," or "It's encephalitis." That's what you can feel when you get the pink slip and it says, "We don't need you any longer on the job." Or when a wife or husband says, "I don't want you any longer."

TWO FINAL LESSONS FOR "LEANERS"

1. There's nothing wrong with leaning, if you lean ultimately and completely on the Lord. In fact, being human you *have* to lean; you can't walk the life of faith alone. That's why you have Christ. You're built to be a leaner. You've got an inner shrine within your heart, and no one can occupy the shrine like He can occupy it. Nothing wrong with leaning, if you're leaning on the Lord.

2. Being stripped of all substitutes is the most painful experience on earth. There is nothing more painful than being stripped of the toys of the heart. So relieve yourselves of them before He has to take them away. Don't make an idol out of your mate or your children. Don't make an idol out of your position. Don't make an idol out of some possession. Enshrine the Lord in your heart and lean only on Him. David needed to learn that all-important principle. Maybe you do, too. It was extremely difficult for him. You can expect the same.

Chapter Seven

For Cave Dwellers Only

D avid had bottomed out.
    In a downward swirl of events, he lost his job, his wife, his home, his counselor, his closest friend, and finally his self-respect. When we left him last, he was dribbling saliva down his beard and scratching on the gate of the enemy like a madman. Realizing that his identity was known by the Philistines, he feigned insanity and then slipped out of the city of Gath. Once more he was a man on the run.

> So David departed from there and escaped to the cave of Adullam. . . .
>
> 1 Samuel 22:1

THE CAVE: HOW IT HAPPENED

This was the lowest moment of David's life to date, and if you want to know how he really felt, just read the song he composed about it, Psalm 142. He had no security, he had no food, he had no one to talk to, he had no promise to cling to, and he had no hope that anything would ever change. He was alone in a dark cave, away from everything and everybody he loved. Everybody except God.

No wonder he wrote this baleful song of sorrow:

I cry aloud with my voice to the LORD;
I make supplication with my voice to the LORD.
I pour out my complaint before Him;
I declare my trouble before Him.
When my spirit was overwhelmed within me,
Thou didst know my path.
In the way where I walk
They have hidden a trap for me.
Look to the right and see;
For there is no one who regards me;
There is no escape for me;
No one cares for my soul.

I cried out to Thee, O LORD;
I said, "Thou art my refuge,
My portion in the land of the living.
Give heed to my cry,
For I am brought very low;
Deliver me from my persecutors,
For they are too strong for me.
Bring my soul out of prison,
So that I may give thanks to Thy name;
The righteous will surround me,
For Thou wilt deal bountifully with me."

Psalm 142

That's the way David felt as a cave dweller. "I don't know of a soul on earth who cares for my soul. I am brought very low. Deliver me, Lord."

Can you feel the loneliness of that desolate spot? The dampness of that cave? Can you feel David's despair? The depths to which his life has sunk? There is no escape. There is nothing left. Nothing.

Yet in the midst of all this, David has not lost sight of God. He cries out for the Lord to deliver him. And here we catch sight of the very heart of the man, that inward place that only God truly sees, that unseen quality that God saw when he chose and anointed the young shepherd boy from Bethlehem.

THE CHALLENGE: WHAT IT INVOLVED

David has been brought to the place where God can truly begin to shape him and use him. When the sovereign God brings us to nothing, it is to reroute our lives, not to end them. Human perspective says, "Aha, you've lost this, you've lost that. You've caused this, you've caused that. You've ruined this, you've ruined that. End your life!" But God says, "No. No. You're in the cave. But that doesn't mean it's curtains. That means it's time to reroute your life. Now's the time to start anew!" That's exactly what he does with David.

David hangs out no shingle. He advertises no need, except to God. He is alone in a cave. And look at what God did. Look who came to join him: "When his brothers and all his father's household heard of it [David's escape to the cave], they went down there to him" (22:1).

Remember, it hasn't been all that long since David's family didn't pay any attention to him. His own father had almost forgotten he existed when Samuel came to the house looking for a possible candidate for the kingship. Samuel had to say, "Are these all your sons?" And Jesse snapped his fingers and said, "Oh, no, I've got a son who keeps the sheep." And later, when he went to the battle and was going to take up arms against Goliath, his brothers put him down, saying, "We know why you're really here. You just want to be seen."

But here he is, broken, at the end, without crutches . . . crushed in spirit. And would you look who comes to him? Those same brothers and his father along with the rest of the household.

Sometimes when you're in the cave, you don't want others around. Sometimes you just can't stand to be with people. You hate to admit it publicly; in fact, you usually don't. But it's true. Sometimes you just want to be alone. And I have a feeling that at that moment in his life, this cave dweller, David, wanted nobody around. Because if he wasn't worth anything to himself, he didn't see his worth to anybody else.

David didn't want his family, but they came. He didn't want them there, but God brought them anyway. They crawled right into that cave with him.

But look! They weren't the only ones.

> And everyone who was in distress, and everyone who was in
> debt, and everyone who was discontented, gathered to him; and

he became captain over them. Now there were about four hundred men with him.

1 Samuel 22:2

What a group! "Everyone who was in distress" came. The Hebrew word here, *zuk,* means not only "in distress," but "under pressure, under stress." So here came hundreds of pressured people.

Second, "everyone who was in debt," made their way there. The Hebrew here, *nashah,* means "to lend on interest, to have a number of creditors." So these were people who couldn't pay their bills.

And third, here came "everyone who was discontented." The Hebrew here, *maar nephesh,* means "to be in bitterness of soul, to have been wronged and mistreated." That group came too.

What does all this mean? Well, in that day the land was aching under the rule of Saul. He had overtaxed the people. He had mistreated them. He was a madman, given to intense depression, and they were suffering the consequences. Some couldn't stand it any longer. So David ended up with a cave full of malcontents. Can you imagine that? It's bad enough to be in there alone feeling like a worm. But to have over 400 more worms crawl in there with you, that's a mess!

But God is at work here. He is rerouting David's life. Sure, the man is in the cave. Sure, he feels worthless. He feels useless. He feels mistreated. He feels misunderstood. That's why he's in the cave. And before he can spit, his brothers come. The rest of his family comes. And then before he can find them a place to sit down, strangers of all sorts begin to drop in. I don't know how the word traveled, but before long there were 400 fellow cave dwellers looking to him as their leader.

That cave was no longer David's escape hatch. If you can believe it, the smelly, dank cave became a place of training for those who were the beginning of the army that would be called "David's mighty men of valor." That's right—this motley crew would become his mighty men in battle, and later they would become his cabinet when he took office. He turned their lives around and built into them order and discipline and character and direction.

David was beaten all the way down, until there was no way to look but up. And when he looked up, God was there, bringing this bunch of unknowns to him little by little until finally they proved themselves to be the mightiest men of Israel. Wow!

What a turning point in David's life, when he made the crucial decision not to walk away. He would accept his situation and make the best of it.

If it was a cave, so be it. If those around him needed leadership, he'd provide it. Who would've ever guessed that the next king of Israel was training his troops in a dark cave where nobody saw and nobody cared. How unusual of God . . . yet how carefully He planned it!

David became a sort of Robin Hood. His Sherwood Forest was the rugged Judean wilderness, with its mountains, caves, and deep wadis. There, he commanded a group of mavericks because God wanted him to become a maverick king. Israel would never see another king like David.

We looked at Psalm 142. Now let's look at two others David wrote, Psalms 57 and 34. We don't know in what order he wrote these, but looking at his life, they seem to fit in this backward order—142 when he was at his lowest moment on his face, Psalm 57 when he's on his knees, and finally Psalm 34 when he's on his feet.

Notice that Psalm 57 is titled "A Mikhtam of David, when he fled from Saul, in the cave" (the descriptive line at the beginning of many of the psalms gives you their author and their context).

> Be gracious to me, O God, be gracious to me,
> For my soul takes refuge in Thee;
> And in the shadow of Thy wings I will take refuge,
> Until destruction passes by.
> I will cry to God Most High,
> To God who accomplishes all things for me.
> He will send from heaven and save me . . . (vv. 1–3).

At this point, David is on his knees. He's still down, but at least he's looking up. He's no longer just looking within. Then he says,

> My soul is among lions;
> I must lie among those who breathe forth fire,
> Even the sons of men, whose teeth are spears and arrows,
> And their tongue a sharp sword . . . (v. 4).

This sounds as though it was written when the strangers began to crowd into the cave. If you've ever worked with malcontents, you know that's true. They are a thankless, coarse, thoughtless body of people, so overwhelmed with their own needs they don't pay attention to anyone else's.

And so David says to God,

Be exalted above the heavens, O God . . .
My heart is steadfast, O God, my heart is steadfast;
I will sing, yes, I will sing praises! . . .
Be exalted above the heavens, O God;
Let Thy glory be above all the earth (vv. 5, 7, 11).

See where David's eyes are now? "O God, You be exalted." In Psalm 142 he's saying, "I'm in the cave, I'm at the end, there's no one on the right hand or left. I have no one who cares." And now in Psalm 57 he says, "Now you be gracious to me, God. I'm stretched, I'm pulled beyond my limits. You meet my needs."

He's crying out his declaration of dependence.

Now look at Psalm 34, which I believe is the third psalm he wrote while in the cave. What a difference. What a change has come over David! He says,

I will bless the LORD at all times
His praise shall continually be in my mouth (v. 1).

Later we learn that David's men became acutely able with the sword and with the bow and arrow. Obviously, they had training practices. They learned how to get their act together in battle. They developed discipline in the ranks. They might have been mavericks, but they are on the way to becoming skilled hunters and courageous fighters.

So David, seeing his men marching in step and using the sword and the spear and the bow with skill, says to them, "Magnify the LORD with me, let us exalt His name together." He's putting their eyes on the Lord. "I sought the LORD, and He answered me, and delivered me from all my fears."

To the distressed among the group he says, "O taste and see that the LORD is good; how blessed is the man who takes refuge in Him!"

To those in debt he says, "O fear the LORD, you His saints; for to those who fear Him, there is no want."

To the discontented he says, "The young lions do lack and suffer hunger; but they who seek the LORD shall not be in want of any good thing."

And finally, he gives sort of a wrap-up lesson to the entire group: "Many are the afflictions of the righteous [dark and lonely are the caves of the righteous]; but the LORD delivers him out of them all."

THE CHANGE: WHY IT OCCURRED

Why did such a major change take place in David's life and attitude?

First, *because David hurt enough to admit his need*. When you are hurting, you need to declare it to someone, and especially to the Lord. David hurt enough to admit his need.

Some years ago, I read one man's moving account of his attempt to get a group of fourteen men and women in the church to communicate with one another at more than a superficial level. Many of these people had been attending the same church for years without knowing anyone else's personal feelings about anything.

In an effort to help them learn how to communicate with one another at a deeper level, this man suggested that various individuals in the group relate some incidents from their past that had helped form their personalities. Much to his disappointment, every one of the fourteen related only positive experiences and feelings.

Near the end of the session, however, one young woman began pouring out her feelings of insecurity, inferiority, and despair. She concluded by stating that all she wanted was what the other people in the group already had.

The man says, "We sat there stunned by the reality which had drawn us irresistibly toward this thin, totally unprotected young woman. It was we who needed what she had: the ability to be open, personal, honest in a vulnerable way. As I looked around the group, I knew that somehow because this theologically unsophisticated, honest woman had turned loose her silence and her pride and had reached out in total honesty that it was safe for us to start becoming one in Christ Jesus."

David hurt enough to admit his need.

Second, *he was honest enough to cry for help*. We have lived under such a veneer for so long in our generation that we hardly know how to cry for help. But God honors such vulnerability. He did then . . . He does now.

And third, *he was humble enough to learn from God*. How tragic it is that we can live in one cave after another and never learn from God. Not David! I love the man's utter humility. If it is to be a cave, then let's not fight it. We'll turn it into a training ground for the future!

As I look at this time in David's life, I cannot help but reflect upon Jesus and His coming from the glories of heaven to accept a body of malcontents and sinners like us.

Some of us are living in an emotional cave, where it is dark and dismal, damp and disillusioning. Perhaps the hardest part of all is that we cannot declare the truth to anybody else because it is so desperate . . . so lonely.

I weary of the philosophy that the Christian life is just one silver-lined cloud after another—just soaring. It is not! Sometimes the Christian life includes a deep, dark cave.

Remember, the conversion of a soul is the miracle of a moment, but the making of a saint is the task of a lifetime. And God isn't about to give up, even when you're in such a cave. He's not through, even though you're the lowest you've ever been.

Sometimes life feels like a dry, barren wind off a lonely desert. And something inside us begins to wilt. At other times it feels more like chilling mist. Seeping through our pores, it numbs our spirit and fogs the path before us. What is it about discouragement that strips our lives of joy and leaves us feeling vulnerable and exposed?

Well, I don't know all the reasons. I don't even know most of the reasons. But I do know one of the reasons: We don't have a refuge. Now think about that. Shelters are hard to come by these days, yet we all need harbors to pull into when we feel weather-worn and blasted by the storm.

I have an old Marine buddy who became a Christian several years after he was discharged from the Corps. Let me tell you, when news of his conversion reached me, I was wonderfully surprised. Shocked is a better word! He was one of those guys you'd never picture being interested in spiritual things. He cursed loudly, drank heavily, fought hard, and chased women. He loved weapons and hated chapel services. In the drill instructor's opinion, he made a GREAT Marine. But God? Well, to put it mildly, he and God weren't on speaking terms when I bumped around with him.

And then one day we ran into each other. As the conversation turned to his salvation, he frowned, looked me right in the eye, put his hand on my shoulder, and admitted: "Chuck, the only thing I miss is that old fellowship all the guys in our outfit used to have down at the slop shoot (that's a term for the tavern on the base). Man, we'd sit around, laugh, tell stories, drink a few beers," he said. "And we'd really let our hair down. It . . . it was great!" And then he paused. "I . . . I just haven't found anything to take the place of that great time we used to enjoy. I ain't got nobody to admit my faults to," he said, ". . . to have 'em put their arms around me and tell me I'm still okay."

You know, my stomach churned when I heard that. Not because I was shocked, but because I really had to agree. The man needed a refuge, someone to hear him out.

That incident reminded me of something I had read several years ago:

The neighborhood bar is possibly the best counterfeit there is to the fellowship Christ wants to give His church. It's an imitation, dispensing liquor instead of grace, escape rather than reality, but it is a permissive, accepting, and inclusive fellowship. It is unshockable. It is democratic. You can tell people secrets and they usually don't tell others or even want to. The bar flourishes not because most people are alcoholics, but because God has put into the human heart the desire to know and be known, to love and be loved, and so many seek a counterfeit at the price of a few beers.

With all my heart I believe that Christ wants His church to be . . . a fellowship where people can come in and say, "I'm sunk!" "I'm beat!" "I've had it!"[14]

Now let me get painfully specific with you. Where do *you* turn when the bottom drops out of *your* life? Or when you face an issue that is embarrassing . . . maybe even scandalous?

You just discovered your son is a practicing homosexual. Where do you go? Your mate is talking separation or divorce. Your daughter has run away for the fourth time . . . and this time you're afraid she's pregnant. How about when you've lost your job and it's your fault. Or, financially, you have blown it. Where do you go when your parent is an alcoholic? Or you find out your wife's having an affair? Where do you turn when you flunk your entrance exam or you mess up the interview? Who do you turn to when you're tossed into jail because you broke the law?[15]

You need a shelter. A listener. Someone who understands. You need a cave to duck into.

But to whom do you turn when there's no one to tell your troubles to? Where do you find encouragement?

David was just such a man, and he turned to the living God and found in Him a place to rest and repair. Cornered, bruised by adversity, struggling with discouragement and despair, he wrote these words in his journal of woes: "In Thee, O LORD, I have taken refuge" (Ps. 31:1).

Failing in strength and wounded in spirit, David cries out his need for a "refuge." The Hebrew term speaks of a protective place, a place of safety and security and secrecy. He tells the Lord that He—Jehovah God—became his refuge. In Him the troubled man found encouragement.

Now, a final, all-important question: *Why do we need a refuge?* As I read through another Psalm (31), I find at least three answers to that question.

First, *we need a refuge because we are in distress and sorrow accompanies us.* You know those feelings, don't you? Your eyes get red from weeping. The heavy weights of sorrow press down. Depression, that serpent of despair, slithers silently through the soul's back door. That's when we need a refuge.

Also, *we need a refuge because we are sinful and guilt accuses us.* You know, there's a lot of pain woven through those words. Embarrassment. Feelings like, "It's my fault." What tough words to choke out! "I'm to blame."

Harried and haunted by self-inflicted sorrow, we desperately search for a place to hide. But perhaps the most devastating blow of all is dealt by others.

That brings me to the third reason we need a refuge. *We need a refuge because we are surrounded by adversaries and misunderstanding assaults us.*

Tortured by the whisperings of others, we feel like a wounded, bleeding mouse in the paws of a hungry cat. The thought of what people are saying is more than we can bear. Gossip (even its name hisses), gives the final shove as we strive for survival at the ragged edge of despair.

Discouraged people don't need critics. They hurt enough already. They don't need more guilt or piled-on distress. They need encouragement. In a word, they need a refuge. A place to hide and heal. A willing, caring, available someone. A confidant. A comrade at arms. You can't find one? Why not share David's shelter? The One he called "my Strength . . . my Mighty Rock . . . my Fortress . . . my Stronghold . . . my High Tower."

We know Him today by another name: Jesus. He's still available . . . even to cave dwellers, lonely people needing someone to care.

CHAPTER EIGHT

Life's Most Subtle Temptation

Though large in stature, Saul was small in character. He was so small, in fact, he couldn't bear to watch someone who was very much his junior in age and experience promoted above him, both in bravery and in popularity. Because of this, David was forced to become a fugitive in the wilderness of Judea, giving his life to training a band of guerrillas now grown to six hundred men. In the meantime, Saul was working overtime to find David . . . and kill him.

> And David stayed in the wilderness in the strongholds, and remained in the hill country in the wilderness of Ziph. *And Saul sought him every day,* but God did not deliver him into his hand.
>
> 1 Samuel 23:14 (emphasis added)

God was preparing David for a new kind of role on the throne of Israel, but David didn't know that. All he knew during these years—*not months, but years*—was that King Saul was dogging his steps every day, waiting for him to be vulnerable so he could wipe him off the earth. And it wasn't just Saul he had to fear; the entire army of Israel was committed to the death of David.

> So Saul summoned all the people for war, to go down to Keilah to besiege David and his men.
>
> 1 Samuel 23:8

Then, just at a moment when it appeared that Saul and his army had David and his band surrounded, Saul got word that the Philistines had raided the land. So Saul broke off his pursuit and returned to take care of the Philistine problem. Once more, Saul's evil plans had been thwarted.

> And David went up from there and stayed in the strongholds of Engedi.
>
> 1 Samuel 23:29

Engedi, which means "spring of the goat," was a perfect hideout for David. I've been to Engedi. It hasn't changed much since the days of David. It was an oasis in the desert wilderness, where there were freshwater springs, waterfalls, lush vegetation, and countless caves in the rocky limestone cliffs, high above the Dead Sea. Engedi was a perfect place to hide. It provided protection and water and a natural lookout spot where he could see for miles around, to guard against any enemy's approach.

David and his men took refuge among the rocks and caves at Engedi. These caves pockmarked the cliffs and were ideal places to camouflage their presence. In battle, the higher location is always superior to the lower, and that's where David was—on the high ground.

So here is David, safe and secure, with a bountiful supply of water. Saul finishes his confrontation with the Philistines and returns to the pursuit of the man for whom hatred burns in his heart.

A UNIQUE SITUATION

> Now it came about when Saul returned from pursuing the Philistines, he was told, saying, "Behold, David is in the wilderness of Engedi."
>
> Then Saul took three thousand chosen men from all Israel, and went to seek David and his men in front of the Rocks of the Wild Goats.
>
> And he came to the sheepfolds on the way, where there was a cave; and Saul went in to relieve himself. Now David and his men were sitting in the inner recesses of the cave.
>
> And the men of David said to him, "Behold, this is the day of which the LORD said to you, 'Behold, I am about to

give your enemy into your hand, and you shall do to him as it
seems good to you.' "

1 Samuel 24:1–4

The Bible is a real book, and this unique story is living proof. In the
midst of his mad rush for vengeance, Saul must answer the call of nature.
So he finds himself crouching in the privacy of a cave—but not just any
cave. He tromps right into the mouth of the cave where David and his
men were hiding. Talk about being vulnerable! Bad enough for the king
to be seen at that moment, but to be in the very presence of the enemy.
Oh, man!

If you ever want to test the carnality of a person, ask him (or her) what
you should do when your enemy is vulnerable. Unless they are men or
women of God, they'll tell you to strike every time.

That's what David's men said. "Hey, here's your opportunity. This is
God's way of providing you a chance to move into the position he's promised you."

These men had been trained to fight, remember. And here was their
enemy at his most vulnerable moment. I mean, he's right there. "Go get
him, David! This is it!"

A SUBTLE TEMPTATION

A moment like that is what I call "the Lord's-will incentive." When
we really want to support our idea, we say, "The Lord led me to do
that." (The Lord gets blamed for all sorts of things He has nothing to
do with.)

They said, "David, God has put him right here. Here's a sword."

So what did David do? He "arose and cut off the edge of Saul's robe
secretly" (24:4).

Can't you see him? (You're smiling.) Saul's there on his haunches,
taking care of his business, looking out of the cave, and David sneaks up
behind him and—*snip*—ever so silently cuts off a piece of his robe!

But instead of later gloating or glorying over what he had done, David
became troubled. It says his "conscience bothered him." He was con-
science-stricken. Why? many may ask. He could have killed Saul, but he
didn't. All he did was cut off part of the king's robe. What's the big deal?
Who cares about part of the robe? So his hem wasn't level anymore. Who's
going to notice?

See, that's the way we rationalize when we yield to temptation. "Who cares if you take a little bit from the company; they've got so much. Man, they made $800,000 profit last year. They won't miss these stamps or a few pieces of stationery."

I have a friend who began to walk with God in earnest, and he said, "When I got to the place that I couldn't even take a paper clip, I knew that God had really gone deep in my life." What belongs to the company doesn't belong to you.

There's no such thing as a small step on the road to temptation or on the pathway to revenge and retaliation. Even a small step in that direction is a wrong step.

David cut off a part of the king's garment, and now he began to experience justified guilt. You see, when you really want to walk with God, you desire to come to terms with every detail. You get bothered by little things. Your conscience bothers you when you snap back, even when it's just a one-sentence statement. You have to make it right. You can't let yourself get away with it. It's when we get away with it and tell ourselves "This doesn't matter" that we're on our way to sliding in neck-deep.

David said, "That wasn't right. Hey, I can't do that." It bothered him.

> So he said to his men, "Far be it from me because of the LORD that I should do this thing to my lord, the LORD's anointed, to stretch out my hand against him, since he is the LORD's anointed."
>
> 1 Samuel 24:6

Years ago, when I was in the Marine Corps, they drilled into us, "You don't salute the man, you salute the rank. If he is a major, even if he's wasted, you salute him because of the rank—he's a major."

That's what David was saying here. "Saul is the king! This is the anointed king. No matter how unfair he has been to me, I haven't any business doing that to him."

So the second thing David did was declare a righteous principle. Had Saul been in the wrong? Absolutely! Was it David's job to make it right? No. *That was God's job.* And David realized that. He saw that even in his little tantalizing mockery, he had been operating in the flesh. "That's not right," he says. "There's a righteous principle here that I am breaking."

And David persuaded his men with these words and did not allow them to rise up against Saul. And Saul arose, left the cave, and went on his way.

1 Samuel 24:7

I love this verse. Here we see a guy who did the right thing and brought a whole group with him. He *persuaded* them with his words. The literal meaning here, strange as it may seem, is "tore apart." He tore them apart with his words. It's from the same Hebrew word used in Isaiah 53 where it says, "He was wounded for our transgressions." It means "pierced through, torn apart, ripped up."

I have a feeling that David's men didn't just stand together and mildly say, "You think you should have done that?"

"No, I really don't."

"Well, we'll really consider that, David."

No, their dialogue must have been heated.

"Don't be a fool, David!"

"Hey, listen man, this wasn't right!"

"DAVID, the guy's done everything but take your life."

"Look, I can't do it!"

Back and forth, back and forth they went, but David stood for a righteous principle until they were persuaded.

Remember this when you are hanging in the balance somewhere. Maybe in your profession. Maybe in the way you've begun to do your business. Perhaps in the way you've done your studies or carried on your lifestyle. You've kind of compromised and sort of waltzed along on very thin wires of rationalization, and you've begun to lean. And God says, "You have no business doing that. Get back where you belong."

"Well, what'll they think?"

Hey, who knows whom you could persuade if you walked with God? Few things are more infectious than a godly lifestyle. The people you rub shoulders with every day need that kind of challenge. Not prudish. Not preachy. Just crackerjack clean living. Just honest-to-goodness, bone-deep, nonhypocritical integrity. Authentic obedience to God.

David persuaded the men because, third, he had absolute confidence in God. He wrestled with his guilt, hung his life on a righteous principle, and then he stood fast in absolute confidence in God to make the situation right, even in face of the opposition. "Vengeance is Mine, I will repay," says the Lord. And David put his confidence in that.

David's son Solomon would later write in his Proverbs, "When a man's ways are pleasing to the LORD, he makes even his enemies to be at peace with him" (16:7). That's a whale of a promise! The word "easy" is not in Proverbs 16:7, however. It's true, but it's not easy.

You say, "I'm gonna live for God, Chuck, as of today." And I'll say to you, "All right, fine, get ready for a battle, because you're surrounded by people who don't." Even in Christian colleges, even in seminaries, you'll be around individuals who operate in the flesh. You can be engaged in cross-cultural work on the mission field and be surrounded by people who live in the flesh. Competitive people. People who are out for what they want. Selfish people. That's where the battle is heated.

"When a man's ways please the LORD, He makes even his enemies to be at peace with him." The whole balance of this story has to do with the outworking of that principle.

Watch what David did about his actions:

> Now afterward David arose and went out of the cave and called after Saul, saying, "My lord the king!" And when Saul looked behind him, David bowed with his face to the ground and prostrated himself.
>
> 1 Samuel 24:8

Saul finishes his business in the cave and goes outside; perhaps he walks down a ravine on the other side. About that time, David chugs out of the cave, clutching the piece of the king's robe in his hand, and calls out to the king across the chasm. He not only alerts the king, his sworn enemy, but then bows before him.

AN UNUSUAL CONVERSATION

> And David said to Saul, "Why do you listen to the words of men, saying, 'Behold, David seeks to harm you'?"
>
> 1 Samuel 24:9

Wait a minute! What's he doing?

This is very, very important. Wrong is being done against David, and when you have been wronged, it is necessary for you to declare the truth. You are responsible for declaring the truth to the enemy, whoever the enemy might be. You cannot change your enemy, but you can be sure he understands the right facts.

Our tendency is to say, "Oh, just leave it alone. It'll all work out." But David didn't leave it alone. He said, "King Saul, you're listening to false counsel. People are telling you lies about me. Why do you listen to them?" Then he said, "Let me give you proof, verbal and visual proof, O King!"

> "Behold, this day your eyes have seen that the LORD had given you today in my hand in the cave, and some said to kill you, but my eye had pity on you; and I said, 'I will not stretch out my hand against my lord, for he is the LORD's anointed.'
>
> "Now, my father, see! Indeed, see the edge of your robe in my hand! For in that I cut off the edge of your robe and did not kill you, know and perceive that there is no evil or rebellion in my hands, and I have not sinned against you, though you are lying in wait for my life to take it."
>
> 1 Samuel 24:10–11

David told Saul the whole unvarnished truth; he told it to the person to whom it mattered most. Not to his comrades or to Saul's friends or to the people of Israel, but to Saul himself. He came to terms with the individual with whom there was the battle. Then he said,

> "May the LORD judge between you and me, and may the LORD avenge me on you; but my hand shall not be against you."
>
> 1 Samuel 24:12

David wasn't dangling his righteousness before Saul. David wasn't built like that. He was a man of integrity. He said, "Saul, I could have taken your life, but I didn't. And here's the proof. When you were vulnerable, I didn't strike. I will let God judge between you and me."

Now look at Saul's response:

> Saul called back, "Is it really you, my son David?" Then he began to cry.
>
> And he said to David, "You are a better man than I am, for you have repaid me good for evil. Yes, you have been wonderfully kind to me today, for when the LORD delivered me into your hand, you didn't kill me.
>
> "Who else in all the world would let his enemy get away

when he had him in his power? May the LORD reward you
well for the kindness you have shown me today."

1 Samuel 24:16–19, LB

Talk about a living example of the proverb, "When a man's ways please
the Lord, He makes even his enemies to be at peace with him."

Now wait a minute. Let's come back to reality. This is one case study.
I wish I could promise you that when you do what is right, your enemy
will always see the error of his ways this quickly and turn and repent and
view you correctly, but I can't make that kind of promise.

You're responsible for telling a person the truth, but it is impossible
to make him change his opinion. He may die believing the lie. But down
inside your heart you will know the fulfillment of that sense of righteous
dealings. Your conscience will be clear.

Saul confessed, "David, you're a better man than I am. I see the whole
picture." He even recognized David as the next king. The handwriting was
on the wall.

> "And now, behold, I know that you shall surely be king, and
> that the kingdom of Israel shall be established in your hand."
>
> 1 Samuel 24:20

Saul recognized, "You're the man, David, not me." And then he asked
David for a favor.

In those days, when a dynasty was overthrown, the new regime would
exterminate everyone in the old regime. So after acknowledging that David
would be the next king, Saul pled for his family.

> "Swear to me by the LORD that you will not cut off my de-
> scendants after me, and that you will not destroy my name
> from my father's household."
>
> And David swore to Saul. And Saul went to his home, but
> David and his men went up to the stronghold.
>
> 1 Samuel 24:21–22

Years later, as we will see, David will keep that promise. For now,
however, David does not return with Saul. Instead, David and his men
went back up to the stronghold, and he was wise to do so. He knew Saul
too well, and he was right. Before long, we will see Saul once again turn
on David.

A PRACTICAL APPLICATION

All this brings me to three helpful principles to live by when it comes to life's most subtle temptation. These are worth remembering when we are mistreated.

First, *since man is depraved, expect to be mistreated.* The same nature that beat in the heart of Saul beats in the heart of every person, yourself included. When we are involved in the flesh, we will respond like Saul.

Or, if you are the person who's doing the mistreatment, the offense, come to terms with it. Call it sin.

Second, *since mistreatment is inevitable, anticipate feelings of revenge.* I'm not saying retaliate. I'm saying anticipate the feelings of revenge, because you can be sure they will come. It's the nature of the beast.

Handling mistreatment doesn't come naturally. Which is why Jesus' truth is so revolutionary: "Do unto others as you would have them do to you,"—*not as they do to you.* Rare is the individual who will not retaliate, or at least not want to.

Third, *since the desire for revenge is predictable, refuse to fight in the flesh.* That's why David came out on top. His men said, "Go get him, David." He almost did, I'm convinced. But when he came near the king, he got cold feet and just cut off a piece of robe instead of plunging his knife in Saul's back. Then he made it right.

Let's leave the ancient scene and bring this truth home to rest today. If you are resentful of the way someone has treated you, if you are holding it against that person, hoping you can retaliate or get back, you need to ask God to free you from that bondage. The secret, plain and simple? Forgiveness! Claim God's power to forgive through Jesus Christ. Begin by asking His forgiveness for excusing and cultivating that deep root of bitterness within your own heart. Ask him to expose it in all its ugliness and put it to death. Jesus Christ, who went through hell for you, can give you the power you need to overcome the worse kind of condition in your life.

The desire for vengeance or revenge—the desire to get even—is, in my opinion, the most subtle temptation in all of life. It might be with an employer who promised you something and didn't come through. It might be with a mate who walked away when you needed him or her the most. It might be with your mom or dad who failed you. It could be with a friend you entrusted with some very intimate information, and the friend not only turned against you and revealed it, but is now telling lies about you. Or maybe a coach who took you off the first string and benched you because of some foolish reason. Or a teacher who refused to hear you out and graded you down. And you live today in the backwash of mistreatment. You have been "done wrong," and you're waiting for the moment to get even.

We call this "my rights," don't we? "I have *my rights!* I'm not a door-mat. I refuse to lie down and let him run his tracks over me anymore. I have *my rights!*"

Or we might call it "justified retaliation." "He's done me wrong, and I'm gonna get back."

But God calls it another word: *vengeance.* And we've seen what he thinks about it in the life of David. Now, check Romans 12 and see what else God says about it: Never pay back evil to anyone. Respect what is right in the sight of all men.

> If possible, so far as it depends on you, be at peace with all men.
> Never take your own revenge, beloved, but leave room for the wrath of God, for it is written, "Vengeance is Mine, I will repay," says the Lord. . . .
> Do not be overcome by evil, but overcome evil with good.
> Romans 12:18–21

How often are you to get revenge? "Never," says God. Not usually. Not sometimes. Not occasionally. Not even once! "Never take your own revenge."

Now, we're not talking about national defense here. We're not talking about defending our shores when the enemy comes. We're not talking about standing up for what is right in the public arena. We're talking about a personal offense where harm was done to us and we didn't like it. It's in the past . . . but we keep fanning the flame by refusing to forgive.

God says, "so far as it depends on you," be at peace with all. In other words, you can't change the other person. All you can do is handle your part, through God's power. "If there's to be any blame," He says, "leave it with Me. Don't you live with it. You do all you can to be at peace." And that starts with forgiveness.

There's a three-step process we go through when we want revenge. First: injury. Second: vulnerability. Third: depravity. When you mix the three together, you get revenge. We saw it in David's life. First, Saul did the injury. Second, he came upon Saul at a vulnerable time. Third, in human depravity he could have plunged in the knife, and it all would have tallied "REVENGE." His colleagues would have applauded, but he would have had that on his conscience for the rest of his life.

Now you may be sitting there under control, thinking, *Why, that's no problem for me. I've got a handle on that.* But before the day is out, it can happen: you suffer a personal injury and you wait in the flesh for the person to be in a vulnerable spot and you'll get in your licks—unless God takes charge.

Let's learn a lesson from David: When life's most subtle temptation attempts to draw you in, refuse to yield. Trust me on this one . . . you'll never regret forgiving someone who doesn't deserve it!

CHAPTER NINE

What to Feed an Angry Man

nger is one of the most debilitating emotions we wrestle with. One reason it is debilitating and paralyzing is that it is so unpredictable—it can be on us almost before we know it . . . and it can wear so many different faces. Sometimes it's just an irritation, or the blurting out of a statement or a word we later wish we hadn't said. Occasionally, however, it comes out with such force that it results in hostile actions.

Another reason it's debilitating is that it's so public. You cannot hide anger; it's on display. It's there for everybody to witness and remember.

The answer, of course, is self-control. But it's one thing to say it, and it's another thing entirely to practice it.

Anger is a choice that easily becomes a habit. One man describes it this way:

> It is a learned reaction to frustration, in which you behave in ways that you would rather not. In fact, severe anger is a form of insanity. You are insane whenever you are not in control of your behavior. Therefore, when you are angry and out of control, you are temporarily insane.[16]

You may be surprised to know how accurately that describes the great man whose life we are examining in this book, a man quoted more often in the New Testament than any other Old Testament character, a man whose biography is the longest of any Old Testament biography.

Yes, David, the remarkable man who modeled patience for years under the spear of Saul, finally lost control and, frankly, for a period of time was temporarily insane with anger. If it were not for a woman named Abigail, the man would have been guilty of murder.

A LITTLE BACKGROUND, PLEASE . . .

In those days most people who were working out in the field were shepherds. They kept the flocks of sheep and the herds of goats that were owned by the wealthy. In our story, the basic problem was one of labor, and the basic conflict had to do with an employer-employee relationship. Basically what happens is that David, the employee, plans to kill his boss.

First, let's set the stage. As we do, you'll see that it's kind of like a one-act play that unfolds in several scenes. First we'll get the background, and then we'll meet the characters, before we encounter the conflict.

Saul was still king, and while the official fighting of Israel was done by the army under his command, David and his six hundred guerrilla fighters had been behind the scenes, fighting various wild tribes in the wilderness of Paran. As such, they were also protecting these shepherds from the attack of wild tribes that would suddenly overrun an area, steal livestock, and assault small villages.

According to the customs of that day, at the time the sheep were sheared it was common for the owner of the animals to set aside a portion of the profit he made and give it to those who had protected his shepherds while they were out in the fields. It was kind of like tipping a waiter. There was no written law saying you had to do it, but it was a way of showing gratitude for a job well done.

David and his men have been faithfully watching out for the flocks of a man named Nabal, and word reached them that he was shearing his sheep. So it's payday. It stands to reason, David thinks, that after the careful protection he and his men have provided it is only fair that they receive some remuneration. The problem is, Nabal is a stingy man and he won't pay up.

LET'S MEET THE MAIN CHARACTERS

When we first meet Nabal, we learn that he "was a man in Maon whose business was in Carmel" (1 Samuel 25:2). Right away that tells us he's probably got some bucks. In fact, it says a little later the man was very rich. Actually, the Hebrew word is *heavy*—the guy was "loaded." Nabal had a lot of money. He had a lot of sheep. He had a lot of goats. In fact, it says he owned 3,000 sheep and 1,000 goats. He was clearly a man of great affluence.

By the way, his name was very appropriate. Nabal means "fool." Understand, that didn't mean a person was simpleminded. In the Scriptures a fool was a person who said, "There is no God." He lived his life as though there were no God. Furthermore, we are told that "the man was harsh" (25:3). The Hebrew word here means "hard, stubborn, belligerent." Furthermore, it says he was "evil in his dealings" (25:3). That means he was dishonest. Quite a combination! Nabal was demanding, deceptive, and unfair.

His wife, however, was just the opposite. Her name was Abigail, and Scripture tells us that she was both intelligent and beautiful (25:3). Literally, it says, she had good understanding and a beautiful form. She was lovely within and without.

Abigail was wise. Her decisions made good sense. She was governed not by her emotions but by good logical thinking. She was a keen-thinking, intelligent woman. And if that weren't enough, she was good-looking. We'll come back to her in a few moments.

Then there's our third character, David, whose well-trained men have been doing their voluntary police work in the fields of Paran in the wilderness near Carmel. In fact, this is the actual report that came back to Abigail from her husband's employees:

> "The men [David's men] were very good to us, and we were not insulted, nor did we miss anything as long as we went about with them, while we were in the fields.
>
> "They were a wall to us both by night and by day, all the time we were with them tending the sheep."
>
> 1 Samuel 25:15–16

That's quite a report. Obviously David and his men had done a great job of protecting Nabal's shepherds from raids by any thieves. They were crackerjack troops who had done their job faithfully, efficiently, and quietly. Unfortunately their employer, Nabal, a foolish man, couldn't have cared less. He lived for one thing: pleasing himself.

NATURAL CONFLICTS THAT OCCURRED

Notice the natural conflicts as this plot begins to unfold. The first conflict, implied in verse 3, is between husband and wife. "The man's name was Nabal, and his wife's name was Abigail. . . . The woman was intelligent and beautiful in appearance, but the man was harsh and evil in his dealings." Their temperaments are different. Their behavior is different. Their attitudes are different. Their philosophies are different. The way they treat others is different. It is interesting to see how this woman handled that conflict with her belligerent, stubborn, hard, deceptive, dishonest husband.

The next conflict is between employer and employee. When it was sheep shearing time,

> David sent ten young men, and David said to the young men, "Go up to Carmel, visit Nabal and greet him in my name; and thus you shall say, 'Have a long life, peace be to you, and peace be to your house, and peace be to all that you have.' "
>
> 1 Samuel 25:5–6

"Shalom, shalom, shalom!" David sends this gracious, peaceful greeting. "Shalom, Nabal! May your tribe, may your flocks, may your profit increase. Enjoy the goodness of life." He also instructs his messengers to say:

> " 'And now I have heard that you have shearers; now your shepherds have been with us and we have not insulted them, nor have they missed anything all the days they were in Carmel.
>
> " 'Ask your young men and they will tell you. Therefore let my young men find favor in your eyes, for we have come on a festive day. Please give whatever you find at hand to your servants and to your son David.' "
>
> 1 Samuel 25:7–8

It's interesting that David didn't go to Nabal himself. Perhaps he didn't want to intimidate the man, didn't want to pull rank or show up with hundreds of horsemen alongside. Instead, he sent a few of his men and said, "Gather up what he brings. Maybe it'll be a load of lambs. Maybe it'll be a few shekels for each of us. Whatever. We'll take what he sends."

So David's men go to Nabal's place, where they communicate David's greeting and then wait for their pay.

> But Nabal answered David's servants, and said, "Who is David? And who is the son of Jesse? There are many servants today who are each breaking away from his master.
>
> "Shall I then take my bread and my water and my meat that I have slaughtered for my shearers, and give it to men whose origin I do not know?"
>
> 1 Samuel 25:10–11

Gracious guy, huh? Notice how many times he says "my . . . my . . . my." Guess where his eyes were: "I . . . my . . . mine."

Now, here's where everything breaks loose. Hold on to your seats. This is David, our hero. The same guy who months before refused to retaliate or fight back, even when Saul was trying to kill him. This is David, master model of patience.

Maybe the men hit David with Nabal's response at a bad time. Let's face it, when men are hungry, they're a little testy. Maybe David's out in the field. He's got the fire going. He can already taste those shish kebabs, the onions and the green peppers and the roasting mutton. But his guys show up empty-handed.

Here's where anger explodes into temporary insanity!

> So David's young men retraced their way and went back; and they came and told him according to all these words.
>
> And David said to his men, "Each of you gird on his sword." So each man girded on his sword. And David also girded on his sword, and about four hundred men went up behind David while two hundred stayed with the baggage.
>
> 1 Samuel 25:12–13

Four hundred men! That'll probably handle Nabal, don't you think? When you overdo something in our house, we have a saying that says, "You're killing a roach with a shotgun." You kill the roach all right . . . but you blow the wall out at the same time. Hey, nobody puts on a sword just to have a discussion, so we have a pretty good idea what's going through David's mind here. But talk about overkill! There's no need to take four hundred men to squash one tightwad. David has lost control.

In his very practical book on the life of David, *The Making of the Man of God,* Alan Redpath writes:

David! David! What is wrong with you? Why, one of the most wonderful things we have learned about you recently is your patience with Saul. You learned to wait upon the Lord, you refused to lift your hand to touch the Lord's anointed, although he had been your enemy for so many years. But now, look at you! Your self-restraint has gone to pieces and a few insulting words from a fool of a man like Nabal has made you see red! David, what's the matter?

"I am justified in doing this," David would reply. "There is no reason why Nabal should treat me as he has. He has repaid all my kindness with insults. I will show him he can't trifle with me. It is one thing to take it from Saul, who is my superior at this point, but this sort of man—this highhanded individual must be taught a lesson!"[17]

This was the third conflict, by the way, between anger and murder. And so far, David has lost the battle. He's completely enraged.

Meanwhile, back at the ranch, put yourself in Abigail's sandals. Candidly, this could be her opportunity to get rid of an obnoxious loser of a husband! She gets word from the servants that David is going to finish him off. She could say something spiritual like, "Oh, I better pray about this." Those thundering hoofbeats are coming down the hill and she's in there praying, "Lord, take him swiftly!" It's her chance! After all, Nabal has set himself up for this! It's time he learned a lesson.

That's the way a carnal wife, or a carnal husband thinks. That's the way a carnal employee thinks. "Oh, boy, now's my chance. He's vulnerable, and it's all his fault anyway. Now's my chance." Depravity on parade.

Instead, observe what happens.

But one of the young men told Abigail, Nabal's wife, saying, "Behold, David sent messengers from the wilderness to greet our master, and he scorned them.

"Yet the men were very good to us, and we were not insulted, nor did we miss anything as long as we went about with them, while we were in the fields.

"They were a wall to us both by night and by day, all the time we were with them tending the sheep.

"Now therefore know and consider what you should do, for evil is plotted against our master and against all his household; and he is such a worthless man that no one can speak to him."

1 Samuel 25:14–17

SUPERNATURAL SOLUTIONS

So here comes the message to Abigail that we mentioned earlier. And note that the messengers come to her, not to Nabal.

Why? Because he wasn't approachable. That's another indication of Abigail's wisdom. She sees her husband for what he is. She knows his weaknesses. And in his weakest moment, Abigail did not fight, she protected. How gracious of her . . . how wise!

> Then Abigail hurried and took two hundred loaves of bread and two jugs of wine and five sheep already prepared and five measures of roasted grain and a hundred clusters of raisins and two hundred cakes of figs, and loaded them on donkeys.
> And she said to her young men, "Go on before me; behold, I am coming after you." But she did not tell her husband Nabal.

1 Samuel 25:18–19

Wow! Two hundred loaves of bread! We do well in our family to get six Big Macs in a hurry. Can you believe this woman? We're talking the world's first catering service. And she didn't even tell her husband!

Some of the very best counsel a man can get comes from his wife, who knows him better than anybody else on earth. The finest kind of constructive help and direction and even exhortation often comes from our mates. They know what to do, when to do it, and they usually do it with the right intention.

Sometimes a wife needs to act in favor of her husband and not say a word to him . . . and here's a classic case in point. For Abigail to approach her obstinate, foolish husband would have been instant suicide. He'd never have let her send this stuff to David. So she went ahead and did it on his behalf. I'm not saying she acted in secret against him. I'm saying she acted without his knowledge, yet in his favor. She ran interference for the man . . . and in doing so, she saved his life, *literally*.

Now, just picture this. David and his men are coming full tilt down the hill. The only thing louder than the horses hoofs are their stomachs growling in hunger. Their anger intensifies with each passing mile.

> And it came about as she was riding on her donkey and coming down by the hidden part of the mountain, that behold, David and his men were coming down toward her; so she met them. . . .
> When Abigail saw David, she hurried and dismounted from her donkey, and fell on her face before David, and bowed herself to the ground.
>
> 1 Samuel 25:20, 23

Abigail had already thought through what she was going to do and what she was going to say. That's the practical side of wisdom. She knew exactly what approach she would take when she encountered David. It wasn't a shoot-from-the-hip. It was a thought-through plan, and three things stand out about it.

Number one, her tact. Number two, her faith. Number three, her loyalty.

First, she fell on her face before David. And look at her tact. Six times she calls herself "your maidservant," and eight times she calls David "my lord." The woman is a study in wisdom.

> "On me alone, my lord, be the blame. And please let your maidservant speak to you, and listen to the words of your maidservant.
> "Please do not let my lord pay attention to this worthless man, Nabal, for as his name is, so is he. Nabal is his name and folly is with him; but I your maidservant did not see the young men of my lord whom you sent."
>
> 1 Samuel 25:24–25

She knew her husband, didn't she? Everyone knew what he was like, so why hide it? Why try to cover up what he had done?

She didn't. And yet she took the responsibility upon herself. "When you sent those ten men and they had that interaction with my husband, I wasn't there to give another kind of response. But I'm here now as an advocate. I'd like to stand as a mediator between this man and all of your men who have been unjustly treated."

"Now therefore, my lord, as the LORD lives, and as your soul lives, since the LORD has restrained you from shedding blood, and from avenging yourself by your own hand, now then let your enemies, and those who seek evil against my lord, be as Nabal.

"And now let this gift which your maidservant has brought to my lord be given to the young men who accompany my lord.

"Please forgive the transgression of your maidservant; for the LORD will certainly make for my lord an enduring house, because my lord is fighting the battles of the LORD, and evil shall not be found in you all your days."

1 Samuel 25:26–28

What faith she had. She says, "David, as I look at you, I'm looking at the next king. Don't ruin your record with a murder. You're bigger than that, David. You have been wronged, but murder isn't the answer. Wait! Wait, David. Take what I've provided and turn around and go back."

"And it shall come about when the LORD shall do for my lord [that's David] according to all the good that He has spoken concerning you, and shall appoint you ruler over Israel [there's her faith], that this will not cause grief or a troubled heart to my lord, both by having shed blood without cause and by my lord having avenged himself. . . ."

1 Samuel 25:30–31

"You'll have to live with that track record, David. You don't need that."

"When the LORD shall deal well with my lord, then remember your maidservant."

1 Samuel 25:31

Oh, what a speech! What a plea!

When you're faced with critical decisions, sometimes you have to do something very creative. Apart from the Bible, there's no handbook that tells you what to do when those times come.

Nabal's life hung in the balance. And depending on how short David's fuse was, that's how long Nabal would live. His wife realized that. She decided, "It will take a lot of food and a pleading message from me to turn that man's heart." And we can be certain that along the way she prayed fervently for God to intervene.

Often when we are faced with a crisis, the standard, garden-variety answer is to sort of tuck your tail between your legs, run into a corner, and let cobwebs form on you. But there is a better way. As long as you have breath in your lungs, you have a purpose for living. You have a reason to exist. No matter how bad that track record might have been, marked by disobedience and compromise through most of your life, you're alive, you're existing. And God says, "There's a reason. And I'm willing to do creative things through you to put you back on your feet. You can lick your wounds if that's your choice. But there's a better way." It will take creativity, it will take determination, it will take constant eyes on the Lord. But when He pulls it off, it's marvelous.

That's what Abigail did with this crisis. She just says, "Remember your maidservant when the tide turns in your life. That's all I ask."

> Then David said to Abigail, "Blessed be the LORD God of Israel, who sent you this day to meet me."
>
> 1 Samuel 24:32

What a guy! Is it any wonder God chose David as a man after His own heart? What a teachable spirit. He's got a sword ready to be unsheathed, and yet he looks at this woman he's never met before and he listens to her without interrupting . . . and he changes his entire demeanor. Talk about a man after God's heart. That's one of the reasons. He was willing to change. (Furthermore, how can any hungry guy get mad at a woman with a crockpot full of hot, delicious chow?)

May God forever keep us flexible and teachable. Someone has a word in season for a blind spot in our lives, and we're nothing more than dummies if we ignore him. David models genuine humility here.

Then he adds,

> "And blessed be your discernment, and blessed be you, who have kept me this day from bloodshed, and from avenging myself by my own hand. . . ."
>
> So David received from her hand what she had brought him, and he said to her, "Go up to your house in peace. See, I have listened to you and granted your request."
>
> 1 Samuel 25:33, 35

Mission accomplished! Everybody wins. David and his men go back full of food and all the wiser.

Fantastic! Abigail goes home, and her husband puts his arm around her and says, "Honey, thanks. You're a great lady . . . more precious than rubies." No. I wish it said that. On the contrary . . .

> Then Abigail came to Nabal, and behold, he was holding a feast in his house, like the feast of a king. And Nabal's heart was merry within him, for he was very drunk; so she did not tell him anything at all until the morning light.
>
> But it came about in the morning, when the wine had gone out of Nabal, that his wife told him these things, and his heart died within him so that he became as a stone.
>
> 1 Samuel 25:36–37

She had stood between her husband and death, but the fool was so drunk she couldn't even tell him about it. So she crawled in bed, pulled up the covers, and went to sleep. I'm sure she poured out her heart to God and got things squared away between herself and the Lord, realizing she might never know what it was like to have a husband who appreciated her.

The next morning, after Nabal sobered up, she told him what had happened. And what was his reaction? The guy had a stroke. Literally. He listened to the story of how 401 guys were on the way to cut off his head, and he got really still, his eyes became glazed. I would imagine! Ten days later, " the LORD struck Nabal, and he died" (25:38).

Isn't it amazing! When you do what is right, without tiring of it, God takes care of the impossible things. As we saw in the previous chapter, "When a man's ways please the Lord, He makes even his enemies to be at peace with him." The same could be said of a woman, of course. There is no impossible situation that God cannot handle. He won't handle it necessarily your way, but He'll handle it.

Seeing Abigail's faithfulness, God let her spend the night depending on Him. And shortly thereafter she buried her husband.

And listen to David's response when he heard that Nabal was dead:

> "Blessed be the LORD, who has pleaded the cause of my re-proach from the hand of Nabal, and so has kept back his ser-

vant from evil. The LORD has returned the evildoing of Nabal on his own head."

1 Samuel 25:29

My, oh my, did David learn a lesson! "Blessed be God. He kept me from murdering this guy—from doing evil. I don't have to fight that kind of battle, that's God's job. If vengeance is required, it is God's to do."

And for both Abigail and David, this story has a happy ending. When he learns that Nabal is dead, David sends a marriage proposal to Abigail, *and she accepts!*

LESSONS LEARNED

Three things strike me as I think about this incident in the life of David . . . and our lives today.

First of all, *whatever you do when conflicts arise, be wise.* If you're not careful, you will handle conflicts in the energy of the flesh. And then . . . you'll be sorry.

What do I mean by being wise? Well, look at the whole picture. Fight against jumping to quick conclusions and seeing only your side. Look both ways. Weigh the differences. There are always two sides on the streets of conflict. Look both ways. Weigh the differences.

The other part of being wise is to pray. Get God's perspective. He gives us the wisdom we need when we ask Him for it.

Second, *take each conflict as it comes . . . and handle it separately.* You may have won a battle yesterday, but that doesn't count when today's skirmish comes. You may have a great measure of patience today, but it makes no difference tomorrow when the attack comes again. God doesn't give you patience on credit. Every day is a new day.

The third thing we can take away from this experience in the life of David is that *whenever you realize that there's nothing you can do, wait.* Wait patiently. Impossible impasses call for a firm application of brakes. Don't keep going.

Restrain yourself from anything hasty. Whenever possible, put on the brakes! Slow down. I've seldom made wise decisions in a hurry. Furthermore, I've seldom felt sorry for things I *didn't* say.

David obviously learned this lesson well, for he writes in Psalm 40,

I waited patiently for the LORD;
And He inclined to me, and heard my cry.

He brought me up out of the pit of destruction, out of the
miry clay;
And He set my feet upon a rock making my footsteps firm.

Psalm 40:1–2

Psalm 40 never says that David's situation changed. It says David
changed. When you wait, your situation may not change, but you will. In
fact, you may discover that the reason for waiting was all for your benefit,
because you're the one who needed to change.

Chapter Ten

Cloudy Days . . . Dark Nights

One of the most famous books ever written was written by a man who was serving his third term in prison. The book he wrote has changed the lives of literally millions of people. The man was John Bunyan, and the book is *The Pilgrim's Progress.*

At one point in this story, while Pilgrim is making the long, arduous journey to the City of God, he falls into a deep, miry, muddy hole called the Slough of Despond. He cannot get out by himself, but when he begins to cry out, Help—a picture of the Holy Spirit—reaches down and lifts him up from his despondency.

If we were to translate Bunyan's Slough of Despond into today's terms, we would call that muddy hole "the pits." There is no way a Christian can go through this life without spending some time in "the pits" . . . and that is where we find David in this chapter.

There is nothing ethically, morally, or spiritually wrong with our experiencing cloudy days and dark nights. They are inevitable. That's why James says, "Consider it all joy WHEN you encounter various trials" (Jas. 1:2). That's not our concern with David.

Our concern is what he did after he fell in the mire. There was a fork in the road, and he took the wrong way. The result was misery, compromise, and, in fact, sixteen long months of disobedience.

WHAT CAUSED THE CLOUDS AND DARKNESS?

Now there were some causes that led to these dark days that David experienced. He didn't just happen to tumble into "the pits." He experienced it because of three things.

Notice, 1 Samuel 27:1 begins, "Then David said to himself. . . ." Oh-oh. There's his first problem. It's important when we talk to ourselves that we tell ourselves the right thing. David didn't. So the very first cause for his dropping into "the pits" is what I would call his *humanistic viewpoint*. He looked at his situation and sized it up strictly from the horizontal. You won't find David praying even once in this chapter. In fact, David never looks up until much later. He wrote no psalms, he asked for no help, he simply pushed the panic button.

David is coming off a spiritual and emotional high. Remember, he could have slain Saul twice, but he didn't. Then he was about to kill Nabal, but Abigail talked him out of that, thankfully. So he's walked in victory for quite some time. He's come off the crest of victory, and, as all of us know, that's a very vulnerable spot.

The second thing that caused David's problem was *pessimistic reasoning*. See what he says to himself: "Now I will perish one day by the hand of Saul" (27:1).

David should have known better. Notice that he says, "I *will* perish." He's talking about something in the future, . . . but the man doesn't know the future. No one does! But pessimistic reasoning continually focuses on the potential downside of the future, and this prompts worry. In the minds of pessimists, the future is inevitably bleak. So we're not surprised to hear his prediction: "I'll perish."

Samuel had anointed him with oil and assured him he would one day be the king. God spoke to him through Abigail and said that the Lord "shall appoint you ruler over Israel" (25:30). God spoke to him more than once through Jonathan, assuring him, "You'll be the next king." Even Saul, his enemy, had said, "I know that you shall surely be king, and that the kingdom of Israel shall be established in your hand" (24:20). But David ignored all of those promises God had given. He now convinces himself, "I'll perish. I'll never rule over Israel . . . never!"

Why are we pessimistic? Because our eyes are on ourselves. You and I have never had the Lord lead us to a pessimistic thought. Never once. They come strictly from within our carnal minds . . . and they can be devastating.

There's a third reason that David was in this deep despondency. It's what we might call *rationalistic logic*.

> Then David said to himself, "Now I will perish one day by the hand of Saul. There is nothing better for me than to escape into the land of the Philistines. . . ."
>
> 1 Samuel 27:1

Can you believe that statement? That's nothing other than rationalism. He thought, "Times are hard. God has deserted me. I thought I could be king, but I'll never be king. I'm gonna die if I keep on the front edge of Saul's army. They'll finally catch up with me. I'll have to escape. The best solution is to go to Philistia."

Well, for sure Saul wouldn't look for him in the Philistine camp! The adversary lived there. What a picture this is of a Christian who deliberately opts for carnality.

We don't hear much about the carnal Christian, do we? We hear a lot about the lost person who's never met Jesus Christ. We hear a great deal about the saved person who's walking in victory. But not much is said about the believer who chooses to disobey God and operate in the flesh. David, at this point in his life, is a clear illustration of a man who is a believer on the inside, but on the outside he looks just like a nonbeliever because of the way he's living his life.

Psychologist Rollo May has said, "Man is the only animal that runs faster when he has lost his way." Isn't it remarkable how when we lose our way, we move quickly in the wrong direction and play into the adversary's hand? That's *exactly* what David did.

Now you might think that this kind of decision doesn't affect anybody but yourself. I've even heard Christians say, "I'll take my lumps. I'll choose this route and I'll live with the consequences." Wait a minute. Nobody takes his lumps alone. You drag others with you. If it's true that no man lives to himself, and no man dies to himself . . . then we can be certain that no man sins to himself either.

HOW EXTENSIVE WERE THE CONSEQUENCES?

Just look at what happened following David's decision.

> So David arose and crossed over, he and the six hundred men who were with him, to Achish the son of Maoch, king of Gath. And David lived with Achish at Gath, he and his men, each

99

with his household, even David with his two wives, Ahinoam
. . . and Abigail. . . .

1 Samuel 27:2–3

When David left his wilderness home in Israel and retreated into Philistine country, he didn't go alone. He's the commander-in-chief of the
guerrilla troops, remember. The men he's trained in the cave of Adullam
are bonded to him. They have lived together and have done battle together
in the wilderness as well as among the border tribes. David surely knew
they would follow him.

But it is not only his fighting men who go with them. They also bring
their households . . . and David's two wives, Ahinoam and Abigail, go along
as well. So now we have David and his family plus six hundred more
households.

You think you can compromise and it won't affect your family? You
do not live independently of everyone else. When you make a decision
that is wrong, when you choose a course that is not God's plan, it affects
those who trust you and depend on you, those who look up to you and
believe in you. Though innocent, they become contaminated by your sinful
choices.

And where did David go? He fled to Gath. Remember Gath? We've
been there before with David. Remember the giant? Remember his home-
town? He was known as Goliath of Gath. Strangely, that's where David's
headed. Can you believe it? Only a few years earlier he slew Goliath in the
Valley of Elah. Now he runs to Gath, the very home of that giant, and
decides he'll live there with Achish, the king—the archenemy of the Israelites. It says,

Now it was told Saul that David had fled to Gath, so he [Saul]
no longer searched for him.

1 Samuel 27:4

The first consequence of David's poor decision, then, was that *it created
a false sense of security* because Saul had stopped following him. "Hey, I'm
safe in here. Saul has stopped dogging my every move, hunting and haunting me. The pressure's gone! What a relief!"

Sin has its temporary pleasures. Disobedience has its exhilarating moments. We're fools to deny it. There are times when we relax and enjoy
disobedience because of those pleasures . . . but they are passing, they are
short-lived . . . they never bring ultimate satisfaction. Never. Never!

Here is a case in point. We often think the pleasures of sin are obvious, overt pleasures. But sometimes it's just a release of pressure. When we're feeling the intensity of responsibility, walking with God, and we opt for the wrong destination, suddenly there's a release of pressure. We think, *This is great! It pays off.* When that happens, watch out. Destruction is near.

The second consequence of David's decision is found in verse 5. If you can believe it, here's the giant-killer talking to the king of Gath. Listen to his words:

> Then David said to Achish, "If now I have found favor in your sight, let them [the citizens of Gath] give me a place in one of the cities in the country, that I may live there; for why should your servant live in the royal city with you?"
>
> 1 Samuel 27:5

The second consequence is *submission to the adversary's cause*. When we choose a disobedient lifestyle, when we give ourselves to carnality rather than spirituality, we begin to serve the adversary's cause. We actually submit to the enemy and willingly serve his wicked cause. Man! I can't believe David calls himself the "servant" of Achish. But that's exactly what he is.

> So Achish gave him Ziklag that day; therefore Ziklag has belonged to the kings of Judah to this day.
> And the number of days that David lived in the country of the Philistines was a year and four months.
>
> 1 Samuel 27:6–7

So the third consequence is *a lengthy period of compromise*. You say, "Oh, it won't hurt. A day or two here, and I can get back into the swing of things. What's a couple months of carnality compared to a lifetime of obedience?" It doesn't work like that. There is something magnetic about slumping into despondency and beginning a lost-world lifestyle. The pull is deadly. Scars are formed in our (and others') memory.

When Abraham went down to Egypt, he stayed for quite a while. When his nephew, Lot, went to Sodom, he pitched his tent nearby, but before long, he was living in the city itself. Erosion set in. Eventually, Lot became one of the elders who sat at the gate of the city. Ultimately, he became identified with Sodom, intoxicated by its shameless lifestyle.

Now David, when he goes to Gath, ends up staying for *sixteen months.*

This is the man known as "the sweet psalmist of Israel" (2 Sam. 23:1). Yet there's not one psalm attributed to those days when he was with Achish in Gath and Ziklag. Of course not! The sweet singer of Israel was mute. He wrote no songs when he was in this slump. He couldn't sing the Lord's song in a foreign land governed by the enemy's influence! As the Jewish captives in Babylon would later ask, "How can we sing the LORD's song in a foreign land?" (Ps. 137:4). There is not much joy flowing out of David's life during this carnal interlude in Gath.

Even Achish saw David's decision for what it was: a desertion; a defection. David, who has walked with God, now walks away from Him. How tragic! Sometime later, Achish pinpoints it like this:

> Then the commanders of the Philistines said, "What are these Hebrews doing here?" Achish said to the commanders of the Philistines, "Is this not David, the servant of Saul the king of Israel, who has been with me these days, or rather these years, and I have found no fault in him from the day he deserted to me to this day?"
>
> 1 Samuel 29:3

DAVID "SOWS THE WIND"

As David opts for this lifestyle, the winds and storms begin to increase in a rather rapid movement of events.

First of all, a *duplicity* begins to mark David's steps. Webster says that duplicity is "deception by pretending." You pretend to entertain one set of feelings, but really you're operating from another entirely.

Deep inside, David is an Israelite. He will always be an Israelite. But he's trying to make the Philistines think that he is on their side. That's what happens when you spend your time in what a pastor friend of mine calls the "carnal corral." Inside, you're a believer, but on the outside you want to look like the rest of the world. There's a lack of absolute allegiance. This miserable dilemma creates the need to compromise.

And that's precisely what David begins to act out.

> Now David and his men went up and raided the Geshurites and the Girzites and the Amalekites; for they were the inhabitants of the land from ancient times. . . .

And David attacked the land and did not leave a man or a woman alive. . . .

1 Samuel 27:8–9

The Geshurites and Girzites and Amalekites were the enemies of Israel, but they were not enemies of the Philistines. Still, they were not their allies either. Sort of like the Russian-American dilemma in the Second World War. While they were enemies of Nazi Germany, they were not really our allies. So when David slaughters these Geshurites and Girzites and Amalekites, he slaughters people who are neither enemies nor allies of Philistia.

Apparently David was accountable to Achish for his actions, and when he returns to the city, the king asks for a report. "Where have you been? Where have you made a raid today?"

Duplicity leads to *vagueness*. David answers, "Against the Negev of Judah" (27:10). *Negev* is a broad Hebrew word meaning "south," so David was saying, "Oh, I was fighting in the southern part of Judah," implying that he was killing the people of Judah, who were Israelites. But he wasn't killing Israelites. He was killing Amalekites and Geshurites and Girzites.

David is more than vague, though. He says he has been fighting against the Negev of Judah "and against the Jerahmeelites and the Kenites." That is a lie. He didn't fight those people. That's why he wiped out those he did fight, so the word wouldn't get back about what he had really done. He was covering his tracks, you see, so nobody would really know where he was or exactly what he had done.

And David did not leave a man or a woman alive, to bring to Gath, saying, "Lest they should tell about us, saying, 'So has David done and so has been his practice all the time he has lived in the country of the Philistines.'"

1 Samuel 27:11

When you operate in the "carnal corral," you also operate under a cloak of secrecy. You don't want to be accountable. You don't want anybody asking. So you cover up.

He must have done a good job, because Achish believed him.

So Achish believed David, saying, "He has surely made himself odious among his people Israel; therefore he will become my servant forever."

1 Samuel 27:12

DAVID "REAPS THE WHIRLWIND"

Because David earlier opted for the wrong fork in the road, he began living a style of life that resulted in incredible inner turmoil. I want you to see the injury and devastation that happened inside David as a result. Ultimately, he came to a point of utter despair.

First, *David loses his identity.*

Achish begins getting flak from the people of Philistia. They want to know why David and his men and all their households are in their midst. "Why in the world are all those Israelites living down in Ziklag?" These people were their sworn enemies. David was, in fact, the man who had killed their mighty champion, Goliath.

Achish defends David. "Hey, everything's okay. David's our guy now."

But the people said, "No, we don't want him down there. We don't trust him."

And so Achish has to confront David with the fact that they can no longer tolerate having him around.

> Then Achish called David and said to him, "As the LORD lives, you have been upright, and your going out and your coming in with me in the army are pleasing in my sight; for I have not found evil in you from the day of your coming to me to this day. Nevertheless, you are not pleasing in the sight of the lords.
>
> "Now therefore return, and go in peace, that you may not displease the lords of the Philistines."
>
> And David said to Achish, "But what have I done? . . ."
>
> 1 Samuel 29:6–8

David becomes a man without a country. He becomes a displaced person. The loss of identity is the first turn in the downward spiral of carnality. Who am I? What is my mission? Where am I going? What's all of this about, this stuff that I believed all my life? Who has my true allegiance? Tough questions . . . no answers.

David is facing a real identity crisis. He's a displaced person. He's become neither Philistine nor Israelite. Like the carnal Christian, he doesn't feel comfortable in the things of God, but he's now losing interest in his life in the pits. It's a battle for identity.

Second, *David loses his satisfaction.*

And David said to Achish, "But what have I done? And what have you found in your servant from the day when I came before you to this day, that I may not go and fight against the enemies of my lord the king?"

1 Samuel 29:8

David now has to wrestle with disillusionment. The few benefits of carnality are being eclipsed by the many liabilities. When one first walks away from God, it feels pleasurable and freeing, maybe even delightful. But after a while the bills come due and you gotta pay the piper. It's when you start paying the piper that disillusionment sets in.

After displacement and disillusionment, *David descends into depression.*

Then it happened when David and his men came to Ziklag on the third day, that the Amalekites had made a raid on the Negev and on Ziklag, and had overthrown Ziklag and burned it with fire. . . .

And when David and his men came to the city, behold, it was burned with fire, and their wives and their sons and their daughters had been taken captive.

Then David and the people who were with him lifted their voices and wept until there was no strength in them to weep.

1 Samuel 30:1–4

Put yourself in David's stirrups. He comes up over the hill on horseback, and there before him in the distance is the city where he and his men have lived for the past year and a half . . . and the entire place is burned to the ground. Worse than the physical destruction, though, was the personal cost. All of their wives and children had been taken away as captives by the enemy—the Amalekites, the same people David had raided earlier.

David and his men wept until they had no more tears. If you've cried that long, then you know the depth of such depression.

Now look at what happened.

David was greatly distressed because the people spoke of stoning him, for all the people were embittered, each one because of his sons and daughters.

1 Samuel 30:6

The fourth step down was distrust. The very people who had looked to David as a guide and a friend and a leader now turned away, embittered at the results. The guys he had trained in the cave, his crack troops from the wilderness of Paran, these guys are now grumbling, "We don't trust David anymore." Mutiny now boarded the bus of carnality.

David had reached the point in life where some people think of taking their own lives. He was so far down the ladder of despair that he'd reached the bottom rung. The last stop. The place where you either jump off into oblivion or you cry out to God for His forgiveness. For rescue. The wonderful thing is that we do have that choice, because God never gives up on His children.

David made the right choice.

> David was greatly distressed.... But David strengthened himself in the LORD his God.
>
> 1 Samuel 30:6

Now you're talking, David. That's the way to handle the Slough of Despond. The pits may seem bottomless, but there's hope above. Reach up! Help is there.

For the first time in sixteen months, David looks up, and he says, "Oh, God, help me." And He does. He always will. He is "a very present help" when needed.

Dark days call for right thinking and vertical focus. That's what David learns at this moment in his life. He finds that the Slough of Despond isn't designed to throw him on his back and suck him under . . . it's designed to bring him to his knees so he will look up.

Perhaps you have known the joys and ecstasies of walking with Christ, but in a moment of despondency you've opted for the wrong fork in the road and you're now in the camp of carnality . . . you're living in the "carnal corral." In the words of the prophet, you've been like those who "sow the wind, and . . . reap the whirlwind" (Hos. 8:7).

But, like David, you've gotten tired of feeling displaced. The disillusionment has bred distrust . . . and the depression is killing you.

Reach up. Come home. The Father is waiting at the door, ready to forgive and willing to restore. It's time to return . . . to strengthen yourself, yet again, in the Lord your God.

CHAPTER ELEVEN

Two Deaths . . . a Study in Contrast

What do you think those who survive you will write as your epitaph? What will your obituary say? What words will be used in the eulogy to sum up your life?

Saul's epitaph was a sad one, summing up the tragic life of this man who played such an important role in David's life. He was a king who could have been David's role model and mentor, but who instead almost became his murderer.

Saul's epitaph, in five words, appears in the twenty-sixth chapter of 1 Samuel.

> Then Saul said, "I have sinned. Return, my son David, for I will not harm you again because my life was precious in your sight this day. Behold, *I have played the fool* and have committed a serious error."
>
> 1 Samuel 26:21 (emphasis added)

"I HAVE PLAYED THE FOOL." How aptly that describes the life of Saul. "I had God on my side, yet I lived as though He did not exist. There was a great, glorious sunrise in my career in which He anointed me as the king, or at least the people did. I was the pick of the litter in Israel. I was a head above all the other men. I was handsome. I was winsome. I was a strong, natural leader. I was the man who could do the job. The people of Israel chose me to lead them. But they didn't know the inside of me. I have played the fool."

J. Sidlow Baxter describes what it means to play the fool.

> A man plays the fool when he neglects his godly friends, as Saul neglected Samuel. A man plays the fool when he goes on enterprises for God before God has sent him, as Saul did. A man plays the fool when he disobeys God even in seemingly small matters, as Saul at first did; for such disobedience nearly always leads on to worse default. A man plays the fool when he tries to cover up his disobedience to God by religious excuses, as Saul did. "To obey is better than sacrifice." A man plays the fool when he tries to persuade himself that he is doing the will of God, as Saul tried to persuade himself, when all the time, deep down in his heart, he knows otherwise. A man plays the fool when he allows some jealousy or hatred to master and enslave and deprave him, as Saul did, toward David. A man plays the fool when he knowingly fights against God, as Saul did in hunting David, to save his own face. A man plays the fool when he turns from God, from the God he has grieved, and seeks an alternative in spiritism, in traffic with spirits in the beyond. The end of all these ways of sin and folly is moral and spiritual suicide. We can only finish any such downgrade course with the pathetic groan of Saul, *I have played the fool.*"[18]

Saul did all of those things, and at this point in time, he knew it. He willfully disobeyed and he offered these words for his tombstone, "I've played the fool. People look at me and think, *My, what a king.* But God sees us from deep within and He says of me: 'What a fool. What a foolish, empty life.'"

But Saul not only lived a foolish life, he died a tragic death. When you read the account, you can hardly believe it's the same Saul of whom Samuel once said,

> "Has not the LORD anointed you a ruler over His inheritance? . . .
>
> "The Spirit of the LORD will come upon you mightily, and you shall . . . be changed into another man.

"And it shall be when these signs come to you, do for
yourself what the occasion requires; for God is with you."

1 Samuel 10:1, 6–7

SAUL'S DEMISE: A PATHETIC TRAGEDY

Here is the sad account of the ending of Saul's life.

> Now the Philistines were fighting against Israel, and the men
> of Israel fled from before the Philistines and fell slain on Mount
> Gilboa.
>
> And the Philistines overtook Saul and his sons; and the
> Philistines killed Jonathan and Abinadab and Malchi-shua the
> sons of Saul.
>
> And the battle went heavily against Saul, and the archers
> hit him; and he was badly wounded by the archers.
>
> Then Saul said to his armor bearer, "Draw your sword and
> pierce me through with it, lest these uncircumcised come and
> pierce me through and make sport of me." But his armor bearer
> would not, for he was greatly afraid. So Saul took his sword
> and fell on it. . . .
>
> Thus Saul died. . . .
>
> 1 Samuel 31:1–4, 6

The scene is the aftermath of battle, a massacre, a place of unimaginable
horror. Bodies litter the ground. The Philistines have come to mop up and
finish off the job. A sadistic bunch those Philistines. They loved bloodshed,
and now they had the enemy king in their sights.

The battle had completely turned against Saul. He and the Israelite
army are in full retreat before the enemy onslaught, and they are overtaken.
The Philistines kill his three sons (one of them being Jonathan, David's
closest friend). All three may have been slaughtered right in front of Saul,
we don't know. Then the archers make a direct hit on the king and he is
badly wounded. The Latin Vulgate reads, "He was wounded in the ab-
domen. It was a mortal wound."

Saul couldn't escape; he was dying. Philistine arrows pierced his body.
His sons lay dead beside him. It's a pathetic sight.

At that moment, he tells his armor bearer, who has remained loyally at his side, "Draw your sword and finish me off."

He does not want to suffer the final indignity of having the hated Philistines make sport of his body or mock him in death. Isn't it interesting, he's very concerned about his image with the enemy but shows little concern for his relationship with God whom he is about to meet?

That happens when disobedience has dulled our senses. We're very, very concerned about what people will say, but somehow we've lost contact with what God thinks and what God might say. There's not a word in the record of Saul's demise about prayer. It says only that Saul fell on his sword and died (31:4).

Saul died an infamous death, but the next scene is even worse.

> And when the men of Israel who were on the other side of the valley, with those who were beyond the Jordan, saw that the men of Israel had fled and that Saul and his sons were dead, they abandoned the cities and fled; then the Philistines came and lived in them.
>
> 1 Samuel 31:7

Thus, the Philistines moved in; they not only sacked the area, they also began to live in the cities in which the Israelites had once lived.

> And it came about on the next day when the Philistines came to strip the slain, that they found Saul and his three sons fallen on Mount Gilboa.
>
> 1 Samuel 31:8

That's normal in battle. When you defeat the enemy, you take all the weapons and equipment you can in the process. It might mean your own survival in days to come if the enemy rallies and the battle rages on. Whatever you take away, their troops cannot use against you in the future. So as the Philistines began to strip the slain, they stumbled upon Saul. Look what follows.

> And they cut off his head, and stripped off his weapons, and sent them throughout the land of the Philistines, to carry the good news to the house of their idols and to the people.
>
> 1 Samuel 31:9

Saul, the man who once knew the joys and blessings of the kingdom, the man who was the representative of God to the chosen people, the man who cared so much about his image, is now dead. His body is mutilated and his severed head is carried from place to place. The Philistines made jest of the man, made light of his death, and, in the process, no doubt, made profane comments about Jehovah, the God of Saul and the Israelites.

> And they put his weapons in the temple of Ashtaroth, and they fastened his body to the wall of Bethshan.
>
> 1 Samuel 31:10

Alfred Edersheim, in his historical writings, has a unique way of expressing in a few eloquent words the truth of scenes like this. He writes:

> And now it was night, a dark Philistine night. The headless bodies of Saul and his sons, deserted by all, swung in the wind on the walls of Bethshan, amid the hoarse music of vultures and jackals.[19]

What a horrible, tragic scene. But the greatest tragedy of all is that it need never have been. This man need never have died like this. But the truth of the matter is he chose his path. He chose inch by inch, day by day to compromise and to live in the light of disobedience. And he spit in the face of the One who gave him grace, as if to say, "I don't need You. I'll live and die as I please." Saul chose his carnal path, so we shouldn't be surprised at the outcome. But it was indeed suffering that need not have been.

F. B. Meyer says,

> This is the bitterest of all—to know that suffering need not have been; that it has resulted from indiscretion and inconsistency; that it is the harvest of one's own sowing; that the vulture which feeds on the vitals is a nestling of one's own rearing. Ah me! This is pain![20]

That is what happens when we inch out compromise or disobedience in our lives, one day after another, nullifying our testimony, living in mediocrity, choosing the easy way, living like the lost world.

When Saul turned off the light at night, the room was filled with guilt and despair and bitterness that ate like acid inside him. But I emphasize again, he *chose* that life. It need not have been.

It's interesting, if you do a little geographical study, you'll find that Bethshan was really not that far from where Saul was inaugurated. Isn't that something? His entire forty years, four full decades as the king, and he made little headway territorially for the nation of Israel. He wound up only a few miles from where he started. His body hung, silhouetted against the moonlit night, a short ride on horseback from where in his heyday the trumpets blasted and he was announced king of Israel. It's a tragic realization; but given his choices, we aren't surprised. Someone, however, did take pity on this man. The inhabitants of Jabesh-gilead, a town east of the Jordan River.

> Now when the inhabitants of Jabesh-gilead heard what the Philistines had done to Saul, all the valiant men rose and walked all night, and took the body of Saul and the bodies of his sons from the wall of Bethshan, and they came to Jabesh, and burned them there.
>
> And they took their bones and buried them under the tamarisk tree of Jabesh, and fasted seven days.
>
> 1 Samuel 31:11–13

CHRIST'S DEATH: A CLASSIC ANALOGY

Behind the great tragedy of Saul's life is a very interesting analogy—an analogy between Saul's death and Christ's death. At first glance, we might say, What in the world would we find common to both Saul and Christ? Actually, there are six analogies worth noting.

First, *Saul's death appeared to be the end of all national hope*. When Saul died, many people must have thought, *That's the end of Israel. The Philistines will surely conquer us now*. In a similar way, Christ's death appeared to be the end of all national *and* spiritual hope. Put yourself in the place of those surrounding the cross. Some of them watching from the safety of the shadows must have thought, *There's no kingdom! We're finished*. Others said, "We believed in a hoax. Our dream was merely a phantom. We're finished." It looked like the end of all national and spiritual hope.

Second, *with Saul's death it seemed that the adversary had won the final victory*. The Philistines marched in triumph, displaying the heads of Saul and his sons, and dangling the bodies for all to see, probably shouting, "We won the victory!" When Christ died, it seemed as though the Adversary of our souls had won. He must have strutted all over the gates of hell declaring, "The victory is mine. I am the conqueror. The Messiah is dead."

Third, *Saul's death paved the way for an entirely new plan of operation and ushered in David's kingly line,* which led to the Messiah. When Jesus Christ died, a whole new operation moved into action and set in motion our great salvation.

Fourth, *Saul's death opened the opportunity for another who would not otherwise have been included in God's line of blessing,* namely David. Christ's death graciously opened the opportunity of salvation's blessing to the Gentile who would never have otherwise been able to enter and come boldly to the throne of grace.

Fifth, *Saul's death ended an era of dissatisfaction and failure.* Christ's death ended an era of law and guilt, introducing an entirely new arrangement based on grace.

Sixth and finally, *Saul's death displayed the foolishness of man.* Christ's death displayed, in human terms, the foolishness of God. Through the "foolishness" of God's plan, He brings to pass the incredible. He takes the preached word and He changes lives because of His Son's death. They bruised and mocked the body of Jesus and soon after His death, His body was hurriedly placed in a grave because the Sabbath was coming. Little did anyone realize that God was on the verge of doing the greatest miracle the world has ever known.

Ruth Harms Calkin puts her finger on our feelings when we go through times like Saul lived and died in. She calls it simply "Take Over."

> At first, Lord, I ask You
> To take sides with me.
> With David the psalmist
> I circled and underlined;
> "The Lord is for me . . ."
> "Maintain my rights, O Lord . . ."
> "Let me stand above my foes . . ."
> But with all my pleading
> I lay drenched in darkness
> Until in utter confusion I cried,
> "No, don't take sides, Lord,
> Just take over."
> And suddenly it was morning.[21]

It is quite possible the Lord is saying to some Sauls who are in the process of living out that kind of need-not-have-been life, "Now is the time to stop." It is time to say, "Lord, don't change sides, just take over." We do, indeed, come before our Lord like sheep, not asking Him to take sides, but just to take control.

OUR DEATH: AN INESCAPABLE REALITY

Like Saul and his sons, we are all going to die. There's no escaping it. That means that rather than denying death, we must come to terms with it.

Sometimes death is sudden. Sometimes it's long and drawn out. Occasionally, it is beautiful, sweet, and peaceful. At other times it is wrenching and hideous, bloody and ugly. There are times, from our viewpoint, it comes too early. On other occasions it seems the cold fingers of death linger too long as some dear soul endures pain and sadness, loneliness and senility. But however it comes . . . *it comes to us all.* There is no escape.

While he was the chaplain of the Senate, Peter Marshall once told this story which underscores death's inescapable reality:

An old legend tells of a merchant in Bagdad who one day sent his servant to the market. Before very long the servant came back, white and trembling, and in great agitation said to his master: "Down in the market place I was jostled by a woman in the crowd, and when I turned around I saw that it was Death that jostled me. She looked at me and made a threatening gesture. Master, please lend me your horse, for I must hasten away to avoid her. I will ride to Samarra and there I will hide, and Death will not find me."

The merchant lent him his horse and the servant galloped away in great haste.

Later the merchant went down to the market place and saw Death standing in the crowd. He went over to her and asked, "Why did you frighten my servant this morning? Why did you make a threatening gesture?"

"That was not a threatening gesture," Death said. "It was only a start of surprise. I was astonished to see him in Bagdad, for I have an appointment with him tonight in Samarra."

Each of us has an appointment in Samarra. But that is cause

for rejoicing—not for fear, provided we have put our trust in Him who alone holds the keys of life and death.[22]

Yes, all of us have our own appointment in Samarra—an appointment we cannot avoid or escape. But here's the good news for Christians: We who know the Lord Jesus Christ carry within ourselves a renewed soul and spirit, that part of us which He invaded at the moment we were born from above—when we became Christians. He has taken up His residence there and has given us a new nature. Though our outer shell hurts and groans and is dying, our inner person is alive and vital, awaiting its home with the Lord. That connection occurs the moment—yes, the very moment—we die.

> Therefore we do not lose heart, but though our outer man is decaying, yet our inner man is being renewed day by day.
>
> For momentary, light affliction is producing for us an eternal weight of glory far beyond all comparison, while we look not at the things which are seen, but at the things which are not seen; for the things which are seen are temporal, but the things which are not seen are eternal.
>
> 2 Corinthians 4:16–18

What role are you playing today? Is it authentic? Is it genuinely Christian? If so, let me return to the questions I asked as you began this chapter. What do you think those who survive you will write as your epitaph? What will your obituary say?

CHAPTER TWELVE

New King, New Throne, Same Lord

Since we have almost come to the halfway point in our study of David's life, it's a good place to stop and take a panoramic view of things.

In considering the details of David's life, we've reached the place where he's about thirty years old. Before we examine the next forty years of his life, let's get a little overall perspective.

A good place to begin this panoramic study would be the last three verses of Psalm 78. Though brief, they provide a general analysis of the life of David.

> He also chose David His servant,
> And took him from the sheepfolds;
> From the care of the ewes with suckling lambs He brought
>   him,
> To shepherd Jacob His people,
> And Israel His inheritance.
> So he shepherded them according to the integrity of his
>   heart,
> And guided them with his skillful hands.
>
> Psalm 78:70–72

You can find all seventy of David's years wrapped up in these three verses. "He chose David His servant" when he was about seventeen. "He took him from the sheepfolds" when he slew the giant and first left the sheep. "He brought him to shepherd Jacob His people" at age thirty. Between the years of seventeen and thirty, you'll recall, David is on the run from Saul. Then, finally, at age thirty he comes to that pinnacle moment in his life when he takes the throne of Israel. And what happened then? "And he shepherded them according to the integrity of his heart and guided them with his skillful hands" for his final forty years.

For the first fifty years of his life, David walked in the integrity of his heart. Though there were a few temporary excursions in the flesh, most of David's young adult years were years of triumph. Then came the tragedy of the last twenty years of his life. The first part of his life is a model of character and integrity, and the last part of his life is a downhill slide until, I believe, David died a broken man with a broken heart.

There's so much more to a life than just chronology, however. When we read a verse like "David was thirty years old when he became king, and he reigned forty years," it is easy to forget what led to his being exalted as the king. Our tendency is to focus on the present moment and to forget the yesterdays or the tomorrows. Some of the yesterdays need to be forgotten and some of the tomorrows need to be left to the Lord without worry, but we need to keep a perspective like God keeps on life.

Our past is like an art gallery. Walking down those corridors of our memory is like walking through an art gallery. On the walls are all of yesterday's pictures: our home, our childhood, our parents, our rearing, the heartaches, the difficulties, the joys and triumphs as well as the abuses and the inequities of our life. Since Jesus Christ our Lord is the same yesterday and today and forever, then we can take the Christ of today and walk with Him into our yesterday and ask Him to remove the pictures that bring bad or defeating memories. In other words, the Christian can let Jesus invade yesterday and deal with those years of affliction—those years which the locusts have eaten (Joel 2:25–26)—and remove those scenes from the corridors of our lives. I have them. You have them. We need to let Him leave the murals that bring pleasure and victory and take down from the walls those things that bring despair and defeat.

Because of David's many mighty acts and the legacy he left, it is easy to forget that for a dozen or more years he lived as a fugitive and spent many hours of discouragement and disillusionment in the wilderness. He was a broken, humbled man during those days as a fugitive. He learned much from those crushing years, but little good would come from his reliving the pain they brought into his life.

Finally, though, he becomes king, the second king of Israel, chosen and anointed by God himself. How did he take the throne? Did he storm into the role and demand everyone to submit to his rule? No. David was a sensitive man. He had learned how to lead and how to rally others around him in the afflictions of his yesterday . . . especially while he was a cave dweller . . . remember?

Often we're better at handling affliction than we are at handling promotions. As Thomas Carlyle, the Scottish essayist and historian, said, "But for one man who can stand prosperity, there are a hundred that will stand adversity."[23] But David was a man faced with success. His predecessor was dead, by his own hand. If there was ever a chance for a person to take life by his own two fists and demand a following, it was now. But he didn't.

After he heard the news of Saul's death . . .

> David inquired of the LORD, saying, "Shall I go up to one of
> the cities of Judah?" And the LORD said to him, "Go up." So
> David said, "Where shall I go up?" And He said, "To Hebron."
>
> 2 Samuel 2:1

FROM FUGITIVE TO MONARCH

David remembered when Samuel anointed him and whispered, "You will be the next king." He remembered that from many years earlier when he was only a teenager, so he asked, "Lord, shall I go up to one of the cities?" He really wanted to know, "Is it time now, Lord?" He didn't rush to the throne and take charge. He waited patiently on God for further instruction. And God revealed His plan to him. He said, in effect, "Begin your reign in Hebron."

In those days the Lord spoke audibly to His servants. Today He speaks from His Word. You might be in a situation where you are wondering, "God has obviously opened the door, and I'm about to walk through it. But . . . is that what I should do?" Our tendency is to race in when there is some benefit that will come our way. Sometimes it's best to begin very quietly . . . to pace our first steps with great care.

Here we see the Lord saying that to the new monarch, David. "No, wait! Even though you are to be king, be humble about it . . . walk carefully. Be sensitive."

"Shall I go up?"

"Go up."

"Where shall I go?"

"Go to Hebron."

And that's precisely what David did. We are told how long he remained in that limited capacity.

> And the time that David was king in Hebron over the house of Judah was seven years and six months.
>
> 2 Samuel 2:11

David is about thirty years old when Saul dies, but he doesn't immediately march into Jerusalem to take over the whole nation. Instead, following God's instruction, he goes to Hebron, where he has a limited reign over the people of Judah for seven and a half years. He doesn't complain. He isn't anxious. He has learned to wait on God.

Surely, at that time there were some satellite kings, some self-appointed hotshots who had been riding on Saul's shirttails, waiting to make their move . . . and David patiently let the Lord take care of every one of them. He just went to Hebron and settled in, knowing that he had the ability to handle the whole nation, but not unless and not until it was God's time. Such humility everyone admires.

Unfortunately, while he was there, David made some decisions he lived to regret. If you turn to 2 Samuel 3, you'll see a couple of them.

> Now there was a long war between the house of Saul and the house of David; and David grew steadily stronger, but the house of Saul grew weaker continually.
>
> 2 Samuel 3:1

Then it goes into what may sound like an uninteresting genealogy, but through it we learn something about the weak side of David's character.

> Sons were born to David at Hebron: his first-born was Amnon, by Ahinoam the Jezreelitess; and his second, Chileab, by Abigail the widow of Nabal the Carmelite; and the third, Absalom the son of Maacah, the daughter of Talmai, king of Geshur; and the fourth, Adonijah the son of Haggith; and the fifth, Shephatiah the son of Abital; and the sixth, Ithream, by David's wife Eglah. These were born to David at Hebron.
>
> 2 Samuel 3:2–5

What does this tell us? David didn't simply have six children . . . he had six children by six different wives. This polygamy was of the one of the dark spots in David's life that later came back to haunt him.

If you chart out a genealogy of David's immediate family, the total size was enormous. Look at the wives that he took in Hebron: Ahinoam, Abigail, Maacah, Haggith, Abital, Eglah. And that's not counting Michal, daughter of Saul, who was his first wife. When David was forced to flee for his life, Saul had given her to another man. Later, during the war between the house of Saul and the house of David, referred to above, David demanded Michal back, even though she was married to another man. After he went to Jerusalem, only one wife is named (besides Michal), and that is Bathsheba, mother of Solomon. But according to 2 Samuel 5:13–16 and 1 Chronicles 3:1–9, David had many other wives and concubines who bore him children in Jerusalem. We don't know anything about most of them.

If I count correctly, David had a total of twenty sons and one daughter, Tamar. She is listed among the children of Maacah in Hebron, who was also the mother of Absalom.

DAVID'S IMMEDIATE FAMILY

I. CHILDREN BORN IN HEBRON—DAVID, AGE 30–37
(2 Sam. 3:2–5, 13–14; 13:1; 1 Chron. 3:1–4)

Wives	*Children*
Ahinoam	Amnon
Abigail	Chileab (Daniel)
Maacah	Absalom and Tamar
Haggith	Adonijah
Abital	Shephatiah
Eglah	Ithream
Michal	(barren)

II. CHILDREN BORN IN JERUSALEM—DAVID, AGE 37–70
(2 Sam. 5:14–16; 1 Chron. 3:5–8; 2 Chron. 11:18)

Wives	*Children*
Bathsheba (Bath-shua)	Shammua (Shimea), Shobab, Nathan, Solomon (Jedidiah)

| Unnamed Wives | Ibhar, Elishua (Elishama), Eliphelet, Nogah, Nepheg, Japhia, Elishama, Eliada (Beeliada), Eliphelet, Jerimoth |

* The total size of David's immediate family is twenty sons and one daughter (excluding concubines and their offspring, who are not named in Scripture, see 2 Sam. 5:13, 15:16; 1 Chron. 3:9)

I want you to keep all this in mind, because David's enormous family becomes an important issue later in his life, especially after his adultery with Bathsheba. He had, along with the wives, some of whom aren't even mentioned, a number of nameless concubines. This sizable family began during his years in Hebron, where he reigned in a limited capacity for seven and a half years.

> Then all the tribes of Israel came to David at Hebron and said, "Behold, we are your bone and your flesh.
>
> "Previously, when Saul was king over us, you were the one who led Israel out and in. And the LORD said to you, 'You will shepherd My people Israel, and you will be a ruler over Israel.' "
>
> So all the elders of Israel came to the king at Hebron, and King David made a covenant with them before the LORD at Hebron; then they anointed David king over Israel.
>
> David was thirty years old when he became king, and he reigned forty years.
>
> At Hebron he reigned over Judah seven years and six months, and in Jerusalem he reigned thirty-three years over all Israel and Judah.
>
> 2 Samuel 5:1–5

DAVID'S AUTHORITY

With his headquarters in Jerusalem, David finally had the limitless reign he had been promised as God's anointed leader. He had great power and great blessing from God.

Now the king and his men went to Jerusalem against the Jebusites, the inhabitants of the land, and . . . David captured the stronghold of Zion, that is the city of David [that's Jerusalem]. . . .

So David lived in the stronghold, and called it the city of David. And David built all around from Millo and inward.

And David became greater and greater, for the LORD God of hosts was with him.

Then Hiram king of Tyre sent messengers to David with cedar trees and carpenters and stonemasons; and they built a house for David.

And David realized that the LORD had established him as king over Israel, and that He had exalted his kingdom for the sake of His people Israel.

2 Samuel 5:6–12

When the blessings began, they overflowed David's cup. Few monarchs have known such remarkable power and prestige.

G. Frederick Owen, a fine historian who writes more like a novelist, describes the reign of David like this:

Everything favored national prosperity for Israel. There was no great power in Western Asia inclined to prevent her becoming a powerful monarchy. . . . The Hittites had been humbled; and Egypt, under the last kings of the twenty-first dynasty, had lost her prestige and had all but collapsed. The Philistines were driven to a narrow portion of their old dominion, and the king of Tyre sought friendly alliance with David.

With a steady hand David set out to force back and defeat Israel's enemies who had constantly crowded, horned, and harassed the Hebrews; Moab and Ammon were conquered; then the Edomites, alarmed at the ever-increasing power of Israel, rose against David, but were routed by Abishai, who penetrated to Petra and became master of the country.

Commercial highways were thrown open and in came merchandise, culture, and wealth from Phoenicia, Damascus, Assyria, Arabia, Egypt, and more distant lands. To his people,

David was king, judge, and general, but to the nations round about, he was the leading power in all the Near Eastern world—the mightiest monarch of the day.[24]

Simply put, that's a lot of clout for any leader to handle, especially for a man as passionate as David. Very few can be trusted with that kind of power, because with it come unique temptations that very few can handle. As we say, "Power corrupts . . . absolute power corrupts absolutely." But remember, the hand of God was with David. Nevertheless, he was still a man. He could still be given to failure. But more on that later. For now, let's enjoy the blessings he enjoys. They have been a long time coming!

David's accomplishments were marvelous. Territorially, he expanded the boundaries of Israel from 6,000 to 60,000 square miles. Incredible! He set up extensive trade routes that reached throughout the known world. And from that, wealth came into Israel like the nation had never known before.

David unified the nation under Jehovah God, creating a national interest in spiritual things. He was not a priest; he was a king . . . but he lifted up the role of the priesthood so that Judaism could operate openly and freely in the land. He destroyed the idol altars.

I say again, David was a remarkable man. He was a brilliant organizer, a brilliant manager, a brilliant planner. He was also a man of brilliant battlefield savvy, who stayed on the leading edge of military defense.

DAVID'S HUMANITY

David was also human—very human—in fact, he had three major failures in his life, three heartbreaking disappointments.

First, *he became so involved in public pursuits that he lost control of his family.* As we saw earlier, the man had too many wives and too many children to lead and rear properly. Being a man of virile passion, he gave himself passionately to these women; the result were too many children who were thrown together to sort of raise themselves. There's little difference between life on the back street and life in the king's palace if there is insufficient parental direction and guidance. A king or queen can produce prodigals and rebels just as easily as those without wealth and rank.

And that's exactly what happened to David. At the height of his reign, when all of these impressive events and accomplishments are happening nationally, it is evident that David had lost touch domestically. He had undisciplined children. As we'll see in chapter 18, Absalom rebelled. He deceived his father and pushed him from the throne. Tragically, David fled like a wounded animal.

Another son, Amnon, raped his own half-sister, Tamar. This horrendous act led to murder and enormous dysfunctional relationships within the royal family. According to the sacred text, David's only reaction was that he "became angry." That was it. He just got mad. Perhaps his own sin and failure with Bathsheba prevented his knowing what to do. Or, if he knew what to do, he didn't do it. Before the public, David was decisive and brilliant; but behind the scenes, within the walls of his own home, he was passive and negligent.

We'll cover it later, but let me mention here that in his later years, when David was an old man, his son Adonijah, like Absalom, also tried to usurp the throne.

> Now Adonijah the son of Haggith exalted himself, saying, "I will be king." So he prepared for himself chariots and horsemen with fifty men to run before him.
>
> And his father had never crossed him at any time by asking, "Why have you done so?"
>
> 1 Kings 1:5–6

Look at that statement! Never once had David "crossed" his son; literally, he had never *pained* his son. What does that mean? Well, how do you pain your child? Obviously, he had failed to train him properly, to discipline him when necessary. Never once had he crossed him, asking, "Why have you done so?" Just as he failed to control Absalom, he also had no control over Adonijah. I could go on (and, later I will), but my point is clear: David became so enamored with public pursuit that he lost control of his family.

David's second failure was that *he indulged himself in extravagant extremes of passion.* Whatever he did, he did it with all his heart. When he fought, he fought to the bitter end, completely vanquishing the enemy. When he loved, he loved with all his heart, and the numerous wives and concubines were examples of this passion.

His appetites also led to inappropriate seasons of leisure. One spring, at the time of year when other kings went out to battle, David stayed at home in Jerusalem. In his passion for leisure, he hung around the house that day, and what an infamous day it proved to be. As you recall, it was the day he fell into sin with Bathsheba. He was indolent. He was lazy. He was indifferent. He became consumed with lust. And his failure to curb his passions for sex led him to uncontrollable desires . . . which resulted in his going to bed with Bathsheba. He then lied to the people around him. When we get to chapter 16, we'll look at those things in greater detail.

J. Oswald Sanders sums it up correctly, "David's greatest fault lay in his yielding to passions of the flesh."[25]

David's third tragic failure was that *he became a victim of self-sufficiency and pride.* In simple terms, David began to believe his own track record.

He said, "Number the people, Joab."

And Joab said, "Why do we want do that?"

And in so many words, David told Joab, "Don't be insolent with me. Don't be insubordinate. You do as I say." So Joab did, and 70,000 died as a judgment from God—judgment against the king's pride. We'll examine all that in chapter 23.

I once heard a seasoned pastor warn a group of ministers about such things. He said that along with the kind of temperament, winsomeness, and charisma it takes to be a dynamic spiritual leader, there also comes a series of easy faults to fall into. To make them easy to remember, he used four words that began with the same letter, "S": silver, sloth, sex, and self. Stop and think of the dynamic leaders who have fallen. Almost without exception, one or more of these four was the avenue of failure.

TWO TIMELESS TRUTHS THAT OUTLIVE KING DAVID

There are at least two timeless principles we can learn from David's reign that apply directly to our own lives.

First, *no pursuit is more important than the cultivation of a godly family.* And second, *no character trait is more needed than genuine integrity.*

In his autobiography *One Life,* the brilliant surgeon who pioneered and performed the first heart transplant, Christiaan Barnard, tells how at the height of his discoveries and his outstanding career, he lost his home.

It was a bright April morning when I drove out of Minneapolis, heading for New York. It seemed a century had passed since I had first arrived . . . a time longer than all the years before it.

125

In New York, I put the car on a boat and caught a plane for South Africa. At Cape Town, a northwest wind was blowing, and we came in over the sea with the waves close below.

[My wife] was there with the children. I had written little in the last two months, yet I was unprepared for her greeting.

"Why did you come back? Why didn't you stay in America and never come home again?"

There was no longer a smile in her eyes, and her lips seemed to wait for nothing.

Oh God, I thought, I've made the most terrible mistake of my life.

"Don't look so surprised," she said. "We gave you up. We decided you were never coming back."

"It was only a little delay." I said. "I wrote you about it. We were building valves, aortic valves."

"You were also building a family," she said, "I mean, once upon a time you were building one, until you dumped it into my lap."

"We have ceased to exist for you. . . ."

I wanted to say that I came home because I loved my children and believed I loved her. I did it because I felt it. What could I say now that would not sound meaningless?

It began to rain. The city was gray under a gray sky. It was winter in Cape Town, and in Minneapolis, spring was already there. How was it possible to lose a whole springtime?[26]

David also lost a whole springtime . . . and much, much more.

When God measured the tree of David's life, however, He didn't condemn it to be cut down for kindling. In His great love, mercy, and grace, He honored the many efforts of this man on behalf of God's people and the name of Jehovah, as well as the integrity of the heart.

After all these years, David's life still casts a shadow across our own lives. Sometimes, in the drab winter months, on the heels of heavy rains and gray skies, we need to take a good long look at the places in our lives that need our attention . . . those places where we are vulnerable to temptation. We need to ask the Lord to clear away those paths that have been scarred with the litter of yesterday. We need to be people of integrity who care enough about yesterday to make it right with our children today.

There is no person or righteous cause that the enemy of our soul will not try to destroy, and he loves to multiply his victories. If David were here, he would tell us to beware—the Enemy is always lurking, relentlessly seeking to destroy.

THREE LASTING LESSONS LEARNED AT DAVID'S EXPENSE

Three lessons linger as I close the pages of 2 Samuel, chapters 1 through 5.

1. *Prosperity and ease are perilous times, not merely blessings.* In C. S. Lewis's *Screwtape Letters,* he says, "The long, dull, monotonous years of middle-aged prosperity or middle-aged adversity are excellent campaigning weather [for the devil]."[27]

   Have you hit the middle-aged strides where you don't have to worry too much about the things that used to take a lot of time? Take heed! Prosperity and ease are more often than not, perilous times.

2. *Gross sin is a culmination of a process, not a sudden act.* Back in 2 Samuel 3, you'll remember, David was already amassing his fortune along with a number of wives. But when was enough enough? When he had a harem full of them and he was still not satisfied, driven by lust for more? Gross sin isn't a sudden action, it's a process that culminates. And one who commits it says to himself in the morning hours that follow, "I can't believe I did that." That's certainly what David must have said.

3. *Confession and repentance help heal a wound, but they will never erase all the scars.* If we're honest enough to admit it, there are times that we sin, saying, "Well, I can do this now and then confess and repent, and God will forgive me." And that's true. But I must warn you, you can never erase the scars. He will heal the wound, but He will leave the scars. And your children may suffer as a result, and their children after them. That's the heartache of it all. Sin has terrible wages.

The only hope we have is daily dependence on the living Lord. It's the only way we can make it. He's touched with our feelings of infirmity, our weaknesses, our inability in the dark and lonely times to say no. He's touched with that. And He says, "I'm ready with all the power you need. Call on Me and I'll give you what you need."

So? Call on Him! Stop this moment and call on Him. He will hear and heed our cry. I know. In recent days I've done just that . . . and He has provided the strength I needed to go on.

CHAPTER THIRTEEN

David and the Ark

When you mention David, most people will immediately make the connection, "Oh, yes, David and Goliath." Or they will picture David as the man who fell into sin with Bathsheba. When some hear the name David, they think of the time that Samuel anointed him to be king, when David was just a teenager. Some think of David the warrior. Or of David and Saul. Or of David's great and loyal friendship with Jonathan. As a father, I tend to think of David as a grieving, broken man, dissolved in tears after hearing of the untimely death of his son, Absalom.

But none of those things are the things that God remembers about His faithful king—His choice, His man. If you want to see what God remembers about David, you'll have to turn to the New Testament, the book of Acts, chapter 13, verse 22. There, the speaker is Paul. He was addressing a group of people who knew their Jewish history. He was developing a message that was going to end with the person of Christ, but in the process, he reminded them of scenes from the past. He tells them how the Israelites asked for a king and God gave them Saul. And then he says,

> "And after He [God] had removed him [Saul], He raised up David to be their king, concerning whom He also testified and said, 'I have found David the son of Jesse, a man after My heart, who will do all My will.'"
>
> Acts 13:22

What an epitaph! Not, "I found David to be a great warrior," or, "I found David to be a faithful shepherd," or, "I found David to be a brilliant king"—none of those things. It says, "I found David to care about the things I care about. He's a man whose heart beats in sync with Mine. When I look to the right, David looks to the right. When I look to the left, David looks to the left. And when I say, 'I care about that,' David says, 'I care about that, too.'" That's being a man, a person, after God's heart.

Some of us look upon life as, "Well, you win some, you lose some. You just pull it off the best you can. Nobody's perfect." Others say, "If God says it, I want to do it." The latter are the ones who are "after God's heart."

In the family of God there are those two categories of people. Those in the first group spend a lot of time in the "carnal corral"—a lot of time moaning and complaining and later recovering from journeys that are far from His plan and will. But the others don't get very far at all before they start taking account of where they are. They keep short accounts. They come back in line quickly, because they're "after His heart." To those people, nothing in their relationship with God is insignificant. Those who live most of their lives in the second category are rare. There are not a great number of people whose hearts are hot after God, who obey God's precepts and honor His principles. But David was like that.

When you drive down the road and you see the sign, "Speed Limit 35 Miles an Hour," that's a precept. It means 35 miles an hour whether it's 3:00 in the morning or 3:00 in afternoon, whether it's an open road or rush-hour traffic. The limit is clearly 35 miles an hour. That's a precept; there's no give or take.

If the sign reads, "Drive Carefully," that's a principle. It means one speed in heavy traffic on a freeway, and it means something entirely different on a deserted road out in the flatlands of Nevada or Montana. You drive carefully and a certain way in traffic. You drive carefully and another way entirely on a deserted highway. That's a principle. It needs to be applied with wisdom.

When it comes to the spiritual life, those who are after God in their hearts care as much about the principles as they do about the precepts. And when they come across a precept that is clearly delineated, they say, "As I look at my life, I see that it's not like that precept. I need to bring my life in line with the precept." And they do just that. That's what David did, according to 2 Samuel, chapter 6 . . . a classic example of why he was "a man after God's heart."

DAVID'S CONCERN: THE ARK

The setting is Jerusalem, and as you know by now, David is king. In fact, he's a new king. Saul is dead, but the results of his life still echo through the land. In the latter part of his forty-year reign, Saul compromised and fiddled around with all kinds of things besides his job. Most of all, (unlike David) he neglected the things of God.

THE ARK: SOME DETAILS WORTH KNOWING

Now understand, back in the days of David the central place of worship was not the believer but the tabernacle. And under Saul's weak, negligent reign, the emphasis on the tabernacle sort of drifted away. During this time a particular piece of holy furniture had gotten separated from the tabernacle. If you can believe it, the enemy had carted off the ark of the covenant.

Now that doesn't mean much to Gentile people today. But in those days the loss of the ark meant that the presence of God had departed, because the Lord dwelt in His glory upon the ark of the covenant. The ark was so important to the Lord that He gave Moses very specific details of how to build it and make it portable so the Israelites could move this house of God through the wilderness and into the land of Canaan as the central place of worship. And everywhere the ark of the covenant was placed, God's glory rested there—meaning the light, the *shechinah* glory of God, rested on the ark of the covenant. That laserlike ray from heaven was central to the worship of Jehovah. Since it represented the presence of Jehovah, it was the holiest place on earth.

Now, when David took over the throne, he realized that there was no ark of the covenant . . . no central place of worship. The spiritual walk of the people of Israel, therefore, had become mediocre. Their heart was anything but hot after God. As their leader, David knew that he needed to put that piece of sacred furniture back in its rightful place. He needed to set it up as God designed it. His heart was after God's, even to the point of locating a small piece of furniture and putting it in a certain place. To David, when it came to God no detail was unimportant.

Second Samuel, chapter 6, tells how he got the ark of the covenant back in Jerusalem.

> Now David again gathered all the chosen men of Israel, thirty thousand.

> And David arose and went with all the people who were
> with him to Baale-judah, to bring up from there the ark of
> God which is called by the Name, the very name of the LORD
> of hosts who is enthroned above the cherubim.
>
> And they placed the ark of God on a new cart that they
> might bring it from the house of Abinadab. . . .
>
> So they brought it with the ark of God from the house of
> Abinadab, which was on the hill; and Ahio was walking ahead
> of the ark.
>
> Meanwhile, David and all the house of Israel were cele-
> brating before the LORD with all kinds of instruments made of
> fir wood, and with lyres, harps, tambourines, castanets and
> cymbals.
>
> 2 Samuel 6:1–5

So here's David rejoicing and celebrating and having the greatest delightful time, knowing that the ark of the covenant was coming back home
where it belonged, in Zion. There was the sound of music and there was
the delight of obedience beating in the heart of David. *The ark is coming
back! Hip, hip, hooray!* Or perhaps, *Shalom, shalom, shalom!*

Now this is a good time to pause and explain the ark of the covenant
because some of you who are reading this might think it was like Noah's
floating barge-like ark . . . but it was nothing like that at all. The name
itself means "box" or "chest." God himself gave the original blueprint to
Moses. The ark was made of wood, rectangular in shape, gold-plated inside
and out. It had a decorative gold border around it, forming a rim.

Another significant part of the ark was its cover. On top of this open
chest was a grate, a see-through covering made of gold, called the mercy
seat. It perfectly matched the dimensions of the chest. At either end of the
cover was a hammered gold cherubim (the word means "angel"). These
golden angels were facing each other, with wings outstretched over the
golden grate. These creatures looked down upon the chest. Apparently
these cherubim were small because a solid gold piece would be extremely
heavy. If they had been very large they would have made the ark top heavy.
It would be awkward to carry it. The whole thing had to be mobile.

Stay with me—there's more. Beneath the plate within the ark were
three objects: a golden jar containing manna from the wilderness, Aaron's
ancient rod, and the tables of the covenant, that is, the tablets of stone.
God had promised that He would meet with His people above the mercy
seat.

To us, this sounds so strange. All of our worship is so open and real-istic. But we see everything now after Christ came and died. Prior to Calvary, however, so many things of God were found in symbols and types and pictures—sort of like looking at your face through a smoky or foggy mirror. You see the image but you don't see the details. That's the way they worshiped. They had a box, and upon that box shone the very glory of God over this golden grate, this mercy seat.

To be sure, this piece of furniture was absolutely holy. It was set apart to God. So careful was God with His instructions about it that He even told them how it was to be carried.

At the base of each of the four corners was a fixed ring of gold, and through these rings were slipped gold-plated poles by which the entire chest was to be carried, so that no human hand ever touched the ark itself. Also, God clearly stated that handling the tabernacle furniture was to be done only by Levites and the poles were to be carried on their shoulders. Every aspect of their worship was important to God, even how the ark was transported from one place to another. And that's where David got into trouble.

You see, David was an expedient kind of man. He was a pragmatist. David was the king, a decision maker. He knew that in order for the people to worship, they needed the ark of the covenant. In order to get the ark of the covenant down the hill from the home of Abinadab, the quickest and best way to do it was on a cart. So David had them get a new cart, put the cart underneath this chest, and told a few men, in effect, "Haul it down to Jerusalem."

So they're bringing it down this way, with two sons of Abinadab, Uzzah and Ahio, leading the cart, when something dreadful happens.

> But when they came to the threshing floor of Nacon, Uzzah reached out toward the ark of God and took hold of it, for the oxen nearly upset it.
>
> And the anger of the LORD burned against Uzzah, and God struck him down there for his irreverence; and he died there by the ark of God.
>
> 2 Samuel 6:6–7

Uzzah reached out to steady the ark so it wouldn't fall. That's all he did. I mean, after all, wasn't that the practical thing to do? Rather than let it fall off the cart and possibly break or get bent, you have to grab it, right?

Well, what's right? Let me tell you what's right. It wouldn't have been in danger if they had carried it exactly as God had commanded. The Levites were the ones to carry the ark, using the poles that slid through the little ringlets at the bottom of the chest, remember? And the poles were to be put up on the shoulders of these specially chosen men, and they were to balance this holy chest as they carried it from one place to another. But David didn't do that. He took a convenient route, and he changed the details to fit the expediency of the hour.

It's like a saying I heard years ago: "It doesn't matter what you do. Just do something, *even if it's wrong!*" That's the most stupid counsel I've ever heard. *Never* do what's wrong!

Do nothing until it's right. Then do it with all your might. That's wise counsel.

But David said, "We need to get it down here! Who cares how we do it, so long as we get it here?"

God does, David. And to prove it, He took Uzzah's life. Now here's David, standing alongside a corpse, and he gets mad.

> And David became angry because of the LORD's outburst against Uzzah. . . .
>
> 2 Samuel 6:8

Wait a minute. We got the cart before the horse (no pun intended). We've got David standing here mad at the Lord, when, in fact, the Lord was angry at David.

About now you might be thinking, "Well, I thought you said he was a man after God's heart?" I did—or, rather, God did. Does that mean he's perfect? It does not. Having a heart for God doesn't mean you're perfect, it means you're sensitive. It means every detail is important. And when you see you're wrong you face it. You own up. You come to terms with it.

Verse 9 says,

> So David was afraid of the LORD that day; and he said, "How can the ark of the LORD come to me?"
>
> 2 Samuel 6:9

The problem was that David had not done his homework. We often get into trouble when we don't do our homework—when we think we see pretty clearly what the Lord's will is, and so in expediency or in convenience (usually in a hurry) we dash off to do it our way. And the Lord says, "Look, I've written a lot of things in My Book about that decision you just made, and I want you to take counsel from Me. That's why it's not working. If you want to have a heart for Me, then you check My Word and you find either a precept or a principle and you go according to that. When you do that, I'll give you joy like you can't believe. If you don't, I will make you miserable." In fact, in David's case, the Lord said, "I'll even take some lives."

Centuries later, Ananias and Sapphira did very much the same thing. They presumed on the Lord and didn't take Him seriously. We see Uzzah the same way, taken from the earth because he touched an ultra-holy article of furniture that was not to be touched, especially by a non-Levite. Who cares about Levites? God does. Who cares about little ringlets and little golden poles that go through ringlets? God does. If He didn't care, He wouldn't have said anything about it. And because He cares, we must also care.

That's the whole point here. When we begin to care about the things God cares about, we become people after His heart, and only then do we begin to have real freedom and real happiness.

Well, David was afraid.

> And David was unwilling to move the ark of the LORD into the city of David with him. . . .
>
> 2 Samuel 6:10

You better believe it. The last time he tried, it cost the life of a man. So David said, "Leave it." And they put it in the home of a man named Obed-edom.

Three months pass. There is no ark in Jerusalem, and with his stomach churning, David is wondering what in the world is happening. "I want the ark of the LORD here. And Obed-edom has it there. What's wrong? Obed-edom is having the time of his life. He's getting all the blessing!"

> Now it was told King David, saying, "The LORD has blessed the house of Obed-edom and all that belongs to him, on account of the ark of God." And David went and brought up the ark of God from the house of Obed-edom into the city of David with gladness.
>
> 2 Samuel 6:12

Well, wait a minute. I thought it said that he didn't touch it. But it says here that he brought it up. Why is it that a few verses earlier he wouldn't touch it, and a few verses later he's saying, "Bring it in."

I'll show you. In a parallel passage in 1 Chronicles 15, we see what happened behind the scenes. When I stumbled over this in my study, it was one of those moments where I yelled, "Glory!" (Usually makes my secretary jump, but that's okay.)

> Now David . . . prepared a place for the ark of God, and pitched a tent for it. Then David said, "No one is to carry the ark of God but the Levites; for the LORD chose them to carry the ark of God, and to minister to Him forever." And David assembled all Israel at Jerusalem, to bring up the ark of the LORD to its place, which he had prepared for it.
>
> And David gathered together the sons of Aaron, and the Levites. . . . Then David called for Zadok and Abiathar the priests, and for the Levites . . . and said to them, "You are the heads of the fathers' household of the Levites; consecrate yourselves both you and your relatives, that you may bring up the ark of the LORD God of Israel, to the place that I have prepared for it. Because you did not carry it at the first, the LORD our God made an outburst on us, for we did not seek Him according to the ordinance."
>
> 1 Chronicles 15:1–13

What happened? Well, one of David's counselors, no doubt, or the Lord himself, spoke to David and said, "You know the Law specifically states that before the ark or any furniture can be moved, it has to be moved a certain way by a certain group of people." And David, who's hot after God, responded, "Really? I didn't know that." "Yeah, David. It has to be done His way." "Well, what's His way?" "Well, there are these little ringlets and you have to put poles in 'em. And you have to put the poles upon the shoulders. And you have to let the Levites carry this thing. And if you do that, David, you're home free."

And being a man after God's own heart, David gets it! Aha! He didn't seek the Lord before. He just sort of dashed out there to get the job done, and that's when he got burned.

Well, David said, "The Lord did that because we didn't seek Him."

What's the big deal, the big message, about the poles and the ringlets? The message is our life. It is the details—the pole and the ringlets—that drive us crazy in our carnal life. We don't want to take the time to get the poles, or we don't want to go to the trouble of putting the poles upon the right shoulders. I mean, it's a lot easier just to use a cart. After all, the American is a pretty pragmatic kind of person. And the Lord can't be that concerned about details, right? Wrong!

Let me tell you something. If the Lord cared enough to write it and cared enough to preserve it, He cares enough about the details to have you and me pull it off precisely His way.

And that's ultimately what David did. I love that about him.

> And so it was, that when the bearers of the ark of the LORD
> had gone six paces, he sacrificed an ox and a fatling.
>
> 2 Samuel 6:13

"One, two, three, four, five, six. Hold it! Anybody got a match? Bring in the ox, bring in the fatling, set fire to it." (Whoosh!) These guys are standing there, watching this thing go up, and David is very careful. "You don't want to fiddle around with something that God got specific about, men." Why does he say that? Because *he's a man after God's heart!* He cares about what God cares about. And when he heard the truth, he wanted to do it, just like God said. "Six paces, fatling. Six paces, fatling."

Finally they get the ark into Jerusalem, and look at what David is doing.

> And David was dancing before the LORD with all his might,
> and David was wearing a linen ephod. So David and all the
> house of Israel were bringing up the ark of the LORD with
> shouting and the sound of the trumpet.
>
> 2 Samuel 6:14–15

Why in the world would they get so excited about it? Because they're free. When you obey, you're free. When you disobey, you're in bondage. All around us we see individuals in bondage because they're in sin, and all they talk about is freedom. *They're not free.* The obedient guy dancing is free. More specifically, because he stuck that pole in the ringlet, because he put the pole on the shoulders of the right men, and because nobody touched the sacred chest, David is free.

The world's system says, "Don't worry about those little details; God's bigger than little golden ringlets." No, He's not. Because He sees the whole scene, He puts our obedience to the test in little things like a ringlet and a pole and a shoulder.

And I should warn you, when you're really free, the people who are not so free will have trouble with your being free. Look at David's wife in verse 16. Her husband is down there dancing and singing and shouting, and there's Michal up there in the second floor flat, frowning down on her husband.

> Then it happened as the ark of the LORD came into the city of David that Michal the daughter of Saul looked out the window and saw King David leaping and dancing before the LORD; and she despised him in her heart.
>
> 2 Samuel 6:16

David is rejoicing before God in obedience. He offers burnt offerings and blesses the people. Then he distributes food to the people in celebration. On the heels of all that, he goes home higher than a kite in ecstasy, walks up the stairs, opens the door, and this is what he hears from dear ol' Michal:

> "How the king of Israel distinguished himself today! He uncovered himself today in the eyes of his servants' maids as one of the foolish ones shamelessly uncovers himself!"
>
> 2 Samuel 6:20

Sarcasm, sarcasm, sarcasm. Jab, jab. These two did not have good chemistry. (They should never have gotten married.)

And notice how David responds. He refuses to let her reaction win the day.

So David said to Michal,

> "It [my rejoicing] was before the LORD, who chose me above your father and above all his house, to appoint me ruler over the people of the LORD, over Israel; therefore I will celebrate before the LORD.
>
> "And I will be more lightly esteemed than this and will be humble in my own eyes, but with the maids of whom you have spoken, with them I will be distinguished." And Michal the daughter of Saul had no child to the day of her death.
>
> 2 Samuel 6:21-23

David got a bit of sarcasm in there himself with his reference to Michal's father, but he did state the truth. And we don't know exactly why it says that Michal had no children. Perhaps David was never again intimate with her. Whatever the reason, she was barren till the day of her death. To be barren, by the way, was the greatest stigma for a Jewish woman to endure.

THE APPLICATION: SOME LESSONS WORTH REMEMBERING

Two things strike me here and both have to do with the whole matter of focus; one is horizontal, and one is vertical. David's eyes were on the Lord; Michal's eyes were on other people. When those opposites mix, an explosion is sure to occur.

First, *the better you know where you stand with the Lord, the freer you can be.* When you do the homework, you find out where you stand with your Lord, and you follow His plan, then you are free. I mean *really* free! Many won't understand, of course. To some, you will be seen as detestable. You'll be misunderstood. Like David with his own wife. But you won't care that much about public opinion either. You'll care about the Lord's opinion. There is no freedom like the kind He provides. In a word, it's *grace.*

Second: *The freer you are before the Lord, the more confident you will become.* When you know where you stand, that is real security.

Some of you might be bound up in a carnal walk, and you're thinking, *Hey, this is really free.* Forget it . . . you're not free. You're enduring the worse kind of bondage. Others of you might be thinking, *Wow, if I've gotten so specific about this business of the Christian life, I must be majoring in the minors.* It's possible, but if it's important to God, it ought to be important to you. If God took the time to put it down and it's a precept, you better believe 35 miles an hour means 35 miles an hour. It never means 38, it never means 45, it means 35. He never changes, and He means what He says.

Some of you might be like Michal, so occupied with what everybody else is thinking or saying, all you can do is view a few people that are genuinely free with jaundiced eyes and say, "They get all the breaks." Now wait. God sets His heart of favor on those whose hearts are following Him. He honors those who honor His Word. He makes them exceedingly happy.

I want to encourage those of you who have become rather concerned about the fine print of your life. I want to commend you for that. You are the ones who make godly husbands and godly roommates and godly wives and godly workmen and godly pastors and godly musicians and godly professionals. You care enough about your life that regardless of your occupation, when you hear something declared from Scripture, you're thinking, *How can I get that into my life?* Good for you! Don't stop. Don't even slow down.

There was a period in my own life when I sort of dinked around with the Christian life. I took some and left some. I bit off the part that was tasty, but I left the part that was painful. Until one man cared enough to tell me the truth by saying, "You are a classic illustration of a heady Christian." I thought that was an insult. I was so proud, I didn't want to listen to what he had to say. Then he said, "Before you walk away I just want to tell you, you have the makings of putting it together, but you're a long ways from it." And he said, "I want to stick around you for a number of months and help you in the process so that you can see how it can be done, so that whether in public or private you're putting it together." He cared enough to do that. Those were some tough years in my life.

Now, like you, I'm still in the process, putting it together. But thank God for that friend who helped me get started by saying, "You need to put those precepts to work in your life. Quit excusing your disobedience."

Knowing where you stand before the Lord leads to true freedom. Being free before the Lord, you will become confident, and that is genuine security.

Has the Lord clearly led you to do something, but you're still saying "No" or "Not now"? Maybe you're trying to bargain with Him, substituting something else in place of his direct advice. Listen to me: Wait no longer—obey! Obey today!

Do you have a stubborn streak within you that causes you to rebel or argue or fight back, even though you know it's against God's leading? Perhaps you've bragged about your strong will or you've cultivated the habit of resistance. Listen to me: Rebel no more—obey! Obey today!

Or have you developed a deceitful technique of hiding your disobedience behind the human masks of lies or rationalization or manipulation or blame? Listen to me: Deceive no further—obey! Obey today!

The very best proof of your love for your Lord is obedience . . . nothing more, nothing less, nothing else.

You want to be like David? You want to become a man or woman "after God's heart"?

It's not rocket science. Pay attention to the things God considers important. Sweat the small stuff. In one word: obey.

CHAPTER FOURTEEN

When God Says No

There's a line in an old hymn that says, "What He takes or what He gives us, shows the Father's love so precious."[28]

Now it is easy for us to sing, "What He gives us shows the Father's love." But it is hard for us to sing the other side, "What He takes from us shows the Father's love." We think of love as something that is giving, but sometimes love involves taking away something that would not be best.

Think of your broken dreams. Think of times you felt that something was the plan of God for your life, only to have it stopped and have the Father reveal to you in some way, "That's not My plan. That may be a noble purpose. In fact, that's a great resolve; but it's not My plan for you." That's hard to hear. King David learned just how hard it was.

A PEACEFUL INTERLUDE

Being a man of war—in fact, a very courageous warrior—David was often involved in battle and stressful situations. However, there was an interlude of calm and quiet in his life. Sometimes a great overture moves from one passionate strain to another, only to pause in the middle, before its grand finale. That's the way I picture the king at this time. There was a very quiet period of time when things were calm and peaceful.

Now it came about when the king lived in his house, and the
LORD had given him rest on every side from all his enemies. . . .

2 Samuel 7:1

First of all, David had *domestic peace*. Over the hearth above his fireplace David could have written, "Shalom." All was at peace, all was well
with his soul. The kids were playing in the rooms around the house. The
wives were happy, and David was at peace in his heart. Perhaps this was
a time when he sat beside the fire in the evening and watched it crackle.
In doing so, he began to muse, began to meditate. Those are some of the
best times in life—the brief interludes, the quiet times. They give us time
to reflect, to think deeply.

Furthermore, David had *national rest*, for "the Lord had given him rest
on every side from all his enemies." I'll tell you, David didn't know that
kind of peace very often. The age-old battle with the Philistines was temporarily settled; all was quiet, at least for a while. There was no giant on
the scene shouting out blasphemies. There was no movement, no strategy
to invade the land. Rugged carts were not hauling battle implements up
close to the wall of Jerusalem—none of that. There was an interlude of
peace.

And David, as he begins to reflect upon the peaceful time inside the
lovely cedar-lined home in which he's living, begins to dream. And he
begins to talk about this dream to Nathan, a prophet.

This is the first mention of Nathan the prophet in the Bible. He was
a confidant of David, in fact, would later be the man who pointed the
finger at the adulterer-king and said, "You are the man! You're the sinner."
He's a close friend. He's a prophet. For now he's a counselor.

So David calls him in and he says to Nathan,

"See now, I dwell in a house of cedar, but the ark of God
dwells within tent curtains." And Nathan said to the king, "Go,
do all that is in your mind, for the LORD is with you."

2 Samuel 7:2–3

Well, that's a good friend. Good friends encourage you, and vice versa.
Nathan encouraged David to follow through on what was in his heart.
What exactly was that?

In the last chapter we saw how David brought the ark of God up to
Jerusalem and back to the people of Israel. But it had begun to bother

him that the ark of God was in a tent while he lived in a beautiful house. So he got the idea in his mind to build a permanent residence for God in which to house all the sacred furniture. David said, "It isn't fitting that the king should live in this lovely cedar dwelling and the ark, the very presence of Jehovah himself, should be in a little tent out there. I will build a house for God. I want to build a temple in His honor." God had never dwelt in a permanent house, but David resolved to change that.

Now I want to emphasize, from everything we know about him, David had no ulterior motive here. He had no selfish ambition. He had no desire to make a name for himself. As a matter of fact, he wanted to exalt no other name but God in building this house.

It is during the interludes of life that we have time to seize a dream or an ideal objective. Some of you in a quiet moment of your life realized the vocation into which God was calling you. Maybe it happened at a camp or a retreat, where you threw a branch of promise on the fire, having determined an objective to follow. Maybe it happened in the quietness of your own room after a church service one evening. Or maybe it was while you were a student in a dormitory. You couldn't go to sleep, so you turned through the Scriptures and landed on some thoughts that began to make sense. Before long, they stretched out a direct arrow toward some new and exciting objective. And you said, "That's it! That's my commitment; that's where I'm going." It's in the interludes of life that those things happen. You have to slow down and become quiet in those special times to hear His voice, to sense His leading.

But let me add this: Sometimes the dream is from God; sometime it's not. Both are noble. Both are great resolves. Both are ideals. But when it's not of God, it won't come to fulfillment . . . nor should it. And it's often hard to determine which is which. It's very hard. In fact, you'll have friends like Nathan who will say, "Go, do all that is in your mind, for the LORD is with you," only to have God show you later that it's not His plan. Interestingly, that is exactly what happened to David.

A HEAVEN-SENT RESPONSE

Look at the divine response from God. Actually, it comes through Nathan, but it's a word from God.

But it came about in the same night that the word of the LORD came to Nathan, saying, "Go and say to My servant David,

143

'Thus says the LORD, "Are you the one who should build Me a house to dwell in?" ' "

2 Samuel 7:4–5

In a parallel passage in 1 Chronicles 17, it is put more directly:

And it came about the same night, that the word of God came to Nathan, saying, "Go and tell David My servant, 'Thus says the LORD, "You shall not build a house for Me to dwell in. . . ." ' "

1 Chronicles 17:3–4

What a hard answer that was to take to the king. Earlier that day Nathan said to David, "The LORD is with you, David. Go ahead and make your plans." Now, only a few hours later, Nathan hears the Lord saying, "No way. No way!"

See, earlier, Nathan wasn't listening to the right voice. It wasn't God's plan for David to build a temple. It was a great idea, a great plan on David's heart . . . but it wasn't God's plan. And that is tough to bear.

But within the refusal of that request, God offers David affirmation.

"Now therefore, thus you shall say to My servant David, 'Thus says the LORD of hosts, "I took you from the pasture, from following the sheep, that you should be ruler over My people Israel." ' "

2 Samuel 7:8

Now that's clear. "David, I've appointed you to be a king. I've gifted you and chosen you to lead My people—not to build a temple."

"And I have been with you wherever you have gone and have cut off all your enemies from before you; and I will make you a great name, like the names of the great men who are on the earth."

2 Samuel 7:9

"David, you're a man of war. Your heart is on the battlefield. You're a soldier and a fighter, not a builder. You're a man for the trenches, and I've blessed you in such a way that all of the enemies have been subdued."

144

"When your days are complete and you lie down with your fathers, I will raise up your descendant after you, who will come forth from you, and I will establish his kingdom. He shall build a house for My name, and I will establish the throne of his kingdom forever."

2 Samuel 7:12–13

Ah! Great breakthrough! "David, you will know the delight of having a son by whom this temple will be built. Not through *your* efforts, but through *your son* the dream will be fulfilled."

Now, please remember, it is not a question of sin here. It is not God's judgment that is coming upon David as a consequence of wrong. It is simply God's redirecting David's plan and saying, "This is a great resolve, but I say 'no' to you and I say 'yes' to your son. Now accept that."

Well, was David wrong to begin with—wrong in thinking of building the temple?

It is not a question of being wrong. It's a question of accepting God's "no" and living with the mystery of His will. We people on this earth package everything. And we expect God to package His plan for us just like we would. We want the logic that we use to be His logic. And when it isn't, we wonder what's wrong because it's not working out like we would have worked it out.

To resolve this question, look for a moment at a parallel section in 2 Chronicles 6. I repeat, it is not sin that is involved here. As a matter of fact, the Lord affirms David for even having the thought. In doing so, He takes the guilt out of the whole thing. David's son Solomon is speaking here:

"Now it was in the heart of my father David to build a house for the name of the LORD, the God of Israel. But the LORD said to my father David, 'Because it was in your heart to build a house for My name, you did well that it was in your heart. Nevertheless you shall not build the house, but your son who shall be born to you, he shall build the house for My name.' "

2 Chronicles 6:7–9

The last part of verse 8 is profound, for God says to David, "You did well that it was in your heart." Rather than seeing his desire to build the temple as something wrong, God says to him, "I commend you for that thought. I commend you for having a heart that is so sensitive to Me that you would want to construct a house of worship for My glory. It is well that it was in your heart. It's not My plan for you to do that, but I commend you for such a thought."

SOME EARTHBOUND WISDOM

When God says "no" it is not necessarily discipline or rejection. It may simply be redirection. You have pursued His will; you have wanted to do His will. You threw that piece of wood on the fire and you saw your selfish desires go up in smoke. With all good intentions you said, "By God's grace I am going to pursue this." And here you are, thirty or forty years later, or maybe only five years later, and it hasn't worked out.

Now if you listen to some people, you'll be put on a guilt trip. "You see there," they say, "you set your heart on God, but you have run from Him. You're out of His will." I don't know how many couples I have talked with who early in their lives had their life's plan all mapped out, but it didn't transpire. As hard as they tried to make it work, it didn't go in the direction they had planned. Usually, they're living in the backwash of guilt because they think they are no longer walking in the will of God. Hey, it was well that it was in their heart, but who is to say that it was, in fact, His will. Perhaps the very road they are traveling is God's will for them . . . and it took His saying "no" to get them on that right road.

The thing we have to do in our walk with God is to listen carefully from day to day. Not just go back to some decision and say, "That's it forever, regardless." We need to look at it each day, keep it fresh, keep the fire hot, keep it on the back burner, saying, "Lord, is this Your arrangement? Is this Your plan? If it is not, make me sensitive to it. Maybe You're redirecting my life."

The second thing I would say is that *God does not call everybody to build temples.* He calls some people to be soldiers. He calls some people to do the gutsy work in the trenches. He calls some people to represent Him on foreign soil, but He doesn't call everyone. God has all kinds of creative ways to use us—ways we can't even imagine and certainly can't see up there around the next bend in the road. Let me add . . . one of the hardest things to hear is that God is going to use someone else to accomplish something you thought was your objective. That's what David had to hear, "It won't be you, David . . . it will be your son, Solomon."

Pause for a few seconds and ponder the paragraph you just read. Some need to let that sink in.

Well, what was David's response? It's beautiful.

Then David the king went in and sat before the LORD. . . .

2 Samuel 7:18

Look at that posture. He just sat down. Isn't that interesting? Maybe he went into his bedroom in his home—or maybe his study. He may have sunk down on the floor and just silently looked up. He had just heard God tell him, "The answer is 'no'. You're not going to execute that dream. I'm pleased to know such a noble thought was in your heart, but it's not in My plan." So he sat down. And just like a child he begins to express grateful questions to the Lord. He says,

"Who am I, O Lord GOD, and what is my house, that Thou hast brought me this far? And yet this was insignificant in Thine eyes, O Lord GOD, for Thou hast spoken also of the house of Thy servant concerning the distant future. . . . And again what more can David say to Thee? For Thou knowest Thy servant, O Lord GOD!"

2 Samuel 7:18–20

Isn't that like a little child? When a child refers to himself, he often calls himself by name. "Daddy, can Noah ride his big-wheel a little bit longer before he comes in for supper?" That's what my grandson would say to his daddy.

Just like a little boy, David sat down before the Lord and said, in effect, "Dad, what is David, that You've blessed my house and You've blessed my life, and You've brought me from leading a little flock of sheep to giving me this magnificent throne? Who am I?"

You know, it's important that every once in a while we sit down, take a long look at our short lives, and just count our blessings. Who are we to have been protected from the rains that fell, leaving hundreds homeless? Who are we that He has blessed our house and kept it safe? Warm in the winter . . . cool in the summer. Who am I, Lord, that You should give me health and strength to be able to hold a job or pursue this career or get this degree? Or to have parents who have encouraged me? Or to have these kids and to see them grow? Who am I?

"Dream or no dream, I'm a blessed person," says David. Here is more evidence that David was a man after God's own heart.

What a powerful moment this is. What a statement of praise David offers to God, even in this moment of what must have been a time of disappointment for him.

"Thou art great, O Lord GOD; for there is none like Thee, and there is no God besides Thee. . . . The word that Thou hast spoken concerning Thy servant and his house, confirm it forever . . . that Thy name may be magnified forever. . . . Thou art God, and Thy words are truth. . . . May it please Thee to bless the house of Thy servant. . . ."

2 Samuel 7:22–29

What a grateful man! Still, we almost have to ask, did David really mean what he said? One more passage will help. We are prone to think, *Well that's great in theory, but did David really support his son in this project that was originally his own dream?*

Yes, he did. In 1 Chronicles 22 David said,

"This is the house of the Lord GOD, this is the altar of burnt offering for Israel."

1 Chronicles 22:1

Do you know what I think is happening here? David has unrolled the plans he's been thinking through, and he's walking around the city, saying, "This is where the house will be, and this is the altar area." Knowing that he's not going to actually build the house of God, he gives support.

So David gave orders to gather the foreigners who were in the land of Israel, and he set stonecutters to hew out stones to build the house of God.

And David prepared large quantities of iron to make the nails for the doors of the gates . . . and timbers of cedar logs beyond number, for the Sidonians and the Tyrians brought large quantities of cedar timber to David.

And David said, "My son Solomon is young and inexperienced, and the house that is to be built for the LORD shall be exceedingly magnificent, famous and glorious throughout all lands. Therefore now I will make preparation for it." So David made ample preparations before his death.

1 Chronicles 22:2–5

What a father! He may have been weak at other times, but at this moment, David stands tall. "Lord, I know You don't want me to fulfill the dream, but, Lord, I'm going to set apart as much as I can to support my son as he fulfills the dream that was on my heart." What an unselfish response. "And I'll see that the nails are there, and that the lumber and the stones are there—all the materials that my son will need. And then I'll back off and I'll say, 'Magnify Your name through the efforts of another.' "

HELPFUL HOPE FOR BROKEN DREAMS

I see two simple truths in all this. First, *when God says "no," it means He has a better way, and He expects me to support it.*

Second, *my very best reaction is cooperation and humility.* He doesn't call everybody to build the temple, but He does call everyone to be faithful and obedient. Some of you who are reading this are living with broken dreams. Sometime in the past you had high hopes that your life would go in a certain direction. But the Lord, for some mysterious reason, has now said, "No." And you've moved along in life and now you're up in years and you find yourself slowly becoming shelved and the younger ones are taking charge and moving on. How quickly age takes over!

James Dobson puts it beautifully. "About the time our face clears up, our mind gets fuzzy." Just about the time we get our act together, we're too old to pull it off. And so we turn it over to the Solomon in our lives. But it takes real humility to say to that person, "May God be with you. I'll do everything I can to support you in seeing that it gets accomplished."

I saw this attitude in Dr. Richard Seume, a man of God who, to me, emulated what a pastor was all about. For over twelve years he pastored at Emmanuel Baptist Church in Richmond, Virginia. God blessed him. He was a member of a number of mission boards and was extremely gifted as a pulpiteer and as a writer. When he left the pastorate in Virginia, he became pastor of Wheaton Bible Church.

He was not there long, however, before he was stricken with a rare kidney disease, which meant he had to live on a dialysis machine six hours a day, three to four days a week. At the zenith of his career, the rug was cut out from under him. He could no longer take the rigors of the pastorate, and as a result, some misunderstood; a few criticized. He left, almost a broken man. But instead of giving up, he accepted Dr. John Walvoord's invitation to return to his alma mater and become the chaplain at Dallas Theological Seminary, a position he held until he died in a car accident several years ago.

At one point during those last years, when he looked so ill, so stooped and jaundiced, he said to me, "Chuck, I would like someday to write an article for *Reader's Digest,* because I think that way it would reach the greatest number of people. I'd like to call it 'Plugged in for Life.'"

And he said with a handsome smile, "You'll never know what it's like, unless you live like I have lived, to go to bed at night not sure that tomorrow morning will come. *I face death every day.*" What a great man of God was Dr. Seume!

This man whose dreams for his own life had been shattered, chose to invest his last years in the lives of younger men, the Solomons of the future, to build the temples he would never see built. He embraced God's alternate plan with all his might. Empty-handed and dependent on his God, he invested himself in hundreds of younger ministers, who are now engaged in fulfilling some of the dreams he once had hoped to accomplish.

One of my all-time favorite poems comes to mind in moments like these.

> One by one He took them from me,
> All the things I valued most,
> Until I was empty-handed;
> Every glittering toy was lost.
>
> And I walked earth's highways, grieving,
> In my rags and poverty.
> Till I heard His voice inviting,
> "Lift those empty hands to Me!"
>
> So I held my hands toward Heaven,
> And He filled them with a store
> Of His own transcendent riches
> Till they could contain no more.
>
> And at last I comprehended
> With my stupid mind and dull,
> That God COULD not pour His riches
> Into hands already full![29]

Do you identify with David? Did you have your hands full of your dreams and your visions, ready to present them to Him on the altar of sacrifice? Did you have your plans all prepared and thought through, only to see them crumble at your feet? And now you're standing there, empty-handed?

I want to say to you that God is ready to fill your empty hands like you would never believe, if you will only lift them up to Him in obedience and praise, as David did. God is still alive and well, and He knows what He's doing.

To some, He says, "yes." To others, "no." In either case, the answer is best. Why? Because God's answers, while surprising, are never wrong.

CHAPTER FIFTEEN

Grace in a Barren Place

The word *grace* means many things to many people. This is certainly epitomized by Lofton Hudson's clever book title, *Grace Is Not a Blue-eyed Blonde*.

We refer to a ballet dancer as having grace. We say grace at meals. We talk about the queen of England bringing grace to events she attends. Grace can mean coordination of movement, it can mean a prayer, it can refer to dignity and elegance. Most importantly, grace can mean unimerited favor—extending special favor to someone who doesn't deserve it, who hasn't earned it, and can never repay it. Every once in a while we come across a scene in Scripture where we see a beautiful illustration of that kind of grace, and we stand amazed at such amazing grace.

We find one of those moments in the life of David. It is, in my personal opinion, the greatest illustration of grace in all the Old Testament. It involves an obscure man with an almost unpronounceable name. Mephibosheth. It's a beautiful, unforgettable story.

GRACE: SEEING AN EXAMPLE OF IT

In the previous chapter, we saw an interlude of peace and quietness in David's life during which he spent time thinking about his past and all the blessings that had been his. As he did so, I'm sure that David thought specifically about his love for his friend Jonathan, lost in battle, and about

Jonathan's father, Saul, David's predecessor. While reflecting upon those two men and the impact they'd had in his life, David began to think about a promise he had made. He pondered it and then he addressed it.

> Then David said, "Is there yet anyone left of the house of Saul, that I may show him kindness for Jonathan's sake?"
>
> 2 Samuel 9:1

Actually, this is a rather unfortunate translation, because "kindness" often smacks of a soft tenderness, but what David was expressing was much deeper than that. The original Hebrew word here could be and should be rendered "grace"—"that I may show *grace* for Jonathan's sake."

Grace is positive and unconditional acceptance in spite of the other person. Grace is a demonstration of love that is undeserved, unearned, and unrepayable. So David ponders, "Is there anybody in this entire area to whom I might show forth that kind of positive acceptance, demonstrate that kind of love?"

Why did he want to do that? Well, he had made a promise. In fact, he had made two promises.

Back in 1 Samuel 20, when David is still running for his life from Saul but is obviously destined for the throne, Jonathan says,

> "If it please my father to do you harm, may the LORD do so to Jonathan and more also, if I do not make it known to you and send you away, that you may go in safety. And may the LORD be with you as He has been with my father.
>
> "And if I am still alive, will you not show me the loving-kindness [there's that word again—the grace] of the LORD, that I may not die?"
>
> 1 Samuel 20:13–14

It was the custom in eastern dynasties that when a new king took over, all the family members of the previous dynasty were exterminated to take away the possibility of revolt. So Jonathan is saying here, "David, when you get to the throne, as surely you will, will you show my family grace? Unlike the common custom of other kings, will you preserve our lives? Will you take care of us and protect us, that we may not be forgotten?"

Without hesitation, David agreed. His love for Jonathan prompted him to enter into a binding covenant with his friend.

So Jonathan made a covenant with the house of David, saying, "May the LORD require it at the hands of David's enemies." And Jonathan made David vow again because of his love for him, because he loved him as he loved his own life.

1 Samuel 20:16–17

Later, you may recall, after David had spared Saul's life in the cave, Saul said to him,

"And now, behold, I know that you shall surely be king, and that the kingdom of Israel shall be established in your hand. So now swear to me by the LORD that you will not cut off my descendants after me, and that you will not destroy my name from my father's household."

And David swore to Saul. . . .

1 Samuel 24:20–22

So David made the promise both to Jonathan and to Saul. Later (recorded in 2 Samuel 9) we find him thinking about that promise. He starts asking the people in his court, "Is there anyone left to whom I might demonstrate grace because of Jonathan?"

I think it's worth noting that he asks, "Is there anyone?" He doesn't ask, "Is there anyone qualified?" Or, "Is there anyone worthy?" He says, "Is there anyone? Regardless of who they are, is there ANYBODY still living who ought to be the recipient of my grace?" That's unqualified acceptance based on unconditional love.

Well, they identified someone.

Now there was a servant of the house of Saul whose name was Ziba, and they called him to David; and the king said to him, "Are you Ziba?" And he said, "I am your servant."

And the king said, "Is there not yet anyone of the house of Saul to whom I may show the kindness of God?" And Ziba said to the king, "There is still a son of Jonathan who is crippled in both feet."

2 Samuel 9:2–3

If you read between the lines here, you will feel an implication in the counsel Ziba was actually giving the king. I think he was implying, "David, you really better think twice before you do this, because this guy's not going to look very good in your court. He doesn't fit the surroundings, this throne room, this beautiful new home in the city of Jerusalem. You know, David, he has a serious disability."

David asks, "Is there anybody?" And this counselor answers, "Yes, but he's crippled."

David's response is beautiful. He moves right on and says, "Where is he?" He doesn't ask, "How badly?" He doesn't even ask how he happened to be in that condition. He just said, "Where's the man located?"

That's the way grace is. Grace isn't picky. Grace doesn't look for things that have been done that deserve love. Grace operates apart from the response or the ability of the individual. Grace is one-sided. I repeat, grace is God giving Himself in full acceptance to someone who does not deserve it and can never earn it and will never be able to repay. And this is what makes the story of David and Mephibosheth so memorable. A strong and famous king stoops down and reaches out to one who represents everything David was not!

David simply asks, "Where is he?"

> And Ziba said to the king, "Behold, he is in the house of Machir the son of Ammiel in Lo-debar."
>
> 2 Samuel 9:4

That last geographical term is interesting. *Lo* in Hebrew means "no," and *debar* is from the root word meaning "pasture or pastureland." So this descendant of Jonathan is in a place where there is unimaginable desolation. He lives out in some obscure, barren field in Palestine.

Since the custom was to kill anyone from a previous dynasty, such individuals were either exterminated or they hid for the rest of their lives. And that's what this man had done. He had hidden himself away, and the only one who knew his whereabouts was an old servant of Saul named Ziba.

David doesn't ask how this man became crippled in both feet, but we are curious, and we find the answer in chapter 4. It's quite a story and only adds to the pathos of the situation. Let's go back for a few moments.

> Now Jonathan, Saul's son, had a son crippled in his feet. He was five years old when the report of [the death of] Saul and Jonathan came from Jezreel, and his nurse took him up and

fled. And it happened that in her hurry to flee, he fell and became lame. His name was Mephibosheth.

2 Samuel 4:4

When she heard that Saul and Jonathan were dead, the nurse picked up the boy who was in her charge and fled, to protect him. As she hurried, she probably tripped, and the boy tumbled out of her arms. As a result of that fall, he was permanently disabled and had been hiding away ever since, fearful of his life. The last thing he wanted was to see an emissary from the king rap on his door. But that was exactly what happened.

Can you imagine the man's shock? We don't know how old Mephibosheth was, but he probably had a family of his own by now, for later we read that he had a young son named Mica. After answering the knock at his door, Mephibosheth is looking into the faces of David's soldiers, who say to him, "The king wants to see you." He most likely thought, *Well, this is the end.*

Then these men take him to Jerusalem, into the very presence of the king himself. I love scenes like this portrayed so vividly in the Bible!

> And Mephibosheth, the son of Jonathan the son of Saul, came to David and fell on his face and prostrated himself. And David said, "Mephibosheth." And he said, "Here is your servant!"

2 Samuel 9:6

What a moment that must have been. This frightened man throws aside his crutches and falls down before the king who has all rights, sovereign rights, over his life. And the king says, "Are you Mephibosheth?" And he said, "It's true; I'm Mephibosheth." He had no idea what to expect. Surely, he expected the worst.

> And David said to him, "Do not fear, for I will surely show kindness [grace] to you for the sake of your father Jonathan, and will restore to you all the land of your grandfather Saul; and you shall eat at my table regularly."

2 Samuel 9:7

Can you imagine what Mephibosheth must have felt at that moment? Expecting a sword to strike his neck, he hears these unbelievable words from King David.

Dr. Karl Menninger, in his book, *The Vital Balance*, talks about what he calls the "negativistic personality," the kind of personality that at first says "no" to almost everything. "These are troubled patients," says Menninger. "These troubled people have never made an unsound loan, they have never voted for a liberal cause, or sponsored any extravagances. They cannot permit themselves the pleasure of giving." He describes them as "rigid, chronically unhappy individuals, bitter, insecure, and often suicidal."[30]

To illustrate, he tells the story of Thomas Jefferson, who was with a group of companions riding horseback cross-country when they came to a swollen river. A wayfarer waited until several of the party had crossed and then hailed President Jefferson and asked if he would carry him across on his horse. Jefferson pulled him up onto the back of his horse and carried him to the opposite bank. "Tell me," asked one of the men, "why did you select the president to ask this favor of?" "The president?" the man answered. "I didn't know he was the president. All I know is that on some of the faces is written the answer 'no' and on some faces is written the answer 'yes.' His was a 'yes' face."[31]

As I mention in my book, *The Grace Awakening*, people who understand grace fully have a "yes" face. I want to suggest that when Mephibosheth looked up, he saw a "yes" written across David's face. Don't you wish you could have been there at that magnificent moment?

David looked at him and said, "Oh, my friend, you're going to have a place of honor like you've never had before. You will become a member of my family . . . you will eat regularly at my table."

And it gets better. Look at it.

> Again he prostrated himself and said, "What is your servant, that you should regard a dead dog like me?"
>
> Then the king called Saul's servant Ziba, and said to him, "All that belonged to Saul and to all his house I have given to your master's grandson. And you and your sons and your servants shall cultivate the land for him, and you shall bring in the produce so that your master's grandson may have food; nevertheless Mephibosheth your master's grandson shall eat at my table regularly." Now Ziba had fifteen sons and twenty servants.
>
> Then Ziba said to the king, "According to all that my lord the king commands his servant so your servant will do." So Mephibosheth ate at David's table as one of the king's sons. And Mephibosheth had a young son whose name was Mica.

And all who lived in the house of Ziba were servants to Mephibosheth. So Mephibosheth lived in Jerusalem, for he ate at the king's table regularly. Now he was lame in both feet.

2 Samuel 9:8–13

What a fantastic account of grace! Every time I read it I get a "yes" face written across mine, because I see a demonstration of what grace is all about.

Picture what life would be like in the years to come at the supper table with David. The meal is fixed and the dinner bell rings and along come the members of the family and their guests. Amnon, clever and witty, comes to the table first. Then there's Joab, one of the guests—muscular, masculine, attractive, his skin bronzed from the sun, walking tall and erect like an experienced soldier. Next comes Absalom. Talk about handsome! From the crown of his head to the soles of his feet there is not a blemish on him. Then there is Tamar—beautiful, tender daughter of David. And, later on, one could add Solomon as well. He's been in the study all day, but he finally slips away from his work and makes his way to the table.

But then they hear this clump, clump, clump, clump, and here comes Mephibosheth, hobbling along. He smiles and humbly joins the others as he takes his place at the table as one of the king's sons. And the tablecloth of grace covers his feet. Oh, what a scene!

GRACE: UNDERSTANDING THE EXTENT OF IT

But that isn't the end of the story. Not really. That story is still going on, reflected in the lives of all God's children. I can think of at least eight analogies to indicate this.

1. Once Mephibosheth enjoyed uninterrupted fellowship with his father, son of King Saul. So with Adam, who walked with the Lord in the cool of the evening and enjoyed an uninterrupted fellowship with his Creator-Father. Like Adam, Mephibosheth once knew what it was like to be in close relationship with the king.

2. When disaster came, the nurse fled in fear and Mephibosheth suffered a fall. It left him crippled for the rest of his days. Likewise, when sin came, Adam and Eve hid in fear. The first response of humanity was to hide from God, to

find reasons for not being with God. As a result, mankind became a spiritual invalid and will be so forever on earth.

3. David, the king, out of sheer love for Jonathan, demonstrated grace to his handicapped son. So God, out of love for His Son, Jesus Christ, and the penalty He paid on the cross, demonstrates grace to the believing sinner. He's still seeking people who are spiritually disabled, dead due to depravity, lost in trespasses and sins, hiding from God, broken, fearful, and confused. We are walking with God today because He demonstrated His grace to us out of love for His Son.

4. Mephibosheth had nothing, deserved nothing, could repay nothing . . . in fact, didn't even try to win the king's favor. He was hiding from the king. The same is true of us. We deserved nothing, had nothing, and could offer God nothing. We were hiding when He found us.

    Some of you can look back to a time when you were addicted to drugs, when you were involved in a futile life, moving from one skirmish to another, from one guilt experience to another, spending one confusing night after another, in one sexual encounter after another, wondering where it all was going to lead. You offered nothing to God. You had nothing that you could give to Him, not one good work that you could say genuinely revealed righteousness. And yet the King set His heart on you. Isn't that great? No—better than that—it's *grace*. That's what God does for us, demonstrating love and forgiveness we can't earn, don't deserve, and will never be able to repay. Yes, that is grace. There's something freeing about grace. It takes away all of the demands and it puts all of the response on God's shoulders as He comes to us and says, "You're Mine. I take you just as you are, crutches and hang-ups and liabilities, and all."

5. David restored Mephibosheth from a place of barrenness to a place of honor. He took this broken, handicapped person from a hiding place where there was no pastureland and brought him to the place of plenty, right into the very courtroom of the king. The analogy is clear. God has taken us from where we were and brought us to where He is—to a

place of fellowship with Him. He has restored us to what we once had in Adam.

6. David adopted Mephibosheth into his family, and he became one of the king's sons. This is what God has done for the believing sinner—adopted us into the family of the heavenly King. He has chosen us, brought us into His family, and said, "You sit at My table, you enjoy My food, I give you My life." Every Christian is adopted as a family member of God.

7. Mephibosheth's disability was a constant reminder of grace. He had nothing but crutches, yet he was given the plenty of the king. Every time he limped from one place to the next, from one step to the next, he was reminded, "I am in this magnificent place, enjoying the pleasures of this position because of the grace of the king and nothing else."

   That's the way it is with the Father. Our continual problem with sin is a continual reminder of His grace. Every time we claim that verse, "If we confess our sins, He is faithful and just to forgive us and to cleanse us," we remind ourselves that grace is available. That's when the Lord covers our feet with His tablecloth and says, "Have a seat. You're Mine. I chose you simply because I wanted to."

8. When Mephibosheth sat down at the table of the king, he was treated just like any other son of the king. That's the way it is now . . . and the way it will be throughout eternity when we feast with our Lord. Can you imagine sitting down at the table with Paul and Peter and John . . . and perhaps asking James to pass the potatoes? And talking to Isaac Watts and Martin Luther, Calvin and Wycliffe? To break bread with Abraham and Esther, Isaiah and, yes, King David himself? Along with Mephibosheth, remember. And the Lord will look at you and He'll say with that "yes" face, "You're Mine. You're as important to Me as all my other sons and daughters. Here's the meal."

It will take eternity for us to adequately express what this truth means to us—that He chose us in our sinful and rebellious condition and in grace took us from a barren place and gave us a place at His table. And, in love, allowed His tablecloth of grace to cover our sin.

I end this chapter with a smile. A "yes" face that says, "Thank You, Father, for finding me when I wasn't looking . . . for loving me when I wasn't worthy . . . for making me Yours when I didn't deserve it."

Grace. It really is *amazing!*

CHAPTER SIXTEEN

The Case of the Open Window Shade

The Bible never flatters its heroes. All the men and women of Scripture have feet of clay, and when the Holy Spirit paints a portrait of their lives, He's a very realistic artist. He doesn't ignore, deny, or overlook the dark side.

Personally, when I step into this chapter of David's life, I am forever grateful that God has finished writing Scripture. There is not a person I know who would want to have his failures and vices recorded for all generations to read and discuss and make movies about and write books on and preach sermons on down through the centuries.

No sin, save the sin of Adam and Eve, has received more press than the sin of David with Bathsheba. Moviemakers exploit the passage with their "David and Bathsheba" films, conveying the idea that this man was some sort of a sexual addict with uncontrollable animallike drives. That's not true. That's not true at all. This is a good time to remember that David was a man who loved God . . . he was still "a man after God's heart." He sinned, but his sin was no greater than your sin or mine; ours simply have not been recorded for all to read. Admittedly, his sin was intensified because of who he was and because of how he mishandled it . . . but it was just sin—an act of disobedience he later came to regret with bitter tears. You and I know such experiences, not in the same details as David, but in the sorrowful aftermath.

I'm not justifying what David did. And as you will see in this chapter, and some that follow, I'm certainly not defending it. I am just trying to put it in proper perspective. If you cluck your tongue or shake your head in shame over David, then you have completely missed the warning: "Let him who thinks he stands take heed lest he fall" (1 Cor. 10:12). Wedged between the words "stand" and "fall" are the words "take heed." We need to do that on a regular basis. If we do not "take heed" by running as fast as we can run from this kind of temptation, we will fall, just as David did. My point: His flesh and our flesh are equally weak. Unless we "take heed" our flesh will lead us into a similar sinful excursion, and our consequences and grief will be as bitter as his. With this in mind, let's see what we can learn from the man's tragic failure.

A DARK BACKDROP

David was now about fifty years old, perhaps a few years older. He had been on the throne approximately twenty years. He had distinguished himself as a man of God, as a composer of psalms, as a faithful shepherd, as a valiant warrior on the battlefield, and as a leader of his people. He not only led the people in righteousness, he gave them the glorious music of the psalms. He was a man of passion as well as compassion. As we just observed, he was the one who took in Mephibosheth, keeping his promise to Jonathan and to Saul, demonstrating grace and showing honor.

So as we look at the next segment in David's life, understand that we're not examining the life of a wild rebel or a sexual pervert. But he is one who fell into a period of sin, and that sin had devastating consequences for his family, his reign, and his nation. *Sin always bears consequences.* That's why we're to take heed lest we fall, whether we are in our fifties or sixties, our teens, or our twenties, thirties, or forties. No one is too young or ever gets too old to fall.

At this point, David's life was like a neglected sea wall standing constantly against the barrage of the tide and the waves and the ever-pounding sea. Unguarded and in a weakened moment, it crumbled at his feet and he paid a terrible price.

David didn't fall suddenly; some chinks had already begun to form in his spiritual armor.

> David realized that the LORD had established him as king over Israel, and that He had exalted his kingdom for the sake of His people Israel.
>
> 2 Samuel 5:12

Clearly, David realized his God-given privilege. He realized the hand of God was on him. He realized that the Lord's blessing was abundant. But there were areas of private neglect beginning to take their toll.

> Meanwhile David took more concubines and wives from Jerusalem, after he came from Hebron; and more sons and daughters were born to David.
>
> 2 Samuel 5:13

Although the blessing of God was on him, on the people, and upon his decisions and leadership, he increased the number of his wives and concubines. This was in direct contradiction to God's commandments. In Deuteronomy 17 we find clearly stated requirements for the king of Israel's life.

> "When you enter the land which the LORD your God gives you, and you possess it and live in it, and you say, 'I will set a king over me like all the nations who are around me,' you shall surely set a king over you whom the LORD your God chooses, one from among your countrymen you shall set as king over yourselves; you may not put a foreigner over yourselves who is not your countryman. Moreover, he shall not multiply horses for himself, nor shall he cause the people to return to Egypt to multiply horses, since the LORD has said to you, 'You shall never again return that way.' Neither shall he multiply wives for himself, lest his heart turn away; nor shall he greatly increase silver and gold for himself."
>
> Deuteronomy 17:14–17

God said there were at least three things the king of Israel must not do: he must not multiply horses for himself or allow his people to return to Egypt to multiply horses; he must not multiply wives for himself; and he must not greatly increase silver and gold for himself. David was faithful in the first and the third; but being a man of passion, he failed in the second. And even though his wives and concubines increased, his passion was not abated. This king who took another man's wife already had a harem full of women. The simple fact is that the passion of sex is not satisfied by a full harem of women; it is *increased*. Having many women does not reduce a man's libido, it excites it . . . it stimulates it. David, being a man with a strong sexual appetite, mistakenly thought, *To satisfy it, I will have more women.* Thus, when he became the king, he added to the harem, but his drive only increased. One of the lies of our secular society is that if you just satisfy this drive, then it'll be abated.

While thinking about the king's harem, who in the kingdom is qualified to blow the whistle on David? Look at his track record. A humble beginning. A giant killer. Two decades of sterling leadership. Choice men in the right places. A military force every foe respected. Enlarged boundaries that now reached 60,000 square miles. No defeats on the battlefield. Exports, imports, strong national defense, financial health, a beautiful new home, plans for the temple of the Lord. Who could point a finger of accusation against such a king? So what if he married a few more women and privately increased the number of his concubines?

So what? Well, first of all, because it turned the heart of the king from the Lord. That's what the Lord was warning about in Deuteronomy. His lust and polygamy secretly began to erode his integrity.

Second, because it made him vulnerable. Between chapters 5 and 11 we see nothing but a success story. David is at an all-time high. He is fresh off a series of great victories on the battlefield. He has reached the peak of public admiration. He has ample money, incredible power, unquestioned authority, remarkable fame. His lifestyle looks like this—an arrow going farther and farther up into the clouds, like the sharp climb of a jet after takeoff as it increases in altitude. Farther and farther and farther up into the clouds went the life of David. And therefore he was vulnerable.

Our most difficult times are not when things are going hard. Hard times create dependent people. You don't get proud when you're dependent on God. Survival keeps you humble. Pride happens when everything is swinging in your direction. When you've just received that promotion, when you look back and you can see an almost spotless record in the last number of months or years, when you're growing in prestige and fame and significance, that's the time to watch out . . . especially if you're unaccountable.

In this situation, David is not only vulnerable, he's unaccountable. Perhaps he's becoming a tad impressed by his own track record, because when you get to chapter 11 he is indulging himself. That's another chink in the armor—indulgence.

Earlier we saw that David indulged his sons, and left the responsibility for his family to others while he was engaged in battle. And when the bills came due, he was too relaxed to face his responsibilities.

A SENSUAL SCENE

It is at this point, at this moment of vulnerability and indulgence in his fifty-year-old life, that we find David in his elegantly furnished bedchamber. Perhaps it was lavishly appointed, with richly woven draperies covering the walls and ornately carved wood framing the windows. It is spring. The rainy season is over, and warm breezes are blowing across Jerusalem. Billowing drapes are hanging over his open windows. Stars are beginning to twinkle brightly in the clear skies above. It was a warm, lovely Jerusalem evening in the springtime, just after sunset . . .

> when the kings go out to battle, that David sent Joab and his servants with him . . . and they destroyed the sons of Ammon and besieged Rabbah. But David stayed at Jerusalem.
>
> 2 Samuel 11:1

David was in bed, not in battle. Had he been where he belonged—with his troops—there would never have been the Bathsheba episode. Our greatest battles don't usually come when we're working hard; they come when we have some leisure, when we've got time on our hands, when we're bored. That's when we make those fateful decisions that come back to haunt us.

That's where David was—indulging himself beyond the boundaries of wisdom. He belonged in the battle; instead, he was in the bedroom. He pushed the bedspread back, stretched himself, yawned a couple of times, sighed, looked around the room. He certainly didn't need any more sleep. He was not suffering the exhaustion of a busy, productive man; he was tired from not being tired.

Perhaps I need to take a walk, he thinks. It looks like a nice night to be out in the air. So he shoves aside the drapes and steps out onto the roof.

Eastern monarchs frequently built their bedchambers on the second story of the palace and had a door that opened onto what you and I would call a patio roof. Often it was elegantly furnished, a place to sit with his family or with his men in counsel. Situated above the public demands and away from the streets, it was secreted so that people could not spot him. And that's where David found himself that unforgettable night.

We read that he walked around on the roof of the king's house. This is a large home, and he's enjoying the scenes and sights. Then, in the distance, he hears some splashing and perhaps the humming on the lips of this very beautiful woman living just beyond the palace, just within clear sight of his own backyard. The verse reads,

> From the roof he saw a woman bathing; and the woman was very beautiful in appearance.
>
> 2 Samuel 11:2

The Bible never pads the record. When it says a woman is beautiful, she's fabulous. When it says she's very beautiful, she's a knock-out, physically attractive beyond description. Rarely will the Scriptures include the word "very," and when it does, rest assured, it is not an exaggeration. Raymond Brown, in his work on David's life, suggests,

> When we read this terrible story we instinctively think of the offence as David's sin, but this attractive woman cannot be entirely excused. Bathsheba was careless and foolish, lacking in the usual Hebrew modesty, or she certainly would not have washed in a place where she knew she could be overlooked. From her roof-top she would often have looked out to the royal palace and must have known that she could be seen. It is not enough merely to avoid sin *ourselves*. The New Testament insists that Christians must ensure that they do not become a stumbling block to others (Rom. 14:12–13). If David had gone to war he would not have seen Bathsheba that night. If she had thought seriously about her action she would not have put temptation in his path.[32]

Without desiring to cast blame, let me linger here and underscore a practical point. It is so very important today in our society where ANYTHING goes to remember that if you want to be part of the answer to the common battles with sensuality rather than part of the problem, you work in cooperation with righteousness. That means that you give thought to your actions, your dress, your "looks," and your conduct. That means when you happen upon some alluring object, you turn away and refuse to linger. Not even David in all his godliness could handle it. It was too big for him. That also means you are modest, careful, and controlled, not leaving even a hint of allurement, lest another be tempted. I believe both David and Bathsheba were at fault on this occasion, but of the two, certainly David was the aggressor. He stopped. He stared. He lusted. He sought her. He lost control of his passion. He lay with her.

In his book, *Temptation*, Dietrich Bonhoeffer wisely strikes at the heart of the problem that you and I, like David, wrestle with.

> In our members there is a slumbering inclination toward desire, which is both sudden and fierce. With irresistible power, desire seizes mastery of the flesh. All at once a secret, smoldering fire is kindled. The flesh burns and is in flames. It makes no difference whether it is a sexual desire, or ambition, or vanity, or desire for revenge, or love of fame and power, or greed for money. . . .
>
> At this moment God is quite unreal to us. [Remember those words.] He loses all reality, and only desire for the creature is real. The only reality is the devil. Satan does not here fill us with hatred of God, but with forgetfulness of God. . . . The lust thus aroused envelopes the mind and will of man in deepest darkness. The powers of clear discrimination and of decision are taken from us. The questions present themselves as, "Is what the flesh desires really sin in this case?" And, "Is it really not permitted to me, yes, expected of me now, here in my particular situation to appease desire?" . . .
>
> It is here that everything within me rises up against the Word of God. . . . Therefore the Bible teaches us in times of temptation in the flesh, there is one command: Flee! Flee fornication. Flee idolatry. Flee youthful lusts. Flee the lusts of the world. There is no resistance to Satan in lust other than flight. Every struggle against lust in one's own strength is doomed to failure.[33]

If you do not run, you will fall. It's only a matter of time. I have given that counsel so many times. When you run from temptation, lust backs off. It is the only counsel that works for me. If you try to fight it, you will fall. Again, it's only a matter of time. Now . . . back to the scene.

David stood on the roof of that palace in the night air, with no one else around, and he lost all cognizance of who he was or what would happen if he fell into that sin. As the smoldering desire down inside burst into flames, God became quite distant and unreal to him. He forgot that he was God's man. He forgot all the lessons he had learned during the days of his youth and during his fugitive years in the wilderness. He forgot God!

Not only did David take a second look, he was staring for an undetermined period of time. In his mind, fueled by lust, he envisioned the pleasure of sex with that beautiful woman. Blinded by desire for her, he became engulfed with imagination. He wanted that woman . . . now! Then, "David sent and inquired about the woman." And notice the report.

> "Is this not Bathsheba, the daughter of Eliam, the wife of Uriah the Hittite?"
>
> 2 Samuel 11:3

I find that statement incredibly significant. This soft-footed servant offered the king a subtle warning of wisdom. Normally in Israel they would give the genealogy of a person without relation to their mate. They would give the name of the person, the father's name, the grandfather's name, and, on occasion, the great-grandfather. But this servant says, "She is Bathsheba, the daughter of Eliam, the wife of Uriah." In other words, "The lady's married."

I believe that the servant knew exactly what David was thinking. He could see her down there. He was a man as well. He knew his master. He'd seen the harem. He'd watched David operate with women, and so he warned him as he answered him.

But it doesn't even seem to register with David. At that moment God was "quite unreal" to David. Out of control, he said no to all the things he should have said yes to, and yes to all the things he should have said no to. By now his desire for sexual pleasure with that woman was paramount. He moved quickly, ignoring any warning and all consequences.

> And David sent messengers and took her, and when she came to him, he lay with her; and when she had purified herself from her uncleanness, she returned to her house.
>
> 2 Samuel 11:4

Now, let's be absolutely realistic here. We would be foolish to think that there was no pleasure in this encounter between David and Bathsheba. This act carried with it an enormous amount of sensual excitement. Stolen waters *are* sweet. I think both of them probably took great pleasure in this private moment. He was romantic and handsome . . . she was lonely, beautiful, and flattered . . . both thoroughly enjoyed it. Nothing indicates otherwise. Nor did David force himself upon this woman. It appears to be a one-time-only adulterous affair, a mutual situation that brought mutual satisfaction. Perhaps before midnight she slipped back to her own home, hoping no one noticed.

But as the writer of Hebrews says, this represented "the passing pleasure of sin." In fact, the pleasure is gone within a matter of weeks, for Bathsheba "sent and told David, 'I am pregnant.'"

It's been my observation over the years that the devil never tips his hand in temptation. He shows you only the beauty, the ecstasy, the fun, the excitement, and the stimulating adventure of stolen desires. But he never tells the heavy drinker, "Tomorrow morning there'll be a hangover. Ultimately, you'll ruin your family." He never tells the drug user early on, "This is the beginning of a long, sorrowful, dead-end road." He never tells the thief, "You're going to get caught, friend. You do this, and you'll wind up behind bars." He certainly doesn't warn the adulterer, "You know, pregnancy is a real possibility." Or, "You could get a life-threatening disease." Are you kidding? Face it, when the sin is done and all the penalties of that sin come due, the devil is nowhere to be found. He smiles as you fall . . . but he leaves you with no encouragement when the consequences kick in.

How the mighty have fallen! F. B. Meyer succinctly states the outcome:

> One brief spell of passionate indulgence, and then—his character blasted irretrievably; his peace vanished; the foundations of his kingdom imperiled; the Lord displeased; and great occasion given to his enemies to blaspheme![34]

And, lest you think David's fall was a sudden, instant event, consider Emily Dickinson's eloquent piece:

> Crumbling is not an instant's act,
> A fundamental pause;
> Dilapidation's processes
> Are organized decays.
>
> 'Tis first a cobweb on the soul,
> A cuticle of dust,
> A borer in the axis,
> An elemental rust.

Ruin is formal, devil's work,
Consecutive and slow—
Fail in an instant no man did,
Slipping is crash's law.[35]

A PANIC PLAN

"David, I am pregnant." When David got that news, he had a decision to make. He could take one of two courses. He could go before God and declare himself completely contaminated, sinful, guilty, and then declare to his counselors and the nation, "I have sinned." Obviously, that was exactly what he should have done. Or he could go the route of deception and hypocrisy. Sadly, David chose the latter, which led him even further into sin—including the horrific act of murder. And let's not forget, his choosing to lie and deceive set in motion an endless series of heartaches within his immediate family in the years to come. What a fool he was to try and cover up his sin!

When we are in the midst of panic, we don't make wise decisions. And that's where David is. He has had his night of passion—so far as we know, he and Bathsheba were only together that one night—and suddenly the news comes back to haunt him: This woman, this wife of another man, is going to have your baby. And he thinks, *What do I do?* Rather than falling on his face before God, rather than openly admitting his adultery, he chose the route of deception and hypocrisy. He came up with a creative idea that backfired on him.

> David sent to Joab, saying, "Send me Uriah the Hittite." So Joab sent Uriah to David.
>
> 2 Samuel 11:6

Now you have to understand something about Joab. He's a swift, clever, tough-minded warrior out there in the field. And he is street smart. Also, David is a little uneasy with this guy and the clout he carries.

So Joab, surrounded by the sounds of battle, gets a message from King David, saying, "Send Uriah home." Now there's not a naive cell in Joab's body. He is bright and quick—suspicious and malicious. So he sees the report and he sends Uriah back . . . wondering why?

When the husband of Bathsheba came home,

> David asked concerning the welfare of Joab and the people and
> the state of the war.
>
> 2 Samuel 11:7

Did David really care about the people or the state of the war or how
Joab was doing? Not for a moment. It's an ad lib, designed to make him
look compassionate. He's merely setting up Uriah. He's trying to put him
at ease. He's faking it, see. When you're in a cover-up mode, you fake it.
So he has Uriah over for a steak dinner with all the trimmings and asks,
"Now how are things going, Uriah?"

We don't know whether Uriah was flattered by all of this or just puz-
zled, wondering, *What's all this about? I should be in the battle, not sitting
here in the king's palace talking about it.* What we do know is that

> David said to Uriah, "Go down to your house, and wash your
> feet." And Uriah went out of the king's house, and a present
> from the king was sent out after him.
>
> 2 Samuel 11:8

Clever idea . . . but it flops. Instead of going home, as David suggested,

> Uriah slept at the door of the king's house with all the servants
> of his lord, and did not go down to his house.
>
> 2 Samuel 11:9

Where did David want Uriah? Why, of course! He wanted Uriah to
spend the night with his wife. If there is a pregnancy and Uriah has slept
with his wife, nobody will ever know what David has done.

But Uriah is a faithful soldier whose heart is with the men in the field.
And if his men are out in the field, then he is not going to seek the comfort
of his own wife and home. When David learned of this, he said to Uriah,
"Why didn't you go home last night?"

> And Uriah said to David, "The ark and Israel and Judah are
> staying in temporary shelters, and my lord Joab and the servants
> of my lord are camping in an open field. Shall I then go out
> to my house to eat and drink and lie with my wife? By your
> life and the life of your soul, I will not do this thing."
>
> 2 Samuel 11:11

What a reproof to David, the great king, the commander-in-chief. He should feel rebuked by the integrity of a foot soldier—a nobody—a man who was from his helmet to his boots committed to the nation and to the God of the nation . . . but David was too insensitive to feel remorse.

Look at how David handled it.

> Then David said to Uriah, "Stay here today also, and tomorrow I'll let you go." So Uriah remained in Jerusalem that day and the next.
>
> Now David called him, and he ate and drank before him, and he made him drunk; and in the evening he went out to lie on his bed with his lord's servants, but he did not go down to his house.
>
> 2 Samuel 11:12–13

A COMPLETE COVER-UP

Now here's a panic-stricken king, frustrated to the point of rage over his failing plan. No matter what he does, he can't pull off his strategy of deception. He can steal the man's wife, but he can't manipulate the woman's husband. Uriah will not cooperate. So David, in greater panic, escalates his plot to the next level.

> Now it came about in the morning that David wrote a letter to Joab, and sent it by the hand of Uriah. And he had written in the letter, saying, "Place Uriah in the front line of the fiercest battle and withdraw from him, so that he may be struck down and die."
>
> 2 Samuel 11:14–15

David wrote the message, sealed it, and said, "Uriah, take this to Joab." Let me ask you, did he trust Uriah? All the way. He sent the man off with his own death warrant in hand.

When Uriah handed over the message on the battlefield and Joab read it, guess who put two and two together. Joab was no fool. I have a sneaking suspicion he figured the whole thing out in a few milliseconds. A panic-stricken king and a ruthless warrior on the battlefront makes for disaster. Unfortunately, innocent Uriah was doomed.

> So it was as Joab kept watch on the city, that he put Uriah at
> the place where he knew there were valiant men. And the men
> of the city went out and fought against Joab, and some of the
> people among David's servants fell; and Uriah the Hittite also
> died. Then Joab sent and reported to David all the events of
> the war.
>
> 2 Samuel 11:16–18

Now get this. Joab knew *exactly* what was most important to the king.

> And he charged the messenger, saying, "When you have fin-
> ished telling all the events of the war to the king, and if it
> happens the king's wrath rises and he says to you, 'Why did
> you go so near the city to fight? Did you not know that they
> would shoot from the wall? . . . ' Then you shall say, 'Your
> servant Uriah the Hittite is dead also.'"
>
> 2 Samuel 11:19–21

Joab knows Uriah, probably knew of his beautiful wife as well as his
family. He also knows David. He knows what David really wants to hear.
So when he sends the report back to the king, he says, "Tell him, 'Mission
accomplished. I did the deed.'" After that, guess who has the tools for
blackmail. Right, Joab has the king right where he wants him, and one
day he'll rise up and make David rue the day he made that decision. So
he set up Uriah to be killed.

The messenger came to the king from the battlefield, and David listened with bated breath for one statement. Finally he hears what he's been
waiting for: "Your servant Uriah the Hittite is dead also." And adding the
ultimate act of hypocrisy,

> Then David said to the messenger, "Thus you shall say to Joab,
> 'Do not let this thing displease you, for the sword devours one
> as well as another; make your battle against the city stronger
> and overthrow it'; and so encourage him."
>
> 2 Samuel 11:25

But it wasn't just Uriah who fell in battle; other soldiers died as well.
Many paid the price for David's sin on that battlefield, yet David says,
"That's all right, Joab! Stay at it! Tell 'em to go on!" Rather than falling
before God, declaring himself guilty of this crime, he moves right on. In

fact, after a few days, Bathsheba's period of mourning for her husband ends, and,

> David sent and brought her into his house and she became his
> wife; then she bore him a son. . . .
>
> 2 Samuel 11:27

Now I want to ask you something. It sounds simple, but it's not. Why in the world did David murder Uriah? What did he gain by it? Think about that. If Uriah had lived and come home from battle and found his wife pregnant, who would have ever connected it to David? It's doubtful she would have ever said a word. Then, after Uriah is killed, David immediately takes her to the palace and marries her—and it's been my observation that most adults can count to nine. So who in the world was David hiding from?

When you act in panic, you don't think logically. In fact, you usually don't think. You react. You overlook and cover up and smear over and cloud over and deny and scheme until you find yourself in the midst of such a maze of lies that you can never escape or get the mess untangled. Until finally, you face someone honest enough to say, "You are the man!" (More about that in the next chapter.)

Meanwhile, at the end of this awful episode we read eleven simple words: "David did what was evil in the sight of the Lord." Period.

In that brief statement we see the raw, open sewage of David's life. As the Puritans said, "All the moisture of heaven had lapsed into drought. Everything was dry and barren in his soul." The sweet singer of Israel was now living a lie, faking his existence in a minor key. This passionate, handsome king, this exemplary leader now lives in the shadows of his own palace. He no longer goes out to battle. He shrivels into something he was never designed to be, because he deliberately compromised with wrong, then deceitfully covered it over with murder.

This story strikes some a lot harder than others. Some people live in the relentless rage of lust. They curse it, but it's there. They don't want it, but it constantly winks at them, like a beast filled with venom. It bites into them and paralyzes their spiritual walk, just as it did with David. I think God tells us these details of David's fall so everyone can see clearly where it all leads and what its consequences are.

Are you keeping count of David's sins? Lust, adultery, hypocrisy, murder. How could a man—a man after God's own heart—fall to such a level? If you are honest about your own heart, it's not hard to understand.

If you are playing with sins of the flesh, you're living on borrowed time as a child of God. There is nothing as stinging, there's nothing as damning to the life, than hidden sins of the flesh. There is nothing that gives the enemy greater ammunition to send those blasphemous statements toward the church of God than that kind of secret compromise. You can also be part and parcel of it indirectly by not taking a stand against it.

And so—the sad, dark chapter of David's fall comes to an end. Or does it? No, not really. The man is now trapped in a swirl of misery, which he describes in detail in Psalm 32:3–4 as well as Psalm 51:3–4. Sleepless nights. Physical illness. A fever. Haunted memories. Loss of weight. Total misery. The worst: feeling so *terribly alone.* So many miles from God. So full of groaning and agonizing. Read the verses from those two psalms for yourself. Let them take shape in your mind. Don't hurry. We need to see afresh the wages of sin.

No, the chapter doesn't end. Not until many months have dragged on. Not until a knock came on the palace door . . . and a friend who cared enough to confront looked the king in the eye and called a spade a spade.

That's next.

It was a visit David would never forget.

Chapter Seventeen

Confrontation!

Three thousand years ago there lived a great man who served a great nation under a great God—Jehovah God of the heavens. The man's name was David. So powerful was David that sixty-two chapters of the Old Testament are devoted to his biography, and no less than fifty-nine references in the New Testament call people's attention to this man— more, by far, than any other biblical character.

Yet, David, the great man of God, committed a series of terrible sins that led to terrible consequences. When he was about fifty years of age, he committed adultery. Then, rather than immediately face it and admit it, he covered it up with premeditated murder. For the better part of a year, he lived a life of hypocrisy and deception. His world became a world of guarded, miserable *secrecy*.

Looking at the situation during that period, as the days and months passed, one might have thought that the holy God of heaven was asleep, or at least was letting it pass—that sin does actually pay, that there are no wages. But that was not the case.

In a marvelous move on God's part He finally brought before David a man of great integrity, a man who told him the truth. I don't think any other confrontation has ever been so brief and so effective. Four three-letter words did the job: "You are the man!" David crumbled in humility. And I think a fresh gush of relief came over his life.

We need to remember that, like many sins, David's were carried out *secretly*—at least for a while. One of the things that accompanies the promotion of individuals to higher positions of authority is an increase in privacy. This closed-door policy maintained by those in high office brings great temptation for things to be done in secret. Unaccountability is common among those in command. So it was with David. Unable to handle the privacy of the office over the long haul, David finally fell and rapidly went about covering his tragic tracks. It was done secretly.

The second thing I would say about the acts of David is that they were done *willfully*. This was not a momentary mistake. He didn't stumble into the sin. He willfully and knowingly walked into the sin with Bathsheba, killed her husband (at least indirectly), and deliberately lived a lie during the months that followed.

MANY MONTHS IN RETROSPECT

During that time, David's sin did not go unnoticed by God. The last verse of the eleventh chapter says, "The thing that David had done was evil in the sight of the LORD." I would like to add in parenthesis, "And don't you forget it!" What was evil 3,000 years ago is evil today, even though many people do it. To cheapen a marriage with an adulterous relationship is still a willful sin, even though many carry it out. This very night, in secret places, people with wedding rings given by another person, will be with individuals that are not their own partners. It is still evil in the sight of the Lord. (And don't you forget it.)

Maybe nobody else noticed, but God did. And He designed a strategy to bring David to his knees. God is awfully good at that. He doesn't settle His accounts at the end of each month or, for that matter, each year. But when He does settle them, well, "Do not be deceived, God is not mocked; for whatever a man [whatever a woman] sows, this he [she] will also reap," writes the apostle Paul (Gal. 6:7).

As one of my mentors once put it, "God's wheels grind slowly, but they grind exceedingly fine."

Lest you think David's life was enjoyable and that he had long delightful nights with his new wife, free of guilt, and lest you think David was in a marvelous state of mind during those months that followed, turn to Psalm 32. I briefly referred to this at the end of the previous chapter, but now I want to examine David's admission a bit closer.

To begin with, the superscription right beneath the title of the psalm reads, "A Psalm of David. A Maskil." The Hebrew word from which the word Maskil is taken means "instruction." It's a psalm designed to instruct. Indeed it does!

How blessed is he whose transgression is forgiven, whose sin
is covered!
How blessed is the man to whom the LORD does not
impute iniquity, and in whose spirit there is no deceit!
Psalm 32:1–2

Now listen to David's admission.

When I kept silent about my sin, my body wasted away
through my groaning all day long.
For day and night Thy hand was heavy upon me; my
vitality was drained away as with the fever-heat of summer.
Psalm 32:3–4

The Living Bible puts it very well.

There was a time when I wouldn't admit what a sinner I was.
But my dishonesty made me miserable and filled my days with
frustration.
All day and all night your hand was heavy on me. My
strength evaporated like water on a sunny day until I finally
admitted all my sins to you and stopped trying to hide them.

In his splendid book, *Guilt and Grace*, Paul Tournier, the brilliant
Swiss writer, physician, and psychiatrist, talks about two kinds of guilt:
true guilt and false guilt. False guilt, says Tournier, is brought on by the
judgments and suggestions of man. True guilt comes from willfully and
knowingly disobeying God.[36] Obviously, David is enduring true guilt.
Someone has described the way people handle guilt by using the picture
of the warning light on the dashboard of the car. As you're driving along,
the red light flashes on, saying, "Take notice! There's trouble under the
hood." At that moment, you have a choice. You can stop, get out of the
car, open the hood, and see what's wrong. Or, you can carry a small
hammer in the glove compartment, and when the red light turns on, you
can knock it out with the hammer and keep on driving. No one will know
the difference for a while—until you burn up the car. And then you look
back and realize what a stupid decision it was to break out the light on
the dashboard.
Some Christians carry imaginary hammers in the glove compartment
of their conscience. When the light of true guilt begins to flash, they bring

out the hammer and knock out the light. They call it false guilt or they say it's just what everybody else is doing and on and on and on. But all the while their internal motor is burning up. Then, somewhere down the road, they look back and realize what a foolish decision it was not to stop, look deeper, and come to terms with what was wrong.

David says, "When I lived in the true guilt of my soul, I could not stay silent down inside. As a matter of fact, I groaned all day." Now you know what that means. "There was this awful oppression, this misery of conscience. Day and night I felt the heavy hand of God on me. It was like running a fever. I couldn't lift my head. I couldn't handle the pressures of my work. I couldn't cope. I was sick. My body wasted away."

Turn to the other psalm I referred to earlier, Psalm 51. Its superscription calls this "A Psalm of David, when Nathan the prophet came to him, after he had gone in to Bathsheba." So David wrote this psalm after Nathan had paid the fateful visit we're going to consider in this chapter. In this psalm David pleads,

> Wash me thoroughly from my iniquity,
> And cleanse me from my sin.
> For I know my transgressions,
> And my sin is ever before me.
>
> Psalm 51:2–3

David wasn't relaxing and taking life easy, sipping lemonade on his patio, during the aftermath of his adultery. Count on it . . . he had sleepless nights. He could see his sin written across the ceiling of his room as he tossed and turned in bed. He saw it written across the walls. He saw it on the plate where he tried to choke down his meals. He saw it on the faces of his counselors. He was a miserable husband, an irritable father, a poor leader, and a songless composer. He lived a lie but he couldn't escape the truth.

He had no joy. ("Restore to me the joy of Thy salvation" Ps. 51:12.) He was unstable. He felt inferior and insecure. ("Create in me a clean heart, O God, and renew a steadfast spirit within me" Ps. 51:10.) Sin does that to you. It's part of the wages that sin inevitably demands. A carnal Christian will dance all around and try to tell you, "Everything's fine. Don't press me. I'm really free . . . really having fun . . . I'm doing well. You just haven't any idea." But down inside it's there. Everything is empty, hollow, joyless, pointless. A true Christian cannot deny that. True guilt is there. Oppressively there. Constantly there. That's why David says, "Renew a steadfast spirit in me," implying, "I haven't had it for a long, long time."

Then Nathan stepped into David's life and told him the truth. It was an incredible confrontation.

A SUDDEN MOMENT OF TRUTH

It is worth noticing that Nathan didn't come on his own; he was sent by God: "Then the LORD sent Nathan to David." I think the most important word in that sentence is the first one, "then." God's timing is absolutely incredible.

When was he sent? Right after the act of adultery? No. Right after Bathsheba said, "I am pregnant"? No. Right after he murdered Uriah? No. Right after he married Uriah's pregnant widow? No. Right after the birth of the baby? No. It's believed by some Old Testament scholars that there was at least a twelve-month interval that passed before Nathan paid the visit. God waited until just the right time. He let the grinding wheels of sin do their full work and *then* He stepped in.

To be totally honest with you, there are times when I really question the timing of God. Times when I just don't know why He's so slow to carry out what I think He ought to do. But every time I have looked back in retrospect, I have seen how beautifully He worked out His plan, how perfectly it had come to pass. God not only does the right thing; He does the right thing at the right time.

In confronting someone in his sin, the timing is as important as the wording. Simply to tighten your belt, grab your Bible and, at your convenience, confront a person who is in sin is unwise. Most importantly, you need to be sure that you're sent by God. Nathan was.

Then the LORD sent Nathan to David. And he came to him, . . .

2 Samuel 12:1

God not only knew the right time, he chose the right person. It was a man who had David's respect. He'd earned it over the years. Nathan the prophet needed no introduction. David knew him well.

Now put yourself in the sandals of that fearless prophet. Think of the difficult commission God had given him. He was to stand before the most powerful man in the nation and tell that man what he had been refusing to tell himself for a year.

No one else in the land would tell David the truth. Oh, there had been some raised eyebrows. There certainly were some whispers. But nobody would be honest and forthright enough to say, "David, you're in sin." So God said to Nathan, "Go to David and tell him." Nathan obeyed immediately.

Before he was on his way to the palace, Nathan must have thought through how he would present this matter to David because his opening words were both thoughtful and brilliant. Because of the story-approach he used, David was drawn in and at the same time disarmed of all defenses.

> He came to him, and said, "There were two men in one city, the one rich and the other poor. The rich man had a great many flocks and herds. But the poor man had nothing except one little ewe lamb which he bought and nourished; and it grew up together with him and his children. It would eat of his bread and drink of his cup and lie in his bosom and was like a daughter to him."
>
> 2 Samuel 12:1–3

By now David is on the edge of his chair listening, thinking that Nathan is talking about something that happened in the city of Jerusalem.

> "Now a traveler came to the rich man, and he was unwilling to take from his own flock or his own herd, to prepare for the wayfarer who had come to him; rather he took the poor man's ewe lamb and prepared it for the man who had come to him."
>
> 2 Samuel 12:4

As a result of the wise words of Nathan, David was in a most vulnerable spot. Moved with compassion over the situation in the story, David sentences himself. We can feel the passion in his response:

> Then David's anger burned greatly against the man, and he said to Nathan, "As the LORD lives, surely the man who has done this deed deserves to die. And he must make restitution for the lamb . . . because he did this thing and had no compassion."
>
> 2 Samuel 12:5–6

When confrontation comes in God's timing, the way is prepared. In that vulnerable, unguarded moment, David stuck his whole head in the noose. All Nathan had to do was give it a pull. And that is exactly what he did in four words:

"*You* are the man!"

I am absolutely convinced, though the narrative doesn't say it, that David's jaw dropped open. He blinked and stared at Nathan as his own sins silently and vividly passed in review. He didn't know that anyone knew what he had done. Certainly he never expected anybody, especially this trusted prophet, ever to confront him about it. Yet Nathan was the very best person to do it. Proverbs 27:6 comes to mind: "Faithful are the wounds of a friend, but deceitful are the kisses of an enemy." Literally, the verse reads in Hebrew: "Trustworthy are the bruises caused by the wounding of one who loves you." Isn't that vivid? The one who loves you *bruises* you, and those lingering wounds are faithful, they're trustworthy. That kind of confrontation is the best thing in the world for the believer who is hiding secret sin. The fact that it is a friend (one who truly loves you) disarms you, and you melt like putty.

At that moment, David's trusted friend and counselor says, "You're the man, David! You're the one who fed that wayfaring thought. You're the one who said to that stranger called lust, 'I'll take someone else's lamb, and I'll satisfy my desires with her.' David, *you are the man.*"

Then, before David could interrupt, Nathan went on, "Thus says the LORD God of Israel." Notice, none of this is Nathan's message; it is God's message. The prophet is just the mouthpiece of God. Look at the moving message he delivered.

"You are the man! . . . It is I [says the LORD] who anointed you king over Israel, and it is I who delivered you from the hand of Saul. I also gave you your master's house and your master's wives into your care, and I gave you the house of Israel and Judah; and if that had been too little, I would have added to you many more things like these!

"Why have you despised the word of the LORD by doing evil in His sight? You have struck down Uriah the Hittite with the sword, have taken his wife to be your wife, and have killed him with the sword of the sons of Ammon.

> "Now therefore, the sword shall never depart from your house, because you have despised Me and have taken the wife of Uriah the Hittite to be your wife." Thus says the LORD, "Behold, I will raise up evil against you from your own household. . . ."
>
> 2 Samuel 12:7–11

In his sin, David had despised the God he served. Now, as a result of that sin, in days and years to come, David would experience grief within his own household. What a prediction! "The sword shall never depart from your house." Meaning? (A quick look ahead reveals the answer.) Turmoil and tragedy. Rape and revenge. An uncontrollable son. A son who betrays him, who actually drives his own father from the throne.

> "Thus says the LORD, 'Behold I will raise up evil against you from your own household; I will even take your wives before your eyes, and give them to your companion, and he shall lie with your wives in broad daylight. Indeed you did it secretly, but I will do this thing before all Israel, and under the sun.'"
>
> 2 Samuel 12:11–12

Whew! Talk about the consequences of sin. David sits there with his mouth still open, leaning back, perhaps staring at the ceiling, listening to the voice of God from Nathan. Once silence fills the room, the king drops to his knees as he looks up into Nathan's clear eyes and says the one thing that is appropriate, "I have sinned against the LORD."

The eminent British biographer Alexander Whyte writes these words with regard to the courage, faithfulness, and skill of Nathan.

> Preaching is magnificent work if only we could get preachers like Nathan. If our preachers had only something of Nathan's courage, skill, serpent-like wisdom, and evangelical instancy. . . . We ministers must far more study Nathan's method; especially when we are sent to preach awakening sermons. Too much skill cannot be expended in laying down our approaches to the consciences of our people. Nathan's sword was within an inch of David's conscience before David knew that Nathan had a sword. One sudden thrust, and the king was at Nathan's feet. What a rebuke of our slovenly, unskilful, blundering work! When we go back to Nathan and David, we forget and forgive

everything that had been evil in David. The only thing wanting to make that day in David's life perfect was that Nathan should have had to come to David. Now, what will make this the most perfect day in all your life will be this, if you will save the Lord and His prophet all that trouble so to speak, and be both the Lord and His prophet to yourself. Read Nathan's parable to yourself till you say, I am the man![37]

If God has called you to be His messenger, then do it skillfully and do it humbly. Do it right or don't do it. If God calls you to be a confronter, confront. People still long for, hunger for the message of God. When you encounter an individual who has willfully stepped onto the wrong path, face it with him. Call it what it is. Certainly at the right time and in the right way, *but do it!* Don't hedge. Don't try to redefine it. Don't explain it away. Call it sin. And in doing so, remember that you, too, have sinned. So, stay humble and full of compassion . . . but speak the truth in love . . . yes *speak the truth!* A tremendous relief comes over the sinner when someone honestly says, "You have been wrong, face it. Do something about it."

Nathan said, "You are the man, David! And this is the result."

And David, realizing he was absolutely guilty, admitted without hesitation, "I have sinned. I've sinned against the LORD." With that admission, restoration began.

Nathan immediately responded,

> "The LORD also has taken away your sin; you shall not die."
>
> 2 Samuel 12:13

What a promise of grace! "You shall not die." And then he stated the first of several consequences . . .

> "However, because by this deed you have given occasion to the enemies of the LORD to blaspheme, the child also that is born to you shall surely die."
>
> 2 Samuel 12:14

At that point, Nathan's mission is complete. End of confrontation.

Nathan stands, turns around, walks to the door, opens it, steps through, closes it—and David is left alone. Perhaps it was that same evening that he wrote Psalm 51. What relief forgiveness provided!

I believe that a gush of relief swept across David as he thought, *Finally, someone knows the truth and the secret is out. Finally, I have the assurance of God's forgiveness. Finally, it is all out in the open before Him so that the pus can run and the infection actually leave.*

I remember as a little boy suffering from a stone bruise. At least that's what we called it in my young years. I had bruised my heel down deep, right to the bone, and the infection caused my heel to swell and swell, until finally I could not wear a shoe on my foot. In fact, I couldn't put any pressure on the heel. The swelling grew as the infection came more and more to the surface, until it was so painful that I could not even endure a sock on my foot.

Afraid of blood poisoning, my parents finally took me to the doctor, who said, "We'll have to lance this."

Although I knew it was coming and dreaded the thought, when the doctor lanced it, I literally felt a gush of relief as the infection poured out. Suddenly there was even a relief of the pain. Though the lancing was painful, the relief eclipsed it. Shortly thereafter, the infection left and healing followed. Spiritually speaking, that's what David must have felt as the door slammed and he was left alone with his thoughts.

TWO SERIOUS AREAS OF APPLICATION

As we think about David's life, at least two lessons reach out to personalize it for us. One has to do with effective confrontation and the second has to do with genuine repentance.

First of all, *to be effective in confrontation we need to equip ourselves with four things.* If not, we can do more damage than good. We need to confront in absolute truth, right timing, wise wording, and fearless courage.

First, *absolute truth.* Don't go on hearsay. Get the facts. It may take time. You may have to investigate. Out of love and concern you will do all that. You won't investigate and spread the word all around; you'll just check it out until you have the facts carefully recorded and correctly arranged. Without absolute truth, you're shooting in the dark. Do not confront if you don't have the truth.

Second, *right timing.* Many people are confronted at the wrong time and as a result are driven deeper into their wrong because thoughtless Christians went off in a hurry to do something in the spurt of emotion. Wait until you are confident that it's God's timing. You will know. If you are sensitive to the Lord and are walking with Him, He will let you know, "Now is the time." It's then you do it. And, like Nathan, do it privately.

In my ministry I've had to deal with some things that, acting in the flesh, I would have loved to have dealt with earlier. But it wasn't the time. When it was God's time, I had green lights flashing all the way and knew it was clear to speak to the person or persons involved. Painful, but clear.

Third, *wise wording.* I'm impressed that Nathan didn't just go up to David and say, "You are in sin . . . I'm ashamed of you!" No, he went about it in a wise manner. He had planned his approach very carefully.

There's a proverb that says, "A word fitly spoken is like apples of gold in pictures of silver. As an earring of gold, and an ornament of fine gold, so is a wise reprover upon an obedient ear" (25:11–12, KJV). The right words are crucial. If you don't have your wording worked out, don't go. Wait. Think it through. Be a "wise reprover."

Fourth, *fearless courage.* Nathan, remember, was sent by God, and that's where courage comes from. You will have nothing to lose if you walk in the strength of the Lord. Don't fear the loss of a friendship. God honors the truth. After all, it is the truth—and only the truth—that sets people free. If the Lord is really in it, you'll be one of the best friends this person ever had by telling him the truth. Remember the phrase: "Faithful are the wounds caused by the bruising of one who loves you"? Be certain you're confronting out of love. One who doesn't love doesn't confront—at least he doesn't confront God's way.

The next lesson we learn is from David's response . . . it is about genuine repentance itself. How can we know that repentance is genuine? I see four things in Psalm 51 that help me identify true repentance.

First of all, when there is true repentance, *there will be open, unguarded admission.* David says, "I have sinned . . . I have not hidden my sin. Against Thee and Thee only I have sinned and I've done evil." And he spells it out.

When a person holds back the truth or tells you only part of it, he or she is not repentant.

Second: when there is true repentance, there is *a desire to make a complete break from sin.* Repentance is turning around, on the basis of truth, and going in the opposite direction, making a complete break with what has been.

David's son Solomon said,

> He who conceals his transgressions will not prosper, but he who confesses and forsakes them will find compassion.
>
> Proverbs 28:13

Forsaking sin follows confession of sin. Both represent genuine repentance—a desire to make a complete break.

Third: when there is true repentance, *the spirit is broken and humble.* David says,

> The sacrifices of God are a broken spirit; a broken and a contrite heart, O God, Thou wilt not despise.
>
> Psalm 51:17

Grief over what you have done, delight over the relief of repentance and release, doesn't leave you standing there stoic. You may cry; you may then laugh out loud; you may groan or fall on your face or shout for joy over the relief. But you won't be defensive or angry or proud or bitter. A contrite heart makes no demands and has no expectations. Broken and humble people are simply grateful to be alive. When there is absolute repentance, resulting in a broken and humble heart, emotions overflow.

Fourth: true repentance is a *claiming of God's forgiveness and reinstatement.* Turning around, going in the other direction, is our claim that He has forgiven and has reinstated us. That's the very first thing Nathan does with his friend, David. "You will not die, but there will be consequences." All sins are forgivable, when confessed and forsaken, but some sins carry tremendous ramifications . . . the awful, sometimes lingering consequences. David died hating the day he fell into bed with Bathsheba because of the constant conflicts and consequences that resulted. But down inside he knew that the God of Israel had forgiven him and had dealt with him in grace. After all, he was allowed to go on living, wasn't he?

Not all confrontations end like Nathan's with David, of course. Sometimes, tragically, there is no repentance.

The work of purging, of confrontation, is the most severe work of the Holy Spirit. Either our lives are clean or dirty. Either we are keeping short accounts with our heavenly Father as His child or we are living a lie.

When we repent, God promises us restitution and forgiveness through the blood of Jesus Christ. He does not promise relief from any and all consequences, but He promises a relief that only the Spirit of God can give.

> If we confess our sins, He is faithful and righteous to forgive us our sins and to cleanse us from all unrighteousness.
>
> 1 John 1:9

A father came to me sometime ago and spelled out the tragic story of his own son. As he described one rebellious act after another being committed by his son, I finally had to level with the man and say, "Look, you're lowering your standard to stay away from the pain of confrontation. This boy is ruling your home. He is out of control. Furthermore, he's lost respect for his mom and dad, though he won't say that out of his own lips. Confront him. Tell him the truth. Stand your ground." I used this story from 2 Samuel 12 as an example. The man took my words to heart. He thought through his wording. He waited for the right time. And I'm happy to say, he firmly confronted his teen-aged son . . . who responded beautifully. Tough task but worth the effort! Tough love pays off.

My hat goes off to any parent who stands that ground. If you happen to be one of them, you will go down in history as some of those quiet, silent heroes for whom God has reserved special rewards. We're living in a day of great compromise, especially in the realm of the home. We need to learn the lesson of confrontation from Nathan. Though the eras pass, though styles and lifestyles change, God's standard never changes. He is still holy. He is still pure. He still honors the truth, even when it is difficult to declare. But that is what He requires of us, His children.

Those who really care, care enough to confront.

Chapter Eighteen

Trouble at Home

A family in trouble is a common occurrence, but it's never a pretty picture. There are two kinds of trouble a family can experience: trouble that comes from without and trouble that comes from within. Though both can be devastating for a family, the more difficult of the two is trouble from within.

When the clammy fingers of death take their tyrannical toll on our lives and bring pain to our hearts, the trouble comes from without. A fire can burn a house to the ground or a flood can wash it off its foundation, causing struggles that are hard to bear. But I've found that those kinds of external troubles often pull a family together rather than separate them.

Not so when troubles come from within. Trouble from within comes in the form of pressure, tension, abuse, neglect, unforgiveness, bitterness, heartbreaking hatred, and all the other difficulties that accompany the carnal life when parents walk in the flesh or act foolishly . . . or when children respond in rebellion and disagreement and disharmony. When there is friction between husband and wife or between parent and child, that's a lot harder to bear than external struggles, especially when it is the consequence of someone's sin in the family.

Before we look once again into the life of David, I want to give you a principle from Galatians 6:7–8. "Do not be deceived" are the first words of these verses—words we read several times in the New Testament. The Lord gives us that warning ahead of time because the devil or the flesh or the world will work havoc on our thinking, deceiving us into doubting the truth God presents. And so ahead of the principle, God says, "Don't be deceived about this. Don't let anyone teach you the opposite. Don't let yourself, or someone else, or some experience lead you to believe that something other than this is the truth. Don't be deceived."

Now, here's the principle:

> God is not mocked; for whatever a man sows, this he will also reap. For the one who sows to his own flesh shall from the flesh reap corruption. . . .
>
> Galatians 6:7–8

We reap what we sow, forgiveness notwithstanding. If there is anything we have been duped into believing in our era of erroneous teachings on grace, it is the thinking that if we will simply confess our sins and claim God's forgiveness, then all the consequences of what we have done will be quickly whisked away. When we fall into the trap of sin, all we have to do is to turn to the Lord and say, "Lord, I confess to You the wrong. And I agree with You that it is wrong. And I declare before You (and You only!) the wrongness of my actions. Now, I claim Your forgiveness and I count on You to get me back on track." And we think at that point everything is hunky-dory and all the consequences are gone.

But that is not what this verse (or any other verse of Scripture) says. The verse is written to people like you and me living in the era of grace, written to the church. It's not a law verse. It's not addressed to Israel. It's written to God's people, children of the King, people who are in Christ, living under grace. And the verse says:

> Do not be deceived, God is not mocked; for whatever a man sows, this he will also reap. For the one who sows to his own flesh shall from the flesh reap corruption [forgiveness notwithstanding]. . . .
>
> Galatians 6:7–8

Grace means that God, in forgiving you, does not kill you. Grace means that God, in forgiving you, gives you the strength to endure the consequences. Grace frees us so that we can obey our Lord. It does not mean sin's consequences are automatically removed. If I sin and in the process of sinning break my arm, when I find forgiveness from sin, I still have to deal with a broken bone.

Isn't it amazing how we will accept that in the physical realm? Not a person reading these words would deny that. A broken arm is a broken arm, whether I have been forgiven or whether I'm still living under the guilt of my sin. But the same happens in the emotional life. When a parent willfully and irresponsibly acts against God's written Word, not only does the parent suffer, but the family suffers as well. And that means internal trouble that seriously affects other family members.

Now let me address the consequence.

> The one who sows to his own flesh shall from the flesh reap corruption. . . .
>
> Galatians 6:8

These are the words I use to describe the consequence: The pain of the harvest eclipses the pleasure of the planting.

Think of your life as being like the life of a farmer. As you walk along, you are planting daily, one kind of seed or another. If you choose to sow the seeds of carnality, you may enjoy a measure of pleasure. Anyone who denies that is a fool. Even Scripture declares that sin has its pleasure. As I mentioned earlier, the pleasures are short-lived, but sin has its pleasure. That's one of the things that draws us into it. It is exciting. It is adventurous. It brings stimulation. It satisfies the body; it stimulates the desires of the flesh.

What we don't like to face, of course, is that the pain that comes in the harvesting of those sinful seeds eclipses the short-lived pleasure. Nothing concerns me more than today's propensity for using grace as a tool to justify sin or to take away the pain of the consequences. Too much teaching on corrective theology and not enough on preventive theology.

By way of example, think of an experience common to all of us. Every parent goes through the experience of teaching the kids to drive. It is a nerve-racking and difficult process, no matter how gifted your kids are. Now parents have a choice in how to teach their children how to drive. They can teach them in a corrective manner or in a preventive manner.

If I chose to teach my oldest grandson how to drive *correctively*, I could say to him, "Now, Ryan, I want to show you first of all, before we get in the car, the insurance policy that I have taken out on the car. So . . . when you have the wreck, which you're surely gonna have, here's the phone number of the agent. And after the accident, Ryan, I want you to be sure to call me." And I go into detail about all the things that need to be done after the wreck. That would be a "Corrective Driving Course."

On the other hand, I could say, "Now, Ryan, we're going to prevent a lot of problems ahead of time. If you drive by these rules and regulations I'm going to teach you, and if you obey these signs, you could very likely go a long period of time without even a slight scrape. Can't guarantee it, but it would sure be better than the other way." That would be a "Preventive Driving Course." I think you'd agree, the preventive method has it all over the corrective, right?

Most of us were taught 1 John 1:9 long before we learned Romans 6. Why? Because we have been trained to sin. Sounds heretical, doesn't it? But look! From our earliest days we have been taught that "If we confess our sins, He is faithful and just to forgive us our sins and to cleanse us from all unrighteousness" (1 John 1:9). So, when you sin, claim it. Claim God's forgiveness.

That's a marvelous verse. I call it our bar of soap in the Christian life. It keeps us clean. It certainly is the answer to the problem of sin once it has happened.

But it's not the best answer. The best answer is in Romans 6: "Therefore do not let sin reign in your mortal body that you should obey its lusts, and do not go on presenting the members of your body to sin as instruments of unrighteousness; but present yourselves to God as those alive from the dead, and your members as instruments of righteousness to God" (vv. 12–13).

Meaning what? Meaning, as I yield myself to God, when sin approaches, I can say, "No." And in the power of Jesus Christ, I can turn away from it. I don't *have* to sin hour after hour, day after day.

Part of the reason we don't get the full truth of Romans 6 is that nobody's talking about the consequences. Grace does not take away the consequences of sin.

If David could rise from the grave today, he would say "Amen" to that last statement. The sin in David's life led to trouble the likes of which few fathers on earth will ever experience.

PROBLEMS IN DAVID'S PALACE

Let me show you some of the stairsteps that went down in David's life, leading him to a life of misery as a result of his sin.

"David," Nathan said, "you are the man!" The prophet stood before the king and told him what no one else would tell him. "You're the one who took Bathsheba. You're the one who had Uriah murdered. You're the one who's lived like a hypocrite. You're the man, David!"

And David said to Nathan, "I have sinned." Three words he should have said the morning after he slept with Bathsheba. I am convinced the consequences would have been much, much less if he had declared his sin, openly confessed it before God and the people and laid his life bare. But he didn't. And now, a year later, Nathan says, "You're the man, David!" And David admits, "I have sinned."

But wait. Wait a minute. Look at the prediction Nathan makes in spite of David's confession. Under the guidance and inspiration of God, the prophet declares, "The sword shall never depart from your house."

Never? NEVER. "I thought he was forgiven," you say. Hey, he was. Nathan says so: "The LORD has taken away your sin; you shall not die." That's forgiveness. But the consequences are still there. "The sword will not depart from the house."

Am I saying that everyone who sins will have the same consequences? No. God, in His sovereign manner, fits the consequence for the person. It's His choice. It's His move. It's His plan. Why He chooses some to go this way and some that, I do not know. That's not our concern here. All I know is, in David's case, He led him down a path of misery so that he would never forget (nor would we in retrospect) the consequences of that series of acts.

> "The sword shall never depart from your house. . . . Behold, I will raise up evil against you from your own household."
>
> 2 Samuel 16:10

Twice, mention is made of David's own house. The Good News Bible renders this passage with this bad news: "I will cause those from your own family to bring trouble on you." The Living Bible speaks of David having to live under a constant threat from his family, since God said, "I will cause your household to rebel against you."

David has been forgiven, but his problems are not over. Trouble will come upon David's household. Remember my words in the opening paragraph of this chapter? There are two kinds of problems a family can endure: trouble from without and trouble from within. For David, the trouble comes from within, and I don't think words can express the awful pain this man lived with as he saw the misery that unfolded as a result of his own sin. No doubt he would have echoed the words of Eliphaz from Job 4:8: "According to what I have seen, those who plow iniquity and those who sow trouble harvest it."

Many years ago, my friend, John W. Lawrence, wrote a small but very insightful volume entitled *Down to Earth: The Laws of the Harvest*, in which he traces the truth of harvesting what we have sown. He says this about David:

> When David sowed to the flesh, he reaped what the flesh produced. Moreover, he reaped the consequences of his actions even though he had confessed his sin and been forgiven for it. Underline it, star it, mark it deeply upon your conscious mind: *Confession and forgiveness in no way stop the harvest.* He had sown; he was to reap. Forgiven he was, but the consequences continued. This is exactly the emphasis Paul is giving the Galatians even in this age of grace. We are not to be deceived, for God will not be mocked. What we sow we will reap, and there are *no exceptions.*[38]

Do you see what faulty theology has led us to believe? We have set ourselves up with a sin mind-set. We have told ourselves that grace means those consequences are all instantly removed, so we let ourselves be sucked under by the power of the flesh, rather than believing what Paul teaches, that *we don't have to sin* day after day after day. We sin because we want to. We have the power in the person of the Holy Spirit to say no to it at every turn in our life. If we choose to say yes against the prompting of the Holy Spirit, we may be certain we will live in the backwash of the consequences. Unfortunately, so will innocent people who are closely related to us. It is those domestic consequences that create what has come to be known as dysfunctional families.

David lived through such consequences. We begin to look at the downward trend in his life in this chapter. In doing so, we see eight steps of consequences in David's misery. The first step was *marital infidelity.*

> "Behold, I will raise up evil against you from your own household; I will even take your wives before your eyes, and give them to your companion, and he shall lie with your wives in broad daylight."
>
> 2 Samuel 12:11

The Hebrew word for "companion" is an intimate term and most likely referred to one of David's own children. In fact, that is exactly what happened years after David's adulterous affair. His own son, Absalom, cohabited with some of David's wives. The grim account is found in 2 Samuel 16, and I want you to notice where it took place.

> Ahithophel said to Absalom, "Go in to your father's concu-
> bines, whom he has left to keep the house; then all Israel will
> hear that you have made yourself odious to your father. The
> hands of all who are with you will also be strengthened."
>
> So they pitched a tent for Absalom on the roof, and Ab-
> salom went in to his father's concubines in the sight of all Israel.
>
> 2 Samuel 16:21–22

Where did David first fall into sin? On the roof of the palace. Absalom's sordid display says, "I'll rub his nose in it." What a shameful thing.
What a consequence to bear!

The second was *the loss of a child*.

> So Nathan went to his house.
>
> Then the LORD struck the child that Uriah's widow bore
> to David, so that he was very sick. . . .
>
> Then it happened on the seventh day that the child died. . . .
>
> 2 Samuel 12:15, 18

It was bad enough to have the experience of marital infidelity. But on
top of that, came the loss of the newborn baby, which added to the grief
of this forgiven man as well as Bathsheba, the mother of the child.

The third consequence is that *one of David's sons rapes his half-sister*.
David married many wives and had many concubines, as we learned earlier.
From these relationships many children were born. While we do not pos-
sess a full genealogical record of all David's wives, children, and concubines,
we do have a record of the relationship between Absalom and Amnon and
Tamar. Those three were David's children, but Absalom and Tamar came
from one mother; Amnon, another.

Amnon was attracted to his half-sister Tamar, the blood sister of Absalom. The reason I mention Absalom is that he later comes to her defense
and this tells you why.

> Now it was after this that Absalom the son of David had a
> beautiful sister whose name was Tamar, and Amnon the son of
> David loved her.
>
> 2 Samuel 13:1

It was a disgraceful, disgusting kind of love. Better defined, it was incestuous lust.

> And Amnon was so frustrated because of his sister Tamar that he made himself ill, for she was a virgin, and it seemed hard to Amnon to do anything to her.
>
> 2 Samuel 13:2

With the help of a friend, Amnon set up a scenario that brought Tamar into his presence, where the boy faked illness.

> "Come, lie with me, my sister."
> But she answered him, "No, my brother, do not violate me, for such a thing is not done in Israel. . . ."
> However, he would not listen to her; since he was stronger than she, he violated her and lay with her. Then Amnon hated her with a very great hatred. . . .
>
> 2 Samuel 13:11–12, 14–15

In embarrassment and disgrace, Tamar went to the family member who loved her, her brother Absalom.

> So Tamar remained and was desolate in her brother Absalom's house.
> But Absalom did not speak to Amnon either good or bad; for Absalom hated Amnon because he had violated his sister Tamar.
>
> 2 Samuel 13:20, 22

Step four, *a brother hates a brother*. Lust has led to rape; rape has led to hatred; and now hatred leads to the next step, which is murder.

Absalom and Amnon did not speak for two years. For two full years this bitterness and hatred ate away at Absalom.

Now I want to ask something. Where in the world was David during all this? The only thing I find in reference to David as it relates to his daughter being violated by his son is this:

> Now when King David heard of all these matters, he was very angry.
>
> 2 Samuel 13:21

That's all! Classic passivity. Incredible paternal preoccupation. His head is somewhere else. It has been for a long time. These kids have raised themselves, without the proper parental authority and discipline. As we discussed earlier, this is just another consequence of sin in David's life.

What kind of palace did David provide physically for his umpteen wives and children? It was fabulous. They probably had every material thing they wanted. But money cannot buy the best things in life. Things couldn't solve the problem within the relationships of that home. Amnon raped and then hated his sister. Absalom hated his brother, and he did so for two full years. They didn't even speak.

What a nightmare of a home the palace must have been! No one has done a more realistic job of describing it than Alexander Whyte, in a piece he wrote on Absalom. Read it and weep!

> Polygamy is just Greek for a dunghill. David trampled down the first and the best law of nature in his palace in Jerusalem, and for his trouble he spent all his after-days in a hell upon earth. David's palace was a perfect pandemonium of suspicion, and intrigue, and jealousy, and hatred—all breaking out, now into incest and now into murder. And it was in such a household, if such a cesspool could be called a household, that Absalom, David's third son by his third living wife, was born and brought up. . . .
>
> A little ring of jealous and scheming parasites, all hateful and hating one another, collected round each one of David's wives. And it was in one of the worst of those wicked little rings that Absalom grew up and got his education.[39]

And the result? After two long years Absalom carries out his deceptive plan. Absalom is quite a guy, and he plays his father for a fool. He suggests a plan where all of them would go to shear sheep together.

> Absalom came to the king and said, "Behold now, your servant has sheepshearers; please let the king and his servants go with your servant."
>
> But the king said to Absalom, "No, my son, we should not all go, lest we be burdensome to you." Although he urged him, he would not go, but blessed him. Then Absalom said, "If not, then please let my brother Amnon go with us." . . .
>
> 2 Samuel 13:24–26

Now if David had been on top of things in his own household, he would have known that Absalom had not spoken to Amnon for two years. He would also have been aware of the hatred brewing among his children. You've got to be rather thick as a father not to know that a son isn't speaking to another son for two years. And talk about lack of control . . .

> But when Absalom urged him, he let Amnon and all the king's sons go with him.
>
> 2 Samuel 13:27

"He urged him." Meaning what? He badgered him. He begged him. He pled. He intimidated. He used guilt. David's children manipulated and intimidated him, and look at what happened.

> And Absalom commanded his servants, saying, "See now, when Amnon's heart is merry with wine, and when I say to you, 'Strike Amnon,' then put him to death. Do not fear; have not I myself commanded you?" . . . And the servants of Absalom did to Amnon just as Absalom had commanded. Then all the king's sons arose, and each mounted his mule and fled.
> Now it was while they were on the way that the report came to David, saying, "Absalom has struck down all the king's sons, and not one of them is left."
>
> 2 Samuel 13:28–30

Tracing the downward steps, we now have Absalom murdering Amnon, *a brother murdering a brother.* "The sword will never depart out of your household, David." And here he is groaning under the ache of it all.

Now if that's not bad enough, after Absalom kills David's son he then flees. So we have step six: *rebellion.*

When Absalom fled, he went to Geshur. That's where his grandfather lived—his mother's father, who was a king in Geshur. He can't live at home, so he'll go stay with granddad while he licks his wounds and sets up his plan later on, to lead a revolt against his daddy. And that's precisely what he does.

Step seven, Absalom *leads a conspiracy against his father.*

> Absalom lived two full years in Jerusalem, and did not see the king's face.
>
> 2 Samuel 14:28

Then, through a chain of events, Absalom wormed his way to the king's doorstep and began to steal the hearts of the people. He stood at the gate of the king, and as people came to seek David's counsel, Absalom intercepted them. He hugged them and kissed them and won their hearts and got them on his side. He said bad things about his father, all of them false and/or exaggerated. And before long, he had the majority vote. And of all things, David abdicates the throne!

> And David said to all his servants, "Arise and let us flee, for otherwise none of us shall escape from Absalom. . . ."
>
> 2 Samuel 15:14

Later, the final step in this devastating chain of consequences comes when *Joab murders Absalom*. The sword has not departed from David's house.

Surely David regrets the day he ever even looked at Bathsheba and carried on a year of deception. And finally, in the backwash of rape, conspiracy, rebellion, hatred, and murder, he's sitting alone in the palace, no doubt perspiring to the point of exhaustion, and in comes a runner bearing bad news.

> The king said to the Cushite, "Is it well with the young man Absalom?" . . .
>
> 2 Samuel 18:32

David feels guilty over this son of his. And despite all that has happened, despite the young rebel's treachery and rebellion, he is concerned for his son.

> The Cushite answered, "Let the enemies of my lord the king, and all who rise up against you for evil, be as that young man!"
>
> 2 Samuel 18:32

Which is a way of saying, "Your boy is dead." And what follows is probably the most grievous and pathetic parental scene in the Old Testament.

> And the king was deeply moved and went up to the chamber over the gate and wept. And thus he said as he walked, "O my

son, Absalom, my son, my son Absalom! Would I had died
instead of you, O Absalom, my son, my son!"

2 Samuel 18:33

David is a beaten man. He's strung out, sobbing as if he's lost his
mind. Every crutch is removed. He's at the bitter end, broken and bruised,
twisted and confused. The harvesting of his sins is almost more than he
can bear.

Do not be deceived, God is not mocked; for whatever a man
sows, this he will also reap.

Galatians 6:7

If you have taken lightly the grace of God, if you have tip-toed through
the corridors of the kingdom, picking and choosing sin or righteousness
at will, thinking grace covers it all, you've missed it, my friend. You've
missed it by a mile. As a matter of fact, it's quite likely that you are
harvesting the bitter blossoms, the consequences, of the seeds of sin planted
in the past. Perhaps right now you are living in a compromising situation,
or right on the edge of one. You are skimming along the surface, hoping
it'll never catch up. But God is not mocked. It will. Trust me on this one
. . . it will.

For the wages of sin is death, but the free gift of God is eternal
life in Christ Jesus our Lord.

Romans 6:23

Turn to Him right now. Turn your life over to Him. Broken and
bruised and twisted and confused, just lay it all out before Him. Ask Him
to give you the grace and strength to face the consequences realistically and
straight on.

I counseled with a young man a number of years ago who sat alone
with me in my office. With a curled lip and a grim face he stared coldly
at me as we talked about his relationships at home. He'd been sent to me
by his parents, in hopes that I might "talk some sense into his head" (their
words). I could hardly break through that thick hide. He was angry . . .
bitter to the core. Obviously, he had deep wounds.

I said to him, "Tell me about your dad."

He uttered an oath and cleared his throat as he turned and looked out
the window. "My dad!" he said. "My one great goal is to kill him." His

voice trailed off as he added, "I tried once and I failed, but the next time I won't."

Seething with emotion, he began to describe time after time after time after time when his father had ridiculed him, embarrassed him, and even beaten him. Now he was taller than his dad, and it was just a matter of time till he got even.

A chill ran up my spine as I listened to this modern-day Absalom vent his spleen. The more we talked the clearer it became . . . this young man, not yet twenty years old, was the product of a tragic set of circumstances in a home most people would consider Christian. But, deep within those private relationships were all the marks of sinful habits: parental neglect, abusive behavior, unresolved conflicts, lack of honesty, forgiveness, understanding, and most of all, true love.

I have often wondered whatever became of that young man. His father, not unlike David, was well-respected in the community and among his professional peers. No one would have guessed there was such trouble at home . . . unless they got close enough to that son to see the scars.

To everyone else, David was king. To Absalom, David was Dad. Wonder how he would describe David if he, being dead, could speak?

Chapter Nineteen

Riding Out the Storm

Some of the most difficult experiences for the Christian emerge in the backwash of sin. This is a subject we do not like to think about or talk about within the family of God, but it needs to be addressed. Matter of fact, it might surprise you to know how often God's Word addresses it.

Back in the Old Testament, for example, tucked away in one of the ancient prophets' writings, the prophet Hosea, there is a verse that clearly addresses it. I mentioned it briefly in an earlier chapter. Announcing a stern message from God to Israel, His rebellious people, Hosea writes,

> They sow the wind, and they reap the whirlwind.
>
> Hosea 8:7

The prophet is describing the nation of Israel. They were the ones who cried out to God as if they knew Him. The nation that "set up kings but not by Me." The nation that appointed princes, but God didn't know the princes. The nation that walked in their own way (sowing the wind), and as a result they suffered the consequences (reaping the whirlwind).

David's life has reached a similar impasse. God loves David deeply . . . and so He disciplines him severely. David needed to learn the unforgettable lesson that we are to take God seriously. That He means what He says about holiness. That we are to reflect our heavenly Father's character. As Peter writes, ". . . like the Holy One who called you, be holy yourselves also in all your behavior" (1 Pet. 1:15). When we choose willfully and deliberately to disobey our holy God, He does not wink at our sin and cover it over lightly, saying that grace allows Him to overlook disobedience. Grace assures us that He will not kill us. Grace is our help during the time of the whirlwind, holding us together, keeping us strong, stabilizing us. But we may be sure that when we drop the seeds of the wind in the ground we will reap the harvest of sin's whirlwind. By God's grace we will survive as we ride out the storm, but the pain will, at times, seem more than we can bear.

There are two kinds of suffering in the midst of the whirlwind: the kind of suffering *we deserve* because we were the ones who disobeyed; and the kind of suffering *we don't deserve* but experience in the backwash of someone else's transgression.

This is also addressed in Galatians 6:7–8, as we saw so clearly in the previous chapter. Hearing the reference to Hosea, some might say, "Well, that's just Old Testament truth. That was only for people under the Law." I know a Greek word that describes my reaction to that erroneous statement: *Hogwash!* In a passage addressed to the people in the church, people under grace, Paul offers the very same principle.

> Do not be deceived, God is not mocked; for whatever a man sows, this he will also reap. For the one who sows to his own flesh shall from the flesh reap corruption. . . .
>
> Galatians 6:7–8

The same truth is underscored toward the end of Proverbs 6. Talk about a strong section of Scripture! It pictures the scene of the man in the street who is met by a harlot, who makes her move toward him, enticing him through fleshly temptations. And Solomon warns: Don't do that! If you indulge in the lustful pleasures of the moment you will pay a lengthy, painful price.

> My son, observe the commandment of your father,
> And do not forsake the teaching of your mother;
> Bind them continually on your heart;
> Tie them around your neck.
> When you walk about, they will guide you;
> When you sleep, they will watch over you;
> And when you awake, they will talk to you.
> For the commandment is a lamp, and the teaching is light;

And reproofs for discipline are the way of life,
To keep you from the evil woman,
From the smooth tongue of the adulteress.
Do not desire her beauty in your heart,
Nor let her catch you with her eyelids.
For on account of a harlot one is reduced to a loaf of bread,
And an adulteress hunts for the precious life.
Can a man take fire in his bosom,
And his clothes not be burned?
Or can a man walk on hot coals,
And his feet not be scorched?
So is the one who goes in to his neighbor's wife;
Whoever touches her will not go unpunished.
Men do not despise a thief if he steals
To satisfy himself when he is hungry;
But when he is found, he must repay sevenfold;
He must give all the substance of his house.
The one who commits adultery with a woman is lacking
    sense;
He who would destroy himself does it.

                          Proverbs 6:20–32

I appreciate the forthright words of Eugene Peterson as he paraphrases this same section. Read this slowly, preferably aloud.

Good friend, follow your father's good advice;
    don't wander off from your mother's teachings.
Wrap yourself in them from head to foot;
    wear them like a scarf around your neck.
Wherever you walk, they'll guide you;
    whenever you rest, they'll guard you;
    when you wake up, they'll tell you what's next.
For sound advice is a beacon,
    good teaching is a light,
    moral discipline is a life path.
They'll protect you from wanton women,
    from the seductive talk of some temptress.
Don't lustfully fantasize on her beauty,
    nor be taken in by her bedroom eyes.

You can buy an hour with a whore for a loaf of bread,
  but a wanton woman may well eat *you* alive.
Can you build a fire in your lap
  and not burn your pants?
Can you walk barefoot on hot coals
  and not get blisters?
It's the same when you have sex with your neighbor's wife:
  Touch her and you'll pay for it. No excuses. . . .
Adultery is a brainless act,
  soul-destroying, self-destructive;
Expect a bloody nose, a black eye,
  and a reputation ruined for good.[40]

That pretty well sums it up, doesn't it? "Bloody nose . . . black eye . . . reputation ruined for good. . . ."

The most tragic part of this, of course, is when an innocent bystander gets caught in the backwash of another's sin. When people around you have to pay the consequence along with the one responsible.

After one of my messages dealing with consequences a few years ago, a woman came up to me and handed me a tightly folded note written on a small square paper. In it, she told how one of her children, now grown, has chosen to walk away from God. The misery and the havoc he created was taking an awful toll on the home. "I've never heard a message where somebody explained how you ride out another's storm when you're not responsible," she wrote. "We raised our son as best we could with what we had. And now he's turned his heels on us and he's kicked over all the traces. He's going his own way . . . and the rest of the family now lives in misery city. How do we handle it?"

How *do* we ride out another's storm? Whether you or somebody else caused it, *what do you do* when you're reaping someone else's whirlwind? How *do* you handle it?

The best illustration in all of Scripture, you may be interested to know, is found in the life of David. David's family answers this question for us. As we have observed in the two previous chapters, David was a great man who compromised, and the result was tragic, affecting not only the man who sinned but his entire family and other people outside the family as well.

DAVID FACES THE TRUTH

David acknowledged the sowing he had done, before God and the prophet Nathan.

> Then David said to Nathan, "I have sinned against the LORD." . . .
>
> 2 Samuel 12:13

"I have sinned. I went in to Bathsheba, I committed adultery, I took the life of her husband, Uriah. I have been guilty of hypocrisy. I have sinned." Without reservation or rationalization, he confessed his sin before God.

> And Nathan said to David, "The LORD also has taken away your sin; you shall not die."
>
> 2 Samuel 12:13

Now there's a promise of grace.

Under the Law, when you committed adultery, you were to be stoned. When you murdered someone, no exception . . . you were to be killed. "An eye for an eye, a tooth for a tooth, a life for a life." Don't tell me there is no grace in the Old Testament! Grace at this moment came to David's rescue. Nathan assured him, "David, you won't die."

> "However, because by this deed you have given occasion to the enemies of the LORD to blaspheme, the child also that is born to you shall surely die."
>
> 2 Samuel 12:14

What an awful thing to hear!

In those days, God spoke audibly to His people. Now that we have the Bible to read and to give us guidelines, God speaks to us directly from His Word. But in those days, God spoke to His people in dreams and visions and through other designated individuals, like judges and leaders and prophets.

So Nathan the prophet, who spoke for God in this instance, said to David, "You are forgiven. You will not die; however, your baby will. And that's only the first in a series of things that will happen, David. All of this that will transpire will be a permanent reminder that one who sows in the flesh (the 'wind') shall from the flesh reap corruption (the 'whirlwind')."

We traced our way through David's "whirlwind" in the previous chapter, so there's no reason to repeat the details again. My desire now is to address how to weather such a storm when it comes our way.

DAVID RESPONDS CORRECTLY

I find in David's response four helpful guidelines for us to follow today when we go through the whirlwind, either because we have caused it or when we are caught in the backwash of someone else who caused it.

David's first response was prayer.

> So Nathan went to his house.
>
> Then the LORD struck the child that Uriah's widow bore to David, so that he was very sick. David therefore inquired of God for the child; and David fasted and went and lay all night on the ground.
>
> 2 Samuel 12:15–16

Today we know too little of that kind of protracted prayer and fasting. More often than not our response to sin is rather glib. We say, "Well, Lord, I've done this, and I've done that. And I agree with You that the blood of Jesus Christ cleanses me from all sin. So, thank You." And we go right on with our lives, until, . . . "Oops, blew it again. Sorry."

But that's not how David responded. When the whirlwind began, when he felt the hot winds of judgment begin to blow upon him, he fell before God and he lay on the ground all night. He fasted. He waited on the Lord. He sought His mind. And he "inquired of God for the child." He hoped for more grace. Undeserving though he was, he knew His God was full of mercy and dealt in grace. He made no demands, understand, but he pled with God for the life of his baby.

> And he said, "While the child was still alive, I fasted and wept; for I said, 'Who knows, the LORD may be gracious to me, that the child may live.' "
>
> 2 Samuel 12:22

What does it mean when it says he "inquired" of God? It probably means that he reasoned with his Lord . . . passionately and sincerely. "Lord,

I call upon You and upon Your grace. I ask You if it be possible for You to alter Your plan, I plead with You, give me this child. Although I do not deserve Your favor nor have I in any way earned the right to be this bold, I ask You to be merciful. I ask that of You because that is the sincere, humble desire of my heart. I've heard what You have said, and I will accept what You send, but I ask, I inquire of You, would it be possible that You could give me this child?"

In other words, David prayed with a contrite heart.

Notice that during the time of prayer, David did not leave his house. He didn't go to the place of worship. We know that because later it says that he washes and changes his clothes before he goes to the house of the Lord and worships. So obviously, until that time later on he doesn't leave.

You know what I learned from that? I learned that when I go through the whirlwind, I should be still and quiet. I should not announce or advertise everything I'm going through. We Christians tend to tell everything, just dump it all out, rather indiscriminately, when, really, it isn't everyone's business.

When the elders came and found David in this condition, they stood beside him in order to raise him up from the ground. But he was unwilling, nor would he eat with them.

"Come on, David," they said. "Come on, get on your feet. You need to eat something."

"No," he said. "I don't want to do that. Please leave me alone."

When we go through periods of deep distress brought on by our own or someone else's sinfulness, it is wise—in fact, *it is biblical*—not to surround ourselves with people, no matter how well-meaning they might be. Solitude is essential. Silence is necessary. Words from others usually distract. Stay in the Lord's presence and seek His mind during this painful time. There is nothing wrong with being alone for soul-searching times. Proverbs says, "Out of the heart proceed all the things of a man." In fact, it describes the condition of the heart by saying that we are to keep it with all diligence, for out of it come the issues of life (Prov. 4:23). Some things are too precious to share. They're too deep. Too personal. Too painful. They're too profound. In the soul-searching of our lives, we are to stay quiet so we can hear Him say all that He wants to say to us in our hearts. David prayed . . . and so must we. In his case, he stayed at it seven full days, virtually uninterrupted.

David's second response was to face the consequences realistically.

> Then it happened on the seventh day that the child died. And the servants of David were afraid to tell him that the child was dead, for they said, "Behold, while the child was still alive, we spoke to him and he did not listen to our voice. How then can we tell him that the child is dead, since he might do himself harm!"
>
> 2 Samuel 12:18

I take it that David's servants were afraid he might commit suicide. They didn't understand, not really. They looked upon his soul-searching time as a deep depression, little more. And they said, "When we lay this final weight on him, he'll harm himself. How can we tell him?"

Now look at this realistic response on David's part. It's a far cry from suicidal thoughts!

> But when David saw that his servants were whispering together, David perceived that the child was dead; so David said to his servants, "Is the child dead?" And they said, "He is dead."
>
> So David arose from the ground, washed, anointed himself, and changed his clothes; and he came into the house of the LORD and worshiped. . . .
>
> 2 Samuel 12:19–20

David has been seven days on his face, alone, before his Lord . . . waiting on God, inquiring of God, wondering if, in grace, He might spare the child, placing himself at God's disposal, abandoning himself in total seclusion. Now he hears the words, "The child is dead." And what is his response? He quietly gets up, takes a bath, changes his clothes, and goes to the house of God . . . and *worships*.

When I read that, I think of Job.

> The Job arose and tore his robe and shaved his head, and he fell to the ground and worshiped.
>
> And he said, "Naked I came from my mother's womb,
> And naked I shall return there.
> The LORD gave and the LORD has taken away,
> Blessed be the name of the LORD."
>
> Job 1:20–21

When you face the consequences of the whirlwind, you must guard against bitterness. Due to the pain that comes your way, especially since you've already confessed your sins to Him and agonized over how wrong you were, you'll have to guard against blaming God. Thoughts will invade, like: "How could You do this to me, Lord? I've served You these many years. I have humbly and sincerely confessed my disobedience . . . and now look at what You've taken from me!" There's none of that in David's response. Instead, he immediately accepted what had happened realistically and then he worshiped the Lord. This is a good time to remind ourselves he is still "a man after God's own heart."

Many would stand in amazement at David's response. His child had just died. God's answer to his seven-day prayer was a firm "no." He heard the news. He arose, cleaned himself up, and went to the place of worship, as if to say, "God did this and God did that, I accept it from Him without hesitation . . . and I will go on from here." Difficult as that may be for some to understand, that is an incredibly mature response. Remember, a contrite heart makes no demands and has no expectations.

David's third response was to claim the truths of Scripture. If you ever want to get into the Word of God on your own, you want to do it when crisis strikes. You cannot let your emotions be your guide or you will do something rash or foolish. I have found there is no counsel like God's counsel. No comfort like His comfort. No wisdom more profound than the wisdom of the Scriptures! David settled his case with God as he rested in the truth of God's Word.

Let me show you. See verse 21? David's servants couldn't understand David's reaction. Others are often amazed when our response is not "normal" (their word). They expect us to fall apart, to wail, to lose it. Look at David's servants' reaction.

> Then his servants said to him, "What is this thing that you have done? While the child was alive, you fasted and wept; but when the child died, you arose and ate food."
>
> 2 Samuel 12:21

David tells them,

> "While the child was still alive, I fasted and wept; for I said, 'Who knows, the LORD may be gracious to me, that the child may live.' But now he has died. . . ."
>
> 2 Samuel 12:22–23

He faces it, he accepts it, he does not deny it. He says, "This has happened. Why should I fast?"

How many people continue to fast *after* a loved one's death, thinking maybe somehow they can get that person back. Or they begin to make plans to contact a medium so they can somehow communicate with the dead. Though an unwise, incorrect and unbiblical route, many take it. The child of God, when he faces the reality, says, "It's permanent. I cannot bring my loved one back. I will not deny it or try to bargain with God. And in the comfort and counsel of God's Word, I will rely on Him to get me through this crisis."

Look at how David puts it. It's one of the few passages that helps us know about the eternal destiny of small children and infants who die.

> "Can I bring him back again? I shall go to him, but he will not return to me."
>
> 2 Samuel 12:23

Now there is promise based on solid theology. If you have lost an infant, this verse says you cannot bring the child back, but *you will see that child in heaven.* You will see that gift from God that He gave you and for reasons known only to Him, He took from you. "I cannot bring him back, but I can go to him."

David said, "While the child lived, he and I were together, I could love him, be with him. But, now that he is gone, I cannot bring him back. The LORD has given . . . the Lord has taken away. Blessed be His name." After claiming the truth of Scripture, it is amazing the stability you will have.

Which leads to *David's fourth response, he refused to give up.*

When suffering the backwash of sin, our tendency is to say, "I am through. I am finished with living. Life isn't worth it any longer." But look at what David did: He "comforted his wife Bathsheba." It's easy to forget that she was also grieving. Both of them went through a period of grief. They wept. And then they went on living.

> Then David comforted his wife Bathsheba, and went in to her and lay with her; and she gave birth to a son, and he named him Solomon. Now the LORD loved him and sent word through Nathan the prophet, and he named him Jedidiah for the LORD's sake.
>
> 2 Samuel 12:24–25

David is once more walking with the Lord as he did in days past.

One of the most pathetic scenes on earth is a child of God who sits in the corner too long, licking his wounds in self-pity. It takes as much (often more) spiritual strength and purpose to recover and move on as it does to go through a crisis. "I will go on, I will pick up the pieces, I will get back on target, I will go back to work, I will begin to enjoy my friends again, I will carry on as I did before. In fact, by God's grace, I will be wiser and even more effective than I was before."

David, in riding out the storm, gives us some beautiful guidelines. He prayed, he faced the consequences realistically, he turned it all over to the Lord as he claimed the scriptural truth concerning death, and then he refused to give up. He moved on, relying on his God for strength.

A BRIEF SUMMARY

Riding out the storm is a *lonely* experience. You will never be more alone emotionally than when you are in the whirlwind of consequences. You will wish others could help you, but they can't. They will want to be there, they will care, but for the most part, you have to ride out the storm alone.

Riding out the storm is also a *learning* experience. Psalm 32—the same psalm that includes David's misery during his months of secrecy and hypocrisy—also says,

> I will instruct you and teach you in the way which you
> should go;
> I will counsel you with My eye upon you.
> Do not be as the horse or as the mule
> which have no understanding,
> Whose trappings include bit and bridle to hold them in
> check,
> Otherwise they will not come near to you.
> Many are the sorrows of the wicked;
> But he who trusts in the LORD, lovingkindness shall surround
> him.
>
> Psalm 32:8–10

Riding out the storm, thank God, is also a *temporary* experience. It may be the most difficult time in your life. You may be enduring your own whirlwind . . . or you may be the innocent bystander caught in the consequential backwash of another's sin. You may feel desperately alone, and it may seem that it will never, ever end. But believe me, the whirlwind is a temporary experience. Your faithful, caring Lord will see you through it.

Finally, let me mention that riding out the storm is a *humbling* experience. Deuteronomy 8:2 is a verse my wife and I frequently quote in times of testing.

> And you shall remember all the way which the LORD your God has led you in the wilderness these forty years, that He might humble you, testing you, to know what was in your heart, whether you would keep His commandments or not.

As it was for the Israelites, the whirlwind is a time when we learn to take God seriously. He means what He says.

As I close this particular chapter, I want to mention something very personal. Because it is too personal for me to include the details, I'll not be able to fill in all the blanks, so let me, instead, be brief and to the point.

At the very time I write these words, Cynthia and I are riding out a storm that is almost too painful to endure. We are suffering under the consequences of another's disobedience, not our own, so my words in this chapter are anything but theoretical. We have identified with David's loneliness and solitude. His pleadings for grace . . . his protracted prayers mixed with fasting . . . his sincere desire for mercy to come to his rescue. We know, firsthand, whereof he speaks.

But our situation is different from David's in one significant way—he lived to see the end of the waiting period; we have not. Not yet. Our waiting and weeping continue. The storm goes on. And so we wait . . . and we wait . . . and we continue to wait.

By faith, we claim His peace. Because of grace, we know His mercy. But in the meantime, our hearts remain broken and our eyes are never far from tears.

The moving lyrics from two beloved eighteenth-century hymns I've sung for decades have brought me comfort as recently as early this morning, long before dawn:

> From every stormy wind that blows,
> From every swelling tide of woes,
> There is a calm, a sure retreat:
> 'Tis found beneath the mercy seat.

Ah! whither could we flee for aid,
When tempted, desolate, dismayed,
Or how the hosts of hell defeat,
Had suffering saints no mercy seat?[41]

and

Come, ye disconsolate, where e'er ye languish;
Come to the mercy seat, fervently kneel;
Here bring your wounded hearts, here tell your anguish;
Earth has no sorrow that heaven cannot heal.[42]

CHAPTER TWENTY

Friends in Need

The poet Samuel Taylor Coleridge once described friendship as "a sheltering tree."[43] What a beautiful description of that special relationship. As I read those words, I think of my friends as great leafy trees, who spread themselves over me, providing shade from the sun, whose presence is a stand against the blast of winter's wind of loneliness. A great, sheltering tree; that's a friend.

For years, in one particular church I attended as a young man, I was taught that if you are really mature, you don't need anybody else—that it's only the weak person who needs others. How wrong was that teaching! No one can ignore the fact that even Jesus our Lord had many friends around him during His earthly sojourn. Furthermore, He had at least three *intimate* friends. If having friends is a sign of immaturity, why did Jesus have so many?

The truth of the matter is this: It is *not* a sign of weakness and immaturity to have a friend or to need a friend. It's a sign of immaturity *to think you don't need a friend*. Coleridge was right: Friends are like sheltering trees.

ONE BROKEN MAN

As we look at the next stage of David's life, we find a man who had not only a sheltering tree, but a whole grove of them. But first, let's look at the situation in which David now found himself.

Personally, he was awash in guilt. He had committed adultery with Bathsheba, and then killed her husband. On the heels of that he lived many months like a hypocrite. As a result of all this, he had lost his baby and was watching his whole world crumble. He was eaten up with guilt. Psalms 32 and 51 confirm this.

Domestically, his home was shattered. As we saw in chapter 18, anger, bitterness, incest, rape, murder, and rebellion among his now-grown children eventually culminated in his son Absalom's leading a conspiracy against him. Is there any pain worse than family troubles?

Politically, David lost his respect and authority as a leader. Not only had he lost touch with his family, he had a growing number of critics in the country. Their hero had feet of clay.

Personally and domestically and politically, then, he's hurting. At this point, Absalom's conspiracy blossoms.

> Now it came about after this that Absalom provided for himself a chariot and horses, and fifty men as runners before him. And Absalom used to rise early and stand beside the way to the gate; and it happened that when any man had a suit to come to the king for judgment, Absalom would call to him and say, "From what city are you?" And he would say, "Your servant is from one of the tribes of Israel."
>
> Then Absalom would say, "See, your claims are good and right, but no man listens to you on the part of the king." Moreover, Absalom would say, "Oh that one would appoint me judge in the land, then every man who has any suit or cause could come to me, and I would give him justice."
>
> 2 Samuel 15:1–4

Sounds like he's running for office, doesn't it. Well, that's exactly what he's doing without saying so. His technique is based on lies and treachery. His father is the king, and he's down there at the gate where the people come to settle their complaints or seek the counsel of the king. It is there Absalom awaits to intercept with lies and innuendoes. "Wait a minute. You know, nobody up there cares about what you've got to say. But I do. Oh, that someone would see the value of my wisdom and let ME occupy that office. I'd show you what justice is all about."

And it happened that when a man came near to prostrate him-self before him, he would put out his hand and take hold of him and kiss him. And in this manner Absalom dealt with all Israel who came to the king for judgment; so Absalom stole away the hearts of the men of Israel.

2 Samuel 15:5–6

Absalom's plan worked perfectly! Little by little he undermined David's reputation and built his own, until he was ready to make his big move.

But Absalom sent spies throughout all the tribes of Israel, saying, "As soon as you hear the sound of the trumpet, then you shall say, 'Absalom is king in Hebron.' "

2 Samuel 15:10

That's exactly what they did. One blast of the trumpet and Absalom was on his way.

Then a messenger came to David, saying, "The hearts of the men of Israel are with Absalom."

2 Samuel 15:13

And with a sigh, this good man is broken, fractured in his spirit. Not only has his son betrayed him, but he's feeling like there's not a friend around.

And David said to all his servants who were with him at Jerusalem, "Arise and let us flee, for otherwise none of us shall escape from Absalom. Go in haste, lest he overtake us quickly and bring down calamity on us and strike the city with the edge of the sword."

2 Samuel 15:14

Just picture the scene. The once-great King David scrambling around, throwing a few things in a bag, preparing to flee from his own son. After all these years, once again he is running for his life. Surely he recalled the years he lived like a fugitive while running from Saul. He's back at it. "Been there, done that!" If ever a man needed a sheltering tree, David did.

Then the king's servants said to the king, "Behold, your servants are ready to do whatever my lord the king chooses." So the king went out and all his household with him. . . . And the king went out and all the people with him, and they stopped at the last house.

2 Samuel 15:15–16

What emotion and pathos are woven into the fabric of those few words. David was leaving the great city of Zion—the city named after him, the City of David. As he came to the edge, at the last house, he stopped and looked back over that golden metropolis he had watched God build over the past years. His heart must have been broken as he stood there looking back, his mind flooded with memories. All around him the people of his household scurried past, leading beasts of burden piled high with belongings, running for their lives.

He was at the last house, and he needed a tree to give him some shelter. Somebody who would say, "David, I'm here with you. I don't have all the answers, but, man, I can assure you of this, my heart goes out to you." When the chips are down and there's nobody to affirm you and you run out of armor and there are no more crutches to lean on, no reputation to cling to, and all the lights are going out, and the crowd is following another voice, it's amazing how God sends a sheltering tree. In fact, God gives David not one but five of them. Interestingly, most folks have never heard of any of them.

FIVE SHELTERING TREES

Now all his servants passed on beside him, all the Cherethites, all the Pelethites, and all the Gittites, six hundred men who had come with him from Gath, passed on before the king. Then the king said to Ittai the Gittite, "Why will you also go with us? Return and remain with the king, for you are a foreigner and also an exile; return to your own place."

2 Samuel 15:18–19

The *first friend is Ittai the Gittite.* Actually, this is the first time he's mentioned in David's biography. He's a friend of the king, but he never gets in the limelight until the chips are down and David has stopped at the last house and there's no more throne, no more glory. Suddenly he comes out of the woodwork and says, "David, count me in. I'm with you all the way." But the most amazing thing is that he's a Gittite.

A Gittite was a man from Gath. Remember Gath, home of Goliath? David had slithered into Philistia and brought some of the people into exile. Instead of hating him, however, they had fallen in love with him. So when David's back is against the wall, Ittai says, "I stand with you, my friend. By life or death, I'm here." That's a true friend. That's a tree with thick branches, lots of leaves, and a solid trunk.

David says, "Take off! This is your chance to run. Go on back."

> "Shall I today make you wander with us, while I go where I will? Return and take back your brothers; mercy and truth be with you."
>
> 2 Samuel 15:20

"Shalom, brother. Go on, get away, it's gonna be hard where I'm going."

> But Ittai answered the king and said, "As the LORD lives, and as my lord the king lives, surely wherever my lord the king may be, whether for death or for life, there also your servant will be."
>
> 2 Samuel 15:21

I repeat, that's a friend. He says, "David, if they string you up, I'm putting my neck in the noose next to you. If the whole world turns against you, I'll stand in your defense." Ol' Ittai was made of sturdy stuff. There are not many friends like that.

So Ittai says, "Come on, Gittites, let's go!" So they go over the hill, leaving Zion behind, on their way with the king to no man's land, without any promise.

When everything else fails and everybody else has turned away, there are precious few who will give you a call and say, "I'm with you. I'm there. Count on me. Call on me any time, day or night, I'll come. I won't kick you when you're down. I'm by your side. I understand." The amazing thing is that sometimes the person who stands that near is a guy from Gath. A person who once was an enemy but is now a friend.

> While all the country was weeping with a loud voice, all the people passed over. The king also passed over the brook Kidron, and all the people passed over toward the way of the wilderness.
>
> Now behold, Zadok also came, and all the Levites with him carrying the ark of the covenant of God. And they set down

the ark of God, and Abiathar came up until all the people had finished passing from the city.

2 Samuel 15:23–24

Zadok and Abiathar are the next couple of trees who stand by to shelter David. These two men are Levites, and they come along carrying the ark of the covenant. They set that heavy, sacred chest down, and they look over at David and say, "Where do we go from here? We're with you, David. We've been with you all along." These men are priests, representatives of God who minister in the house of God.

And the king said to Zadok, "Return the ark of God to the city. If I find favor in the sight of the LORD, then He will bring me back again, and show me both it and His habitation. But if He should say thus, 'I have no delight in you,' behold, here I am, let Him do to me as seems good to Him."

2 Samuel 15:25–26

What a teachable, humble spirit David has. That's how to ride out the whirlwind of consequences. "Lord, if You choose to finish me off, no problem. But if, on the other hand, you want to use me, I'm thrilled. But whatever happens, I abandon my future into Your hands."

I cannot help but mention once again, through his obedience, David reveals that he is a man after God's own heart. He knows that the ark does not belong to him. Out of sheer respect, he lays it all at the Lord's disposal.

David reveals a true understanding of the connection between the ark and God's presence with his people. He knows that possession of the ark does not guarantee God's blessing. . . . He also recognizes that the ark belongs in the capital city as a symbol of the Lord's rule over the nation, . . . no matter who the king might be. David confesses that he has no exclusive claim to the throne and that Israel's divine King is free to confer the kingship on whomever he chooses.[44]

"Take the ark back to the city," he tells his buddies, Zadok and Abiathar. "Go back. You're needed there." Out of respect, that's exactly what they did. No argument. No resistance. Not even a discussion. They were there to help David, regardless. If that meant going back, so be it.

"Return to the city in peace with your two sons, . . . See, I'm going to wait at the fords of the wilderness until word comes from you to inform me." Therefore Zadok and Abiathar returned the ark of God to Jerusalem and remained there.

2 Samuel 15:27–28

Raymond Brown, in his fine little book, *Skilful Hands, A Biography of David*, writes of this moment:

Their duty at that moment was to obey the king's instructions and to trust his wisdom. It meant that they were going into a life of hardship, insecurity, privation, suffering, and possibly death, but *they would be with the king*, and that was enough.[45]

Sometimes, when you are really in need, you will have a few friends who will say to you, "I'll do whatever you wish. I'm available." They're the Zadoks and Abiathars of your life. No one will ever know about them, but they'll run interference for you. They'll be down there at the front lines, where it isn't really pleasant, protecting you from the blast, shielding and encouraging you just by their presence there. It may work against them; they may get beat up by those who have turned against you . . . but there they stand, in your corner. They are friends.

And David went up the ascent of the Mount of Olives, and wept as he went, and his head was covered and he walked barefoot. Then all the people who were with him each covered his head and went up weeping as they went.

2 Samuel 15:30

Picture that. The mighty king of Israel, barefooted, head covered, and weeping aloud as he ascends the Mount of Olives. And everybody traveling with him is also dissolved in tears. It's a pathetic sight . . . but realistic.

It happened as David was coming to the summit, where God was worshiped, that behold, Hushai the Archite met him with his coat torn, and dust on his head.

2 Samuel 15:32

Who is Hushai? Well, verse 37 calls him "David's friend." That's all it says. The third friend who shelters David is Hushai, the Archite.

When he met David, the man's coat was torn and his head was covered with dust. That's what people did in those days to express total bankruptcy. That's why Job tore his garments and threw dust on his head. It was as if to say, "I have nothing left. I'm finished. I am bankrupt." For Hushai, these were marks of his compassionate feeling for David. And David spotted it immediately.

Sometimes when the pain is so great and you have come to the last house, your own personal Hushai arrives . . . and with his presence wraps himself or herself around you. That warm, speechless embrace says all that needs to be said. He's there. He's there for you. No sermon. No great messages of hope or verse of Scripture. He may not even pray. Just a hug says it all.

So David gives this loyal friend a very significant task.

"Hushai, if you go with me, you'll be a burden," David tells him honestly. "But if you return to the city, you can be of great service to me."

> "If you return to the city, and say to Absalom, 'I will be your
> servant, O king; as I've been your father's servant in time past,
> so I will now be your servant,' then you can thwart the counsel
> of Ahithophel for me."
>
> 2 Samuel 15:34

You're probably thinking, *Who in the world is Ahithophel?* Well, he's now Absalom's counselor. He has joined himself to that band of conspirators. So David is saying, "Hushai, you can help me the most by being my spy in Absalom's camp. You will be the supply line of communication from his headquarters. By claiming loyalty to him, you will be on hand to find a way to turn that throne against him." Here's David—the consummate military strategist. In the midst of all his misery, he is still able to strategize wisely. What he predicted is exactly what happens.

As a matter of fact, a whole line of communication was set up that led to the overthrow of Absalom: Hushai, Zadok, Abiathar, an unknown girl who took a message, Jonathan, Ahimaaz, an unnamed woman who hid two messengers, and finally the errand boy that ran the message to David. These are friends of David we never hear about because few ever bother to cover this segment of David's life. But when the chips were down and they were at the last house, these people rallied around their friend, David. God bless those unknowns!

The fourth group of trees who sheltered David are Shobi, Machir, and

Barzillai. Again, more nobodies who became a group of somebodies in David's corner.

> Now when David had come to Mahanaim, Shobi the son of Nahash . . . Machir the son of Ammiel . . . and Barzillai the Gileadite . . . brought beds, basins, pottery, wheat, barley, flour, parched grain, beans, lentils, parched seeds, honey, curds, sheep, and cheese of the herd, for David and for the people who were with him, to eat; for they said, "The people are hungry and weary and thirsty in the wilderness."
>
> 2 Samuel 17:27–29

"David had come to Mahanaim." If you check your concordance, you'll find the first mention of Mahanaim is in Genesis 32:2; it is the name Jacob gave the place where the angels came and ministered to him. Centuries later, here is David out in the middle of nowhere. Mahanaim and the angels come in the form of three men who bring them all the food and supplies that they need out there in the wilderness.

When you're hungry and weary and thirsty in the wilderness, that's when a friend comes through. You don't even have to ask. When you've got a friend like this, he knows you're hungry. He knows you're thirsty. He knows you're weary. The beautiful thing about sheltering friends is that they don't have to be told what to do . . . the practical stuff. They just do it. This is faith in action. This is rubber-meets-the-road Christianity.

Shobi, from the sons of Ammon, could have said, "David has fought my people, and he has been so cruel. There's no way I'm gonna take even a morsel of bread to David."

As for Machir, he was the son of Ammiel from Lo-debar. Remember Lo-debar? Mephibosheth, the handicapped son of Jonathan, lived in Lo-debar. When Mephibosheth had fled for his life, after the death of his father and grandfather, he finally wound up in the middle of the desert (*Lo-debar*, remember, means "no pastureland"). And Machir was the man who took Mephibosheth into his home. Machir was the kind of guy who took care of people when they were in need. So he could have thought, *I fulfilled my responsibility. I've paid my dues.* (I hate that line!) *David is going to have to take care of himself.*

Then there's Barzillai. If you check in the next chapter, you'll discover that he is eighty years old. He could have said, "I'm retired. I'm old . . . already served my time. Let somebody younger do it." But he didn't say that.

Instead, Shobi, Machir, and Barzillai voluntarily got their heads together, worked hard, and loaded up every supply they could think of and headed off to help David, their friend in need. What great guys! No remuneration. No applause. No big deal. Just faithful-to-the-end friends.

All David's friends came through for him when he needed them, big time. They had no agenda, like gaining political clout. They were there to help with his physical and emotional needs.

Some time later, after a horrendous series of events, David receives word that his rebellious son, Absalom, is dead—MURDERED. This happened before he had a chance to clear up several unresolved conflicts between father and son . . . before he and his son could sit down and come to terms with their differences. Even before David could tell him how sorry he was for being so busy, so preoccupied, so negligent as a dad—BOOM! The news of Absalom's death hits him in the face. And the world caves in around him. We see his sorrow, and we hear his anguish in one of the most poignant scenes in all of Scripture. Read it slowly and with feeling. It is dripping with emotion . . . the emotion of a heartbroken father:

> And the king was deeply moved and went up to the chamber over the gate and wept. And thus he said as he walked, "O my son Absalom, my son, my son Absalom! Would I had died instead of you, O Absalom, my son, my son!"
>
> 2 Samuel 18:33

Soon thereafter, David needed a friend. Memories of his failed past swamped him. Guilt assaulted him. He couldn't get past his grief. He was caught in an emotional vortex that paralyzed him.

Sometimes grief does that to you. It's like you're in a dungeon and somebody locks the door from the outside, and you can't get out. You try your best (you may even fake it), but you're still in there. And all of a sudden a friend finds a way to climb in. *A friend like Joab.*

> Then it was told Joab, "Behold, the king is weeping and mourns for Absalom." And the victory that day was turned to mourning for all the people, for the people heard it said that day, "The king is grieved for his son."
>
> 2 Samuel 19:1-2

The people were seeing Absalom's death as God's deliverance. "God took care of Absalom! Now David, you get back on the throne where you belong. God has vindicated you. This is your chance." But David was so absorbed in his own personal grief in the dungeon, where it was so dark and so empty, he couldn't take that in. He was all alone, lost in the swelling tide of guilt-ridden torment. He had nobody around to say, "Come on, David, get BACK! Your leadership is needed."

It was at that point that Joab came in and rather forcefully confronted him. Had he not, David would not have even heard him.

> And the king covered his face and cried out with a loud voice, "O my son Absalom, O Absalom, my son, my son!"
>
> Then Joab came into the house to the king and said, "Today you have covered with shame the faces of all your servants, who today have saved your life and the lives of your sons and daughters, the lives of your wives, and the lives of your concubines, by loving those who hate you, and by hating those who love you. For you have shown today that princes and servants are nothing to you; for I know this day that if Absalom were alive and all of us were dead, you would be pleased.
>
> "Now therefore arise, go out and speak kindly to your servants, for I swear by the LORD, if you do not go out, surely not a man will pass the night with you, and this will be worse for you than all the evil that has come upon you from your youth until now."
>
> 2 Samuel 19:4–7

What is he doing? He is being a true friend! He is speaking the truth in love. "Come on, David, get on your feet, you've got to get past this grief. There are people out there who have risked their lives in their loyalty to you. They have believed in you and defended you. You've licked your wounds long enough, David. Your heart may be broken, but you are still the king of Israel and there's a job to be done!"

Joab was a friend to David. He cared enough to confront him. He cared enough to tell him the truth and prevent him from compounding the damage that had already been done by making an even greater mistake. We have to hand it to David here. Though gripped by grief, he listened . . . and he took his friend's advice.

So the king arose and sat in the gate. When they told all the people saying, "Behold, the king is sitting in the gate," then all the people came before the king. . . .

2 Samuel 19:8

The gate of the city was where the king or the leaders went to give an audience, to judge, to counsel, to meet with the people. So when David went to the gate, the people knew he was back in leadership. Joab's sheltering friendship, like all the others who had ministered to him earlier, had helped lift David up when he bottomed out.

THE TRUTH ABOUT TRUE FRIENDS

Friendship is indeed a sheltering tree. Friendship is where we find the hands of God ministering, encouraging, giving, and supporting through relatively unknown heroes of the faith . . . nobodies like Ittai the Gittite, Zadok, Abiathar, Hushai, Shobi, Machir, Barzillai, and Joab.

You may be surprised to know, as I was, that the words *friends, friendly,* and *friendship* appear over a hundred times in the Scriptures. God says a lot about friends. As I read all the verses and think about true friendship, I believe it all boils down to four things.

First, friends are not optional; they're essential. There is no substitute for a friend—someone to care, to listen, to feel, to comfort, and, yes, occasionally, to reprove. True friends do that best.

Second, friends are not automatic; they must be cultivated. The Bible says, "A man that hath friends must shew himself friendly" (Prov. 18:24, KJV). Samuel Johnson wrote: "One should keep his friendship in a constant repair."[46] As with trees, friendship needs cultivation.

Third, friends are not neutral; they impact our lives. If your friends lead good lives, they encourage you to become a better person. If your friends lead disreputable lives, they lead you down the same path—or worse. Scripture says, "Be not deceived: Bad company corrupts good morals" (1 Cor. 15:33). So choose your friends carefully and wisely. Gossips usually gravitate to gossips. Rebels run with rebels. You want to be wise? Choose wise friends.

Fourth, friendships come in varying degrees, some of whom play more significant roles in our life than others. We have many acquaintances, some casual friends, several close friends, and a few intimate friends.

Acquaintances are people with whom we have spasmodic contact and superficial interaction. We just skate over the surface with acquaintances.

"How are ya?" "Fine, fine! Great!" (I'm really not fine, but I can't tell you that because you're only an acquaintance.)

Casual friends are people with whom we have more contact, with whom we have common interests, and with whom we may have more specific conversations. Every once in a while we will even seek the opinion of a person who is a casual friend, although there is still a safe distance between us.

Close friends are those people with whom we share similar life goals and with whom we discuss the hard questions. We do projects together, exercise together, socialize together, and sometimes even vacation together.

Intimate friends are those few people with whom we have regular contact and a deep commitment. We are not only open and vulnerable with these people, we anxiously await their counsel. Intimate friends are just as free to criticize and to correct as they are to embrace and encourage, because trust and mutual understanding has been established between them.

All of these levels of friendship are important, but the most important, of course, is the last. Those who have no intimate friends have to be the loneliest people in the world. All of us need at least one person with whom we can be open and honest; all of us need at least one person who offers us the shelter of support and encouragement and, yes, even hard truths and confrontation. Sheltering trees, all!

Thankfully, David had a grove of such trees. As a result he made it through the toughest days and loneliest hours of his life.

Do you? If so, it is a good time to call them up and enjoy their shelter. If not, it's a good time to get a shovel and plant a few. You'll never regret it.

Just ask David.

CHAPTER TWENTY-ONE

Being Big Enough to Forgive

While taking this in-depth journey through the life of David, I don't want to just give you just geography and genealogy. My desire is not to have you walk away with a notebook full of chronological and biographical facts. My hope is to have you see David as a real person and then to see comparisons and opportunities in your own life so that you begin to emulate the qualities that made him a man after God's own heart.

One of those qualities is a *forgiving spirit*. This attribute also happens to be one of the most difficult to acquire. In fact, instead of fully forgiving someone, most folks opt for one of three different responses.

Instead of complete forgiveness, we offer *conditional* forgiveness. "I will forgive you IF . . ." or, "I will forgive you AS SOON AS . . ."; "If you come back and make things right, I'll forgive you," or, "If you own up to your part of the problem, then I'll forgive you." That's conditional forgiveness. It says, "I'm waiting, waiting like a tiger swishing his tail. You make your move, and I'll determine whether it's time to back away or pounce and bite."

The second kind of forgiveness that's less than perfect is *partial* forgiveness. "I forgive you, but don't expect me to forget." Or, "I forgive you, but just get out of my life." Or, "I'll forgive you until that happens again." There are a lot of people we are willing to forgive . . . just so we don't have to see them again.

The third response is *delayed* forgiveness. "I'll forgive you, but just give me some time. Someday, sometime I'll follow through, I'll forgive you." This is a common reaction of someone who has been deeply hurt . . . and has nursed that hurt over the years.

Most of us would rather sit on a judgment seat than a mercy seat. If somebody "did us wrong," we'd rather watch him squirm in misery than smile in relief.

Yet forgiveness isn't just about the other person; it's also about us. When we are unforgiving, it has a dramatic, downward effect on our own life. First of all, there is an *offense*. And if there isn't forgiveness after the offense, then resentment begins to build. And if there isn't forgiveness following that resentment, then *hatred* comes to take its place. Sustained hatred leads to *grudge*. And grudge ultimately settles into *revenge*. "I'm just biding my time. And when I have my chance I'll get back."

I openly confess, several years ago I couldn't have written this chapter. I hadn't really come to terms with these things in my own life. Thank God, since He has helped me deal with this, today I can honestly say I do not know of an individual I have not forgiven . . . and I write that with no sense of pride. Who am I to brag, having nursed an unforgiving spirit far too long?

I say it with thankfulness and relief. I say it in humble honesty to encourage you to know that it can happen. Now let me go another step further. While I don't feel resentment toward anyone, I still wrestle with this issue on a regular basis. Every week, it seems, I have to come to terms with not letting some offense linger and lead me back into resentment. I have to deal with it at the offense level or I'm a goner. If I didn't, before realizing it, I'd be all the way to revenge.

AN EXAMPLE OF COMPLETE FORGIVENESS

Now, let's look at forgiveness in the life of David. This is a great place to do it, because we're at a point where David's life has reached low ebb. As we saw in the previous chapter, he has never been lower—never. This could be compared to the time before he was on the throne when Saul was pursuing him and he was so depressed, so low.

David sinned with Bathsheba and that set off a whole chain reaction. Nathan said, "Your baby will die." And that happened. "Your wives will be taken advantage of in public." And that happened. "Your family will turn against you." And that happened. His son Absalom conspired against him and usurped the throne. Now Absalom is reigning as the king and David is on the run. He is at his lowest ebb. He's at the bottom.

It may very well have been at this moment in his life that he wrote these words.

> I waited patiently for the LORD;
> And He inclined to me, and heard my cry.
> He brought me up out of the pit of destruction, out of the
> miry clay;
> And He set my feet upon a rock making my footsteps
> firm. . . .
> For evils beyond number have surrounded me;
> My iniquities have overtaken me, so that I am not able to see;
> They are more numerous than the hairs of my head;
> And my heart has failed me.
>
> Psalm 40:1–2, 12

He was in "the pit of destruction!" Have you ever felt like that? Of course you have. And in that desperate moment, with guilt crushing in on top of David, in the pit of self-depreciating thoughts, a man named Shimei came out of nowhere to add to his misery. We met some of David's "sheltering trees" in the last chapter. Shimei is no sheltering tree. To put it bluntly, he's a jerk, a third-rate klutz who hits another while he's down. This guy is a real loser. Alexander Whyte calls him "a reptile of the royal house of Saul."[47]

> When King David came to Bahurim, behold, there came out from there a man of the family of the house of Saul whose name was Shimei, the son of Gera; he came out cursing continually as he came. And he threw stones at David and at all the servants of King David; and all the people and all the mighty men were at his right hand and at his left.
>
> And thus Shimei said when he cursed, "Get out, get out, you man of bloodshed, and worthless fellow! The LORD has returned upon you all the bloodshed of the house of Saul, in whose place you have reigned; and the LORD has given the kingdom into the hand of your son Absalom. And behold, you are taken in your own evil, for you are a man of bloodshed!"
>
> 2 Samuel 16:5–8

The Living Bible reads,

"Get out of here, you murderer, you scoundrel!" he shouted at David. "The Lord is paying you back for murdering King Saul and his family [that was a lie]; you stole his throne [another lie] and now the Lord has given it to your son Absalom [that's a third lie—the Lord never gave David's son the throne; Absalom took the throne]! At last you will taste some of your own medicine, you murderer!"

Shimei was your basic reprobate—the kind of person who kicks you while you're on your face, down and out. You're at the very ultimate, lowest pit and along comes a Shimei. Boom! Hits you below the belt. And when you squirm, he comes back with another blow.

Then along comes someone else to give counsel to David.

> Then Abishai the son of Zeruiah said to the king, "Why should this dead dog curse my lord the king? Let me go over now, and cut off his head."
>
> 2 Samuel 16:9

That's a pretty direct game plan, I'd say. "Lemme at him. I'll slice his throat so fast he won't know it 'til he sneezes!" You always have somebody who will say stuff like that. "Hey, you don't have to take that. Let me handle him. Boy, I'm good at this. I mean, you got your rights. Stand up for yourself. Don't let 'em walk all over you. Just cut 'em off at the knees. Sue the guy!" (Sound familiar?)

Now, Shimei has come at David at a hard moment. He's not only thrown rocks and cursed David, he has lied three times in his personal attack. He is way out of line. David has done nothing to warrant these public assaults. But they have come, nevertheless. David now has a choice. He can be offended and become resentful and take revenge on this man— or not.

> But the king said, "What have I to do with you, O sons of Zeruiah?"
>
> 2 Samuel 16:10

If David said that once in his lifetime, he must have said it a half-dozen times. Sons of Zeruiah were all built with a short fuse. Every one of them carried a chip on his shoulder, always ready to fight. But David refuses to retaliate. He stays calm and does not allow Shimei's short fuse to cause an explosion. With a wave of his hand, David responds:

> "What have I to do with you, O sons of Zeruiah? If he curses, and if the LORD has told him, 'Curse David,' then who shall say, 'Why have you done so?' . . .
> "Perhaps the LORD will look on my affliction and return good to me instead of his cursing this day."
>
> 2 Samuel 16:10, 12

Get the picture? It's an amazing study in self-control! David's at rock-bottom, and along comes Shimei who boots him. But instead of fighting back, David says, "The LORD's in it." He never got offended. He never took it personally. He didn't even yell! How in the world could he do that?

Soft heart and thick skin. That's the ticket, plain and simple. Not sensitive skin, so delicate that the slightest pinprick will damage it, but really thick. Rhinoceros thick. So that you can get punched around and punched around. Let me tell you, if you hope to be used of God, *you need that kind of skin.* Count on it—Shimeis are out there by the dozens! The people who get the job done are those who are able to overlook all sorts of hurtful little comments people are going to make. When you walk through thorns, you have to have on heavy boots. You don't walk through thorns barefooted . . . at least not very far. If you are called into leadership, where you must deal with people, you have to be well-shod and armor-plated. If not, you're doomed to failure.

Now that doesn't mean a thickness toward God. It means you have a protective coating against the slings and arrows of people like this Shimei. If you haven't already, it won't be long before you will meet up with a Shimei. It's only a matter of time. Such "reptiles" proliferate. And you'll have to decide: Am I going to be offended or not? Am I big enough to forgive . . . or will I reduce myself to his size and sling rocks back?

Now, let's jump ahead in the story. Some time has passed. Absalom has been brutally murdered. Although this is not what David wanted, the awful event has removed Absalom from the throne, and the people are turning back to David as their leader. They are moving his household goods back over the Jordan to Jerusalem, in a hurry to get the rightful king back on the throne. It's a day of coronation. David has come from the lowest level back up to the highest mountaintop, and he is rejoicing as he is about to be enthroned once again as the king.

Wouldn't you know it? Once again, here comes Shimei.

> Then Shimei the son of Gera, the Benjamite who was from Bahurim, hurried and came down with the men of Judah to meet King David. And there were a thousand men of Benjamin with him, with Ziba the servant of the house of Saul, and his fifteen sons and his twenty servants with him; they rushed to the Jordan before the king.
>
> Then they kept crossing the ford to bring over the king's household, and to do what was good in his sight. And Shimei the son of Gera fell down before the king as he was about to cross the Jordan.
>
> So he said to the king, "Let not my lord consider me guilty, nor remember what your servant did wrong on the day when my lord the king came out from Jerusalem, so that the king should take it to heart. For your servant knows that I have sinned; therefore, behold, I have come today, the first of all the house of Joseph to go down to meet my lord the king."
>
> 2 Samuel 19:16–20

Shimei said the three hardest words in the English language, "I have sinned." They must have rung a bell in David's mind. It hadn't been too many years ago that he had said those same words to Nathan. Forgiveness comes easier when we remember times in our own past when we failed and were forgiven.

Before we look at David's response to this, let's look at the other side of the equation and think about times we might have been in Shimei's shoes. He's not just some Old Testament character or caricature; his actions and reactions are real. We now know because we've all had similar experiences, haven't we? We've done or said something that could easily offend another person. We now know what we did was wrong, and we know the other person is hung up on that. So the ball is in our court. It's our serve. It's now our move, and we need to come to terms with it, but that's tough, isn't it? And it's even tougher when we know that we were 100 percent in the wrong. Well, that is where Shimei finds himself in this scene.

Let's turn once again to David's side of the matter. After what Shimei had said to him earlier, David could have been indifferent to his confession.

He could have just ignored him. Some people would do that . . . just sort of looked past him with a shrug.

George Bernard Shaw wrote wise words, "The worst sin toward our fellow creatures is not to hate them, but to be indifferent to them: that's the essence of inhumanity. . . ."[48]

Indifference is certainly not forgiveness. Indifference is RAGE controlled.

So Shimei is spread out on the ground before David, saying, "I have sinned." What he's really saying is, "Will you please forgive me?"

> But Abishai the son of Zeruiah answered and said, "Should not Shimei be put to death for this, because he cursed the LORD's anointed?"
>
> 2 Samuel 19:21

Abishai doesn't tell David to ignore Shimei. He says, "No way, David. He kicked you when you were down. Kick him back, kick him hard. Finish him off—he's a loser." But David says,

> "What have I to do with you, O sons of Zeruiah, that you should this day be an adversary to me? Should any man be put to death in Israel today? For do I not know that I am king over Israel today?"
>
> And the king said to Shimei, "You shall not die." Thus the king swore to him.
>
> 2 Samuel 19:22–23

Here's another "son of Zeruiah" with that typical short fuse! But David isn't swayed by his counsel any more than he was swayed by Shimei's earlier insults. What magnificent, merciful control he demonstrates! His strength and ability to forgive is a shining example to us.

How could David forgive a "reptile" like this Shimei? Well, first of all, *he kept his vertical focus clear.* "God, You and I can handle this. You take care of that offense. You're good at offenses." I have discovered great strength in taking any offense immediately to God. I mean, immediately. There is something very stabilizing in getting vertical perspective on a situation before seeking any horizontal counsel.

Second, *David was very much aware of his own failure.* The humbled forgiven make good forgivers. David knew only too well what it meant to be a sinner. He knew what it meant to be forgiven by the Lord. He knew the heartache of having done wrong . . . the cleansing feeling—the relief, the sense of burden lifted—that follows repentance and forgiveness. Those horrible months when he was humbled before his God seasoned David and made him merciful. Being well aware of his own shortcomings gave him great patience with another's wrongdoing.

The proud have a hard time forgiving. Those who have never recognized their own failures have a tough time tolerating, understanding, and forgiving the failure of others.

If we are to develop a spirit of forgiveness in our own lives, if we are to put forgiveness into action, we need to do several things.

SOME SOUND ADVICE TO HELP US FORGIVE

First, *we must cultivate a thicker layer of skin*, a buffer to take those jolts that come our way. We need to ask for God's help with this. "Lord, help me not to be so sensitive, so thin-skinned. Lord, take away this delicate china-doll mentality of mine and give me depth. Toughen my hide. Calm my responses. Make me patient with those who speak too quickly. Make me like Christ." This will help us keep our sense of balance so that the slightest push does not send us toppling over, and so that we can bounce back from whatever hits us.

Second, *we can try to understand where the offender is coming from*. This takes a lot of grace, but, again, God is good at grace. Try to see beyond the offense and find the little boy inside that man lashing out at you . . . or the little girl inside that woman who is striking back. Try to find out what is behind their offensive words or behavior. You may be surprised how helpful that can be! Who knows? David may have seen a touch of his old immature self in Shimei as those rocks came whizzing by.

Sometimes we make things more complicated than they really are. Maybe the critics have been saving up their own offenses and have chosen this moment to use you as a punching bag. Maybe they are just having a bad day. A guy gets yelled at at work. He goes home and screams at his wife. She then becomes angry with one of the kids. The kid walks out and boots the cat. And the cat prowls all night trying to find some innocent creature to bite! That's the kind of chain reaction that happens when we don't stay calm and deal honestly and act graciously with each other. I'm not saying it is easy or suggesting it comes naturally. But neither is it impossible. Putting ourselves in the other person's shoes often helps us objectify their reaction. Our Savior did that even while hanging on the cross. He looked at His accusers and prayed, "Father, forgive them, for they do not know what they are doing" (Lk. 23:34). In that one statement, we realize how our Lord viewed His enemies.

Third, *we should recall times in our own life when we have needed forgiveness and then apply the same emotion.* All of us, at one time or another, have done or said something dumb or extreme or offensive and have needed someone's forgiveness. This happens between friends, in families, at work, at school, and, yes, even at church. We must be candid about this—nobody is above the drag of humanity. When it kicks in, we can be as ugly or vile or ornery as the other guy.

I pray for this kind of authenticity all the time. "Keep me authentic, Lord. Take every phony-baloney cell out of my body. Just keep me real."

Fourth, *we need to verbalize our forgiveness.* Say it, don't just think it. Spoken words of forgiveness and graciousness are marvelously therapeutic to the offender, no matter how small or great the offense. Saying our feelings removes all doubt. Stuart Briscoe writes:

> Some years ago a fashionably dressed woman came to my study, very distressed. She had made a commitment to the Lord a few days earlier but had asked to see me because something was troubling her. She poured out an unpleasant story concerning an affair she had been having with one of her husband's friends. Then she insisted that her husband should know, and that I should tell him! That was a new experience for me!
>
> After some discussion with the woman, I called the husband. When he arrived at my study, I told him what had happened. His response was a remarkable and beautiful thing to behold. Turning to his tearful and fearful wife, he said, "I love you. I forgive you. Let's make a new start."
>
> Many things had to be straightened out and much hurt had to be healed, but his response of forgiveness, made possible by his own understanding of the forgiveness of God, became the basis of a new joy and a new life.[49]

Our typical human response to offense is to try all the wrong things: silence, resentment, grudge, indifference, even plotting a way to maneuver and manipulate to get our offender in a vulnerable spot so we can twist the verbal knife, once we've plunged it in. None of this pleases God . . . nor does it work!

Cultivating a forgiving spirit is a very real problem that every one of us wrestles with. We need a heart of full forgiveness and grace in our family relationships, in our work and school relationships, certainly in our church relationships. We need to put feet to the hope that is within us.

In his book, *You Can Win with Love*, Dale Galloway tells a story about John D. Rockefeller, the man who built the great Standard Oil empire. Not surprisingly, Rockefeller was a man who demanded high performance from his company executives. Then, one day, one of those executives made a two million dollar mistake.

Word of the man's enormous error quickly spread throughout the executive offices, and the other men began to make themselves scarce. Afraid of Rockefeller's reaction, they didn't even want to cross his path.

One man didn't have any choice, however, since he had an appointment with the boss. So he straightened his shoulders and tightened his belt and walked into Rockefeller's office.

As he approached the oil monarch's desk, Rockefeller looked up from the piece of paper upon which he was writing.

"I guess you've heard about the two million dollar mistake our friend made," he said abruptly.

"Yes," the executive said, expecting Rockefeller to explode.

"Well, I've been sitting here listing all of our friend's good qualities on this sheet of paper, and I've discovered that in the past he has made us many more times the amount he lost for us today by his one mistake. His good points far outweigh this one human error. So I think we ought to forgive him, don't you?"[50]

Whether it's a two million dollar mistake or a one-sentence off-the-cuff comment, we need to respond with Christlike grace and complete forgiveness. Like David, we need a soft heart and thick skin, we need vertical focus . . . and we need an awareness of our own failures and our own need for forgiveness.

CHAPTER TWENTY-TWO

A Song of Triumph

The long shadows of age and pressure are beginning to fall across David's face. He has lived a full life and experienced both the heights and the depths. He has entered what we might call his twilight years. David often had to trust God in impossible circumstances, but it seems as though recently things have occurred that have kept him on his knees. Long before he was a king, David was a singer of songs, and in 2 Samuel 22 we find what I am convinced is the last song he ever sang. Three major events in David's life provided preparation for this song.

David suffered the anguish and grief of the premature death of his son, Absalom, who was murdered following the conspiracy he led against his father. The second blow that drove David to his knees was a three-year famine that struck the land, adding calamity to humility. And finally, they were back at war with their age-old enemy, the Philistines.

> Now when the Philistines were at war again with Israel, David went down and his servants with him; and as they fought against the Philistines, David became weary.
>
> 2 Samuel 21:15

The NIV concludes that verse, "and he became exhausted."

I would imagine. After all he'd been through, who wouldn't feel exhausted? He's only human. A person can take only so much. The loss of a son, the suffering brought on by famine, the misery of battle—it all wears on him until he begins to crack. Thus, the weary David lifts his hands to God and declares his feelings in a song, which covers no less than 51 verses in 2 Samuel 22. But the tone is not what one might expect, given his circumstances. It is not a dark, somber dirge, but a psalm of praise that the gifted, aging composer "sang to the LORD" (22:1).

These were hard times for David: times of violence (v. 3), days when "torrents of destruction overwhelmed" him (v. 5), days of calamity when he was surrounded by frightening foes and powerful enemies (vv. 18–19). But out of it all the Lord delivered him, as David testifies in this song.

ONE LIFE . . . FOUR THEMES

David sums up his life in four themes, four expressions that weave their way through this psalm of praise. These, then, are the themes of David's full life.

Theme 1: When times are tough, God is our only security (vv. 2–20).

> And he said, "The LORD is my rock and my fortress and my
>   deliverer; My God, my rock, in whom I take refuge;
> My shield and the horn of my salvation, my stronghold and
>   my refuge. . . ."
>
> 2 Samuel 22:2–3

Each of these poetic expressions carries a unique and powerful meaning in which David describes the Lord as a secure heavenly Father. "Times are tough. I've lost my son. I'm losing my nation. My army is in disarray. My land and my people must once again face warfare as the Philistines come upon us. And yet I find that the LORD continues to be a shield, my stronghold, and my refuge."

Feel what David is describing in the following words.

> In my distress I called upon the LORD,
> Yes, I cried to my God;
> And from His temple He heard my voice,
> And my cry for help came into His ears.
>
> 2 Samuel 22:7

To him, God was no distant Deity, preoccupied with other galaxies or concerned with the changing of the seasons. His God heard his voice!

Those guttural cries came into His ears! Watch God's involvement in the movement of David's psalm.

> And my cry for help came into His ears.
> Then the earth shook and quaked, the foundations of heaven
>   were trembling and were shaken, because He was angry.
> Smoke went up out of His nostrils, and fire from his mouth
>   devoured; coals were kindled by it.
> He bowed the heavens also, and came down with thick
>   darkness under His feet.
> And He rode on a cherub and flew; He appeared on the
>   wings of the wind.
> And He made darkness canopies around Him, a mass of
>   waters, thick clouds of the sky.
>
> 2 Samuel 22:7–12

What is God doing? He is responding to those cries. He's bringing rain. He's answering the call for help in the drought and the famine.

> From the brightness before Him
> Coals of fire were kindled.
> The LORD thundered from heaven,
> And the Most High uttered His voice.
> And He sent out arrows, and scattered them,
> Lightning, and routed them,
> Then the channels of the sea appeared,
> The foundations of the world were laid bare,
> By the rebuke of the LORD,
> At the blast of the breath of His nostrils.
> He sent from on high, He took me;
> He drew me out of many waters.
> He delivered me from my strong enemy,
> From those who hated me, for they were too strong for me.
> They confronted me in the day of my calamity. . . .
>
> 2 Samuel 22:13–19

Isn't that just like an enemy? When David is beaten and broken, the hateful enemy invades and confronts and deals harshly, without feeling, without tenderness. But tenderly the Lord brings reprieve and relief.

But the LORD was my support.
He also brought me forth into a broad place;
He rescued me, because He delighted in me.

2 Samuel 22:19–20

Isn't that magnificent? Absolutely fantastic! We have no trouble believing the business about calamity and strong enemies and distress and death and destruction and violence, but at those times it is so difficult to believe that the Lord delights in us. Yet He does. That's the whole message of grace. The LORD dispatches His angels of hope who bring invincible help because He finds delight in us. He cares for us. He feels our ache. He feels it deeply. Even though we resist it, it's true. He delights in us. Believe it, my friend . . . *believe it!*

Are times hard? Are days of trouble upon you? When times are tough, the Lord is our only security. David assures us in his song that the Lord delights in us; He sees and cares about what is happening in our lives, this very moment.

The LORD is our support. In tough times He is our only security. He rescues us because He delights in us. What encouragement that brings as the battle endures and exhausts us. David's song of triumph begins on this easily forgotten theme. I am thankful he reminds us of it.

Theme 2: When our days are dark, the Lord is our only light (vv. 21–31).

For Thou art my lamp, O Lord;
And the LORD illumines my darkness.

2 Samuel 22:29

That reminds me of a scene from my boyhood days. When I was just a lad, my dad and I used to go floundering, a popular pastime on the Gulf Coast. We'd carry a lantern in one hand and a two-pronged spear in the other (called a gig) as we walked along, knee-deep in the shallow water along the shore. As we walked, we'd swing the lantern back and forth as we searched the soft sand for the flounder that came up close to the shore in the evening to eat the shrimp and the mullet. The little lantern provided just enough light to reveal the fish down in the sand beneath the water . . . and just enough so that we could see a few feet ahead as we waded through the water. Actually, it was all the light we needed. It penetrated just enough of the darkness so that we could see where to walk, but not beyond that.

The same is true of the light we receive from God. At times we flounder along, trying to peer too far into the darkness ahead. Yet He gives us just enough light so that we can see to take the next step. That's all He gives and, in reality, that's all we need.

Charles Allen's touching yet uplifting words are appropriate here:

> When a person is suddenly alone, often panic and fear come. I distinctly remember my mother saying to me after my father's death, "I cannot go on without him. I depended upon him for everything." My mother believed that, but she did go on without him. In fact, she lived twenty-five wonderful years after my father died. I remember that one of the things that bothered my mother was that she could not drive a car. She learned that she could live without driving a car. I feel that the most creative years of my mother's life were the years when she was forced to depend upon herself. She had her anxious moments, but somewhere along the way she learned the old expression, "Life by the yard is hard, but life by the inch is a cinch."[51]

That's what David is saying in this psalm. "You are my lamp, Lord, and You give me just enough inches to let me see the next step, and that's all You give me, but that's enough. You are the One who illumines my darkness."

And look at what he says in verse 30.

> For by Thee I can run upon a troop;
> By my God I can leap over a wall.

"I can see my way, Lord. I can get over the hurdles because You are the lamp that gives me that direction."

Remember the encouraging words from that other psalm of light, Psalm 27? "The LORD is my light and my salvation." Actually, we can read that last word as *deliverer* or *deliverance*, since it's the very same word. "The LORD is my light and my deliverance; whom shall I fear? The LORD is the defense of my life; whom shall I dread?" He goes all the way down to describe different experiences and circumstances in which the LORD gives deliverance. He even says, "For my father and my mother have forsaken me, but the LORD will take me up" (Ps. 27:10). It's true—the Lord enlightens our way even more than our parents could provide. The light of the Lord provides both direction and deliverance, so why should we fear?

All of us have our own particular fears. Fear of darkness. Fear of failure. Fear of the unknown. Fear of heights. Fear of financial disaster. Fear of sickness. Fear of death. You name it, we entertain it. Yet, He promises to deliver us from all our fears . . . and so it stands to reason that we can rest in Him. He shields us when we take refuge in Him. What a wonderful song of hope!

> The word of the LORD is tested;
> He is a shield to those who take refuge in Him.
>
> 2 Samuel 22:31

Theme 3: When our walk is weak, the LORD is our only strength (vv. 32–40).

> For who is God, besides the LORD?
> And who is a rock, besides our God?
> God is my strong fortress. . . .
>
> 2 Samuel 22:32–33

Clearly, David is not describing himself as strong. He was exhausted from the battle, remember? He's saying, "The Lord is my strength."

> He makes my feet like hinds' feet [the feet of a deer],
> And sets me on my high places.
> He trains my hands for battle,
> So that my arms can bend a bow of bronze.
>
> 2 Samuel 22:34–35

That's strength, friends and neighbors! We can face *whatever* life throws at us when our strength is sourced in Him.

> Thou hast also given me the shield of Thy salvation
>   [victorious deliverance],
> And Thy help makes me great.
>
> 2 Samuel 22:36

David then goes on to describe in vivid terms specific instances of weakness in which the Lord gives strength. When times are tough, the

Lord sees us through. When days are dark, the Lord is the light. When our walk is weak, the Lord is our strength.

The apostle Paul echoes the same thing in 2 Corinthians 12.

> And because of the surpassing greatness of the revelations, for this reason, to keep me from exalting myself, there was given me a thorn in the flesh, a messenger of Satan to buffet me— to keep me from exalting myself!
>
> Concerning this I entreated the Lord three times that it might depart from me. And He has said to me, "My grace is sufficient for you, for power is perfected in weakness." Most gladly, therefore, I will rather boast about my weaknesses, that the power of Christ may dwell in me.
>
> Therefore I am well content with weaknesses, with insults, with distresses, with persecutions, with difficulties, for Christ's sake; for when I am weak, then I am strong.
>
> 2 Corinthians 12:7–10

That's the secret: "God's great power is perfected in our utter weakness. MY power is best displayed when YOU are weak." Isn't that hard to put into action, though? We want to be strong. And yet a key principle in the Christian life is that God is never stronger in His work than when we are, admittedly, weak. When we come to an end, He steps up and shows Himself strong.

"Thy help makes me great," says verse 36, in David's song of triumph. And that is the truth. When times are tough, the Lord is our only security. When days are dark, the Lord is our only light. When our walk is weak, the Lord is our only strength.

Theme 4: When our future is foggy or fuzzy, the Lord is our only hope (vv. 50–51). Look at how David brings his song to its grand finale:

> Therefore I will give thanks to Thee, O Lord, among the
>   nations,
> And I will sing praises to Thy name.
>
> 2 Samuel 22:50

Despite all that David has been through, he is not bitter or resentful. What a man! David approached the end of his life with a song on his lips, not bitter grumblings or regrets on his heart. Why? Because,

He [God] is a tower of deliverance to His king
And shows lovingkindness to His anointed,
To David and his descendants forever.

2 Samuel 22:51

I have noticed that as we get older and the years start to stack up, the future becomes far more significant than the present. When we are in our fifties and sixties, we begin to wonder about what our seventies and eighties will be like, should we live that long. David promises us in this psalm, from both experience and faith, that the Lord will show lovingkindness to His anointed and even take care of their descendants forever. That's a hope-filled vision—our only hope—the Lord's being our only source of true hope.

A number of years ago my sister, Luci, gave me a volume I treasure . . . and in the front of the book she wrote these words from an old poem— words I immediately memorized and have never forgotten:

Whom have we Lord, but Thee,
Soul-thirst to satisfy?
Exhaustless spring,
The water is free,
All other streams are dry.[52]

We Christians, I have observed, frequently have trouble believing He is our only hope, security, light, and strength because we are so prone to try everything else. We automatically depend upon everything *except* the Lord. Yet still He waits there for us—patiently waiting to show Himself strong.

He is our light and our salvation; whom should we fear? He hears our cry. He lifts us up out of a horrible pit; He places our feet upon a rock and establishes our going. He proves Himself strong in our weakness; He sheds light in our darkness; He becomes hope in our uncertainty and security in our confusion. He is the Centerpiece of our lives. Thank you, David, for leaving us this reminder in your final song of triumph. More than that, thank you, Lord, for being there throughout our lives . . . never letting us down . . . never making us feel foolish because we are weak.

Whom have we, Lord, but Thee?

CHAPTER TWENTY-THREE

When the Godly Are Foolish

Age alone is no guarantee of maturity or freedom from error. As Elihu said to Job, "The experts have no corner on wisdom; getting old doesn't guarantee good sense" (Job 32:9).

In his book, *Spiritual Leadership*, J. Oswald Sanders has a chapter called "The Cost of Leadership" in which he makes this statement:

> No one need aspire to leadership in the work of God who is not prepared to pay a price greater than his contemporaries and colleagues are willing to pay. True leadership always exacts a heavy toll on the whole man, and the more effective the leadership is, the higher the price to be paid.[53]

When a spiritual leader wanders from the things of God, the consequences are often devastating and always far-reaching. When men and women who claim to model the message of Christ defect from that message, either by their actions or the statements that fall from their lips, they leave a destructive wake in the body of Christ.

It would be wonderful if I could announce that as we grow older we automatically grow up, or that the longer we walk with the Lord the more we are guaranteed immunity from sin. That is not the case, however. We will NEVER be immune from sin's appeal. Often those who fall the hardest are those who have walked with God the longest. Not until we are "with the Lord" will we be what we ought to be. There is no such thing as outgrowing sin.

In 2 Samuel 24 (and its parallel passage, 1 Chronicles 21), we are given a vivid account of a tragic example of this when David, in the latter years of his life, committed a sin that affected thousands of lives. This event probably took place on the heels of a war between Israel and her age-old enemies—the Philistines. Interestingly, we find a parallel here between David's last battle (or one of his last battles) and his first battle. Both were with the Philistines, and both involved giants. David killed Goliath in that first battle; in this last one, a brother of Goliath was killed, as were several others who are called "descendants of the giants in Gath."

EXPLANATION OF A BAD DECISION

David was victorious in his first battle, and he was victorious in this one. After the battle and the victory, however, David was vulnerable. As we saw earlier in this book, we are most vulnerable immediately after victory. That's when Satan sets his traps. Look at what happened to King David.

> Now again the anger of the LORD burned against Israel, and it incited David against them to say, "Go, number Israel and Judah."
>
> 2 Samuel 24:1

God was angry with Israel. We don't know exactly why He was angry with the nation, but whatever the reason, it had David ticked off, too. Upset and hassled, he commanded, "Go, number Israel and Judah."

> And the king said to Joab the commander of the army who was with him, "Go about now through all the tribes of Israel, from Dan to Beersheba [that's north to south], and register the people, that I may know the number of the people."
>
> 2 Samuel 24:2

David said, "I want to know how many we have in this land." Bible scholars suggest that his motive was to learn the strength of his army. In other words, his unstated motive was pride. He wanted to see how big his land really was, how vast his kingdom, how impressive his army.

At this point he received some wise counsel—which he ignored, unfortunately.

> But Joab said to the king, "Now may the LORD your God add
> to the people a hundred times as many as they are, while the
> eyes of my lord the king still see; but why does my lord the
> king delight in this thing?"
>
> 2 Samuel 24:3

This was a gracious way of saying, "Oh, David, I hope that God multiplies the nation of Israel a hundred times during your lifetime, but why do you insist on doing this?"

By raising this question, Joab offered wise counsel, but David never got it. Or if he did, his response is not revealed. He seems to have pulled rank and said to Joab, "You do as I said."

In 1 Chronicles 21, we are given more insight into the decision.

> Then Satan stood up against Israel and moved David to number Israel.
>
> 1 Chronicles 21:1

That's a mind-boggling statement: that the Enemy was directly responsible for impressing David's mind with this wayward thought. It's not surprising, though, since we know that the real battle for our lives occurs in the mind. When the apostle Paul wrote of Satan's work, he said, "We are not ignorant of his schemes" (2 Cor. 2:11). The Greek term rendered "schemes" has in its root the word "mind." A paraphrase might read, "we are not ignorant of his ability to get into our minds and direct our thoughts."

And that's exactly what is happening to David. Satan nudged David in his private thoughts and said, "Why don't you number these people? Let's see how big the kingdom is. Why not inventory how vast your land has become?"

Joab warned him against doing it, but "the king's word prevailed" (1 Chron. 21:4). This suggests that there might have been something of an argument between the two men and David won out; kings prevail against generals.

David had reached such a peerless position as the king of Israel that he answered to nobody. He could do whatever he wanted, virtually without challenge. Even when it came to somebody like Joab, who was the commander of his entire army, David could say, "Just do it!" Right or wrong, his word stood. I need to repeat here something I mentioned earlier. An unaccountable life is a dangerous life regardless of the high-ranking position anyone holds. It's a precarious place to be. But that's the way David was.

If you find yourself in that trusted and precarious position of being un-questioned in your authority, be very, very careful. In fact, I would counsel you to select a small group of trusted people to whom you voluntarily make yourself accountable. Carte blanche, free-wheeling leadership is dangerous. Few people can handle it . . . in this case, not even an aging, godly king named David. His decision to number the people reveals this. In fact, this de-cision reveals a couple of weaknesses in David's life at this point.

The first weakness is that *David was out of touch with God*. We do not find David praying, seeking God's counsel, or searching the Scriptures before he made this decision. He simply decided to do it. The second weakness is that *David was unaccountable to anyone around him*—a dan-gerous oversight.

Yet look at what follows David's sinful decision.

EXPLANATION OF A TROUBLED HEART

> Now David's heart troubled him after he had numbered the people. . . .
>
> 2 Samuel 24:10

That's why David was a man after God's heart. He wasn't perfect, but to the end of his days he had a sensitive heart for God. "His heart *troubled* him." The Hebrew term is *nakah*, and it's a severe word. It means "to be attacked, to be assaulted." On occasion it is used in reference to a city that is destroyed or slaughtered. It conveys the idea of being wounded or crip-pled. In other words, deep inside David's inner man was a disturbing reminder of God's displeasure in what he had done.

When that happens, we are on our way to recovery. But many are the stubborn saints who knowingly step out against God's will only to run faster and faster, refusing to listen to the troubled heart down inside. Re-grettably, those in greatest power are often those who listen the least to that inner, aching voice.

David was such a sensitive man. When he got the census numbers from Joab, he began to study the report. As he did, perhaps the Lord brought back to his mind Joab's original counsel, and that question began to haunt him. *Why have I done this thing?* The longer he thought about it, the louder the answer pulsated through his brain. *The only reason is my own pride.*

Have you ever been troubled by something in your spiritual walk? If so, what have you done about it? Have you ignored it and just kept going in the same direction? Or did you come to a dead stop and say, "I was wrong. I was WRONG! God is dealing with me about this, and I know what He wants me to do about it."

David's heart was troubled after he had numbered the people, and once again we find the man saying those hard words:

> "I have sinned greatly in what I have done. But now, O Lord, please take away the iniquity of Thy servant, for I have acted very foolishly."
>
> 2 Samuel 24:10

Turning once again to 1 Chronicles, we get more details:

> And God was displeased with this thing, so He struck Israel.
>
> 1 Chronicles 21:7

I suspect that's what began to trouble David's heart. When we have done wrong and we begin to see the devastation that results from our sin, we cannot let it rest—at least not very long if we are sensitive to God's dealing with us.

> "I have sinned greatly, in that I have done this thing. But now, please take away the iniquity of Thy servant, for I have done very foolishly."
>
> 1 Chronicles 21:8

That's pretty honest, isn't it? "I have sinned . . . I have done very foolishly."

After this genuine declaration, David has a choice to make. This is a most unusual section of Scripture. It's the only time I know of in the Bible where a person is given the opportunity to choose the consequences of following wrong. God gives David three choices.

> And the LORD spoke to Gad, David's seer [one of the prophets that surrounded David's throne], saying, "Go and speak to David, saying, 'Thus says the LORD, "I offer you three things;

choose for yourself one of them, that I may do it to you." ' "

So Gad came to David and said to him, "Thus says the LORD, 'Take for yourself either three years of famine, or three months to be swept away before your foes, while the sword of your enemies overtakes you, or else three days of the sword of the LORD, even pestilence in the land, and the angel of the LORD destroying throughout all the territory of Israel.' Now, therefore, consider what answer I shall return to Him who sent me."

1 Chronicles 21:9–12

Now that's tough, isn't it? Any one of the three is awful. But what a clear reminder for us: One does not sin without making waves and causing a wake. Even if David chooses the three days, as he does, it is a never-to-be-forgotten event.

What a deterrent to sin it would be if, before the fact, we could be given a glimpse of its impact—the sorrow and grief it will bring to others . . . the toll it is going to take. I am not at all surprised to read what David said to Gad: "I am in great distress" (2 Sam. 24:14).

David was "in great distress." The Hebrew word here, *tsarar,* means "to be tied up, restricted, cramped." His stomach was cramped up and churning inside. We would say he was tied up in knots. (We've all felt that way; we've said those words.) David heard this account, and the tremendous guilt he felt down inside was almost more than he could bear.

"I am in great distress; please let me fall into the hand of the LORD, for His mercies are very great. But do not let me fall into the hand of man."

1 Chronicles 21:13

Wise choice. If you want grace, fall into the hands of God. If you want judgment, fall into the hands of fellow human beings. David knew that. He made the best choice. "I'll take three days of the sword of the Lord," says David. But even that was horrible to endure. Oswald Sanders' words I quoted at the beginning of this chapter come to mind here. This was the "high price" to be paid . . . except in this case, those who were under David's leadership were the ones who had to pay the price. How miserable David must have felt, knowing *his* failure caused *their* pain and loss.

A pathetic scene follows as David sees the movement of God's scythe across the land of Israel, cutting people down, one after another. It's almost more than he can bear, the devastation of his own act of foolishness.

> So the LORD sent a pestilence upon Israel from the morning
> until the appointed time; and seventy thousand men of the
> people from Dan to Beersheba died.
>
> 2 Samuel 24:15

Then God sends an angel to destroy Jerusalem. Think of it. God is
going to destroy that great capital city—David's city.

> But as he was about to destroy it, the LORD saw and was sorry
> over the calamity, and said to the destroying angel, "It is
> enough. . . ."
>
> 1 Chronicles 21:15

As David saw the death angel sweep across the land, he

> . . . lifted up his eyes and saw the angel of the LORD standing
> between earth and heaven, with his drawn sword in his hand
> stretched out over Jerusalem. Then David and the elders, cov-
> ered with sackcloth, fell on their faces.
> And David said to God, "Is it not I who commanded to
> count the people? Indeed, I am the one who has sinned and
> done very wickedly, but these sheep, what have they done? O
> LORD, my God, please let Thy hand be against me and my
> father's household, but not against Thy people that they should
> be plagued."
>
> 1 Chronicles 21:16–17

Sin pays a terrible wage. Those who have been raised in church have
heard that so long and so often that it no longer has much impact. But it
should! As one man has so eloquently expressed:

> Sin does not serve well as gardener of the soul. It landscapes
> the contour of the soul until all that is beautiful has been made
> ugly; until all that is high is made low; until all that is promising
> is wasted. Then life is like a desert—parched and barren. It is
> drained of purpose. It is bleached of happiness. Sin, then, is
> not wise, but wasteful. It is not a gate, but only a grave.[54]

David sees every ounce of payment that sin demands. He sees its ugliness, its devastation, its horror. He is a broken man facing the responsi-

bility of his own iniquity, and he throws himself upon the mercy of God.

The Lord has a plan. He wants David to build a never-to-be-forgotten memorial.

> Then the angel of the LORD commanded Gad to say to David, that David should go up and build an altar to the LORD on the threshing floor of Ornan the Jebusite.
>
> 1 Chronicles 21:18

It is amazing how obedient one becomes after suffering sin's terrible consequences. There was no hesitation, not even a question asked. David would have gone anywhere or done anything that God required.

> So David went up at the word of Gad, which he spoke in the name of the LORD.
>
> Now Ornan turned back and saw the angel, and his four sons who were with him hid themselves. And Ornan was threshing wheat. And as David came to Ornan, Ornan looked and saw David, and went out from the threshing floor, and prostrated himself before David with his face to the ground.
>
> 1 Chronicles 21:19–21

David's sin was not public knowledge. Ornan still saw his king as a man of God. That's part of the peril of spiritual leadership. People think only the best . . . they put leaders on a pedestal and continually lay benefits at their feet. David could have taken advantage of this, but he knew only too well the dark side of his own life, and he was still, in spite of all he'd been through, a man after God's heart.

For us to get the full picture of this encounter, let's go back and look at the parallel passage in 2 Samuel.

> And David went up according to the word of Gad, just as the LORD commanded. And Araunah [a different rendering of the name Ornan] looked down and saw the king and his servants crossing over toward him; and Araunah went out and bowed his face to the ground before the king.
>
> And Araunah said, "Why has my lord the king come to his servant?" And David said, "To buy the threshing floor from you, in order to build an altar to the LORD, that the plague may be held back from the people."

And Araunah said to David, "Let my lord the king take and offer up what is good in his sight. Look, the oxen for the burnt offering, the threshing sledges and the yokes of the oxen for the wood. Everything, O king, Araunah gives to the king." . . .

2 Samuel 24:19–23

Little did Araunah realize the sinfulness of his king's life. In childlike innocence, he felt honored to let David have anything he owned. What trust . . . what respect! How it must have pained David to hear those words. Broken, knowing the ugly truth of his own life, by the grace of God he was able to stand there and reject Araunah's [Ornan's] offer.

However, the king said to Araunah, "No, but I will surely buy it from you for a price, for I will not offer burnt offerings to the LORD my God which cost me nothing." So David bought the threshing floor and the oxen for fifty shekels of silver.

2 Samuel 24:24

David says, "I cannot take what you offer as a gift, but I will pay you for it." So David bought the land and the oxen, and that was where he constructed the altar, as God had commanded him to do.

And David built there an altar to the LORD, and offered burnt offerings and peace offerings. Thus the LORD was moved by entreaty for the land, and the plague was held back from Israel.

2 Samuel 24:25

And the LORD commanded the angel, and he put his sword back in its sheath.

1 Chronicles 21:27

With David's obedience, the pestilence was over. The plague was ended. What a relief to read that the angel put his sword back into its sheath. The scent of David's offering was a sweet fragrance in heaven, and the Lord determined "that's enough judgment." What grace!

APPLICATION FOR US TODAY

Now I can just hear someone respond to all this, "How can God do such things?" Frankly, I wonder instead, "How can God stop where He does, knowing what we deserve?" We deserve NONE of the benefits that come our way; they are all benefits of His magnificent grace. If sinful folks like us got what we really "deserved," it would be nothing short of hell itself.

Though the sword was back in its sheath, there were still 70,000 fresh graves in Israel, 70,000 grieving families whose lives were marked by David's compromise with pride. Every spiritual leader would do well to read this story once a year!

David's experience offers us three warnings.

1. *To live an unaccountable life is to flirt with danger.* Accountability is one of the things God uses to keep His people pure. We all need to be held accountable by someone. Had David listened to Joab he would never have numbered the people . . . or been the cause of such devastation. To ignore accountability is to flirt with danger.

2. *To ignore sin's consequences is to reject God's truth.* The Bible is filled with the reality of the consequences of sin.

    Sin is really a selfish act. It's all about bringing ourselves pleasure, caring little about the toll it will take on someone else.

3. *To fail to take God seriously is to deny His lordship.* In the midst of the fun and the delight of living—and no one believes in that more than I do—it is tempting to go too far and take the edge off His holiness. No need to take ourselves all that seriously . . . but when it comes to God, we need to take Him *very* seriously, not play games with Him. And when we do take Him seriously, He gives us the delight and satisfaction of a full life.

I believe if somehow we could bring David back from beyond and interview him today, one of his strongest pieces of advice would be directed toward those who are spiritual leaders . . . who have earned the respect of people . . . whom others follow and trust. If asked what one thing he would want us to remember, I think he would mention this segment from his own experience and warn against falling under the subtle spell of pride.

If a man as great and godly as David could foul up his life so near the end of his days, so can anyone else. That includes you. That includes me. God help us all.

CHAPTER TWENTY-FOUR

The End of an Era

John Wycliffe could be called the beginning of an era. It was through the efforts of this dedicated Christian scholar, preacher, and Bible translator that the Reformation got its start.

Some time before his death in 1384, he was standing alone against verbal and physical attacks. He stayed at the task of translating both the Old and New Testaments of the Bible into the English vernacular . . . a project so unpopular it led to his martyrdom. Until Wycliffe's heroic work, the Scriptures were chained to ornate pulpits, written in Latin, a language only the clergy could read. While threats were being hurled against him for his defiance, Wycliffe finished his monumental task, then wrote these words in the flyleaf of his own translation of the Bible:

> This Bible is translated and shall make possible a government
> of the people, by the people, and for the people.

Little did Wycliffe realize that almost 500 years later his words would be lifted from the page of his Bible and immortalized by a president in the New World who would promise "a new birth of freedom" based on "a government of the people, by the people, and for the people."

Less than a year and a half later, President Lincoln was killed. Among the hundreds who reported his death, one put his finger on the truth when he wrote, "The death of Lincoln marks the end of an era."

Some lives are so significant in courageous accomplishments, they form the beginning of an era. Others bring with their death, the end of an era. Their thinking, their creative ideas, their magnificent model leave a veritable chasm across life's landscape. This person's shoes are so big that after his or her death, nobody can fill them.

The death of David, the greatest king Israel ever had, marked the end of an era, the closing out of a period of time on earth that could never be duplicated. As great as Solomon became, he never took the place or equaled the reign of his father, David. In a very real sense he both began and ended an era.

G. Frederick Owen splendidly summarizes the essence of David's life.

> David satisfied the people throughout Israel, he quieted the Philistines for all time to come, then in the midst of peace and plenty wrote many psalms of praise to Jehovah. The elderly king gathered vast stores of stone and iron, brass, and cedar for the erection of the temple of God, gave his parting charge, and closed the most successful royal career recorded in the annals of history.[55]

David's life and death formed the end of an era. I suppose we would say that God broke the mold when David died.

Before we look at the record of the end of David's life in the Old Testament, let's read Paul's summary of the great king's life, as he looked back on it centuries later.

> For David, after he had served the purpose of God in his own generation, fell asleep, and was laid among his fathers, and underwent decay.
>
> Acts 13:36

Now, take away the name of David and put your own name there.

> For _____ (your name), after he/she served the purpose of God in his/her own generation, fell asleep, and was buried and passed away from the face of this earth.

Every individual has a purpose for living—every one of us. Not many have as great a purpose as David, but no one God brings to life on this earth is insignificant. The tragedy of all tragedies is that we should live and die having never found that purpose, that special, God-ordained reason for serving our generation. You have, like no other person on this planet, particular contributions that you are to make to this generation. They may not be as great as your dreams, or they might be far beyond your expectations; but whatever they are, you are to find them and carry them out. Then, when your twilight years come and your life is ended, you can be satisfied that you have served God's purpose with your life.

David's purpose was to serve as a king and to perpetuate the righteousness of Israel. In 1 Chronicles 28 and 29, we find both the record of the end of his life and his last recorded words. In this closing chapter of his years on earth, David was involved in four activities: he reflected on the temple; he spoke to his son, Solomon; he prayed before the Lord; and then he rejoiced with the assembly. Following these significant activities, Israel's greatest king died, ending an era.

REFLECTING ON THE TEMPLE: AN UNFULFILLED DREAM

After four decades of service to Israel, David, old and perhaps stooped by the years, looked for the last time into the faces of his trusted followers.

> Now David assembled at Jerusalem all the officials of Israel, the princes of the tribes, and the commanders of the divisions that served the king, and the commanders of thousands, and the commanders of hundreds, and the overseers of all the property and livestock belonging to the king and his sons, with the officials and the mighty men, even all the valiant men.
>
> 1 Chronicles 28:1

What an awesome gathering that must have been! The group probably numbered in the hundreds. Each face represented a memory in the old man's mind. There they all were, surrounding this beloved and aged king, who was to give them the final parting words of his life. Perhaps his voice quivered as he lifted his hand to quiet the assembly.

> Then King David rose to his feet and said, "Listen to me, my brethren and my people; I had intended to build a permanent home for the ark of the covenant of the LORD and for the footstool of our God. So I had made preparations to build it."
>
> 1 Chronicles 28:2

As I read this verse, I can feel the immediacy of the truth of this long-past dream in David's life. He lived and died with a frustrated desire, because if there was one legacy David wanted to leave, it was to build the temple of God.

I feel that immediacy in both the words and the spirit of this verse, because I know that beating in the heart of every thinking person is a dream, a desire. When nobody is around and when we're able to be absolutely honest with ourselves before God, you and I entertain certain dreams, certain hopes. You want very much by the end of your days to have _____ (you fill in the blank). That's your own personal desire. It's your secret dream. However, on the basis of the experience in David's life, I must say that it may very well be that you will die with that desire unfulfilled. And that will be one of the hardest things in the world for you to face and accept.

David faced this reality as a man after God's own heart would face it. What a remarkable man! He had this deep desire to build the temple, but the Lord's answer was no. His response was acceptance. He heard the Lord's "no" and he didn't resent it.

> "But God said to me, 'You shall not build a house for My name because you are a man of war and have shed blood.'"
>
> 1 Chronicles 28:3

When Solomon was born, he was given the name that means "peace." The familiar Hebrew term known all around the world, *shalom,* is directly related in root form to the name "Solomon." So the Lord chose David's son, a peacemaker, a diplomat, not a man of war, to build His house. He wanted a man of a different temperament than David to fulfill that dream. David recognized this and quietly accepted God's "no." That's awfully hard to do. Dreams die hard, but look at his response.

> "Yet, the LORD, the God of Israel, chose me from all the house of my father to be king over Israel forever. For He has chosen Judah to be a leader; and in the house of Judah, my father's house, and among the sons of my father He took pleasure in me to make me king over all Israel."
>
> 1 Chronicles 28:4

What is David doing here? He is focusing on what God *did* allow him to do. It is so easy for us to be disappointed, to get so distraught over a frustrated desire that we forget the things God has given us, the good things He has accomplished through our efforts and through our hands. During the closing years of his life, rather than pining away over this unfulfilled desire, David focused on the good things God had given him. I exclaim once again, what a man! He *really* looked at life from God's point of view. Look at how positively he states God's plan:

> "And of all of my sons (for the LORD has given me many sons), He has chosen my son Solomon to sit on the throne of the kingdom of the LORD over Israel. "And He said to me, 'Your son Solomon is the one who shall build My house and My courts; for I have chosen him to be a son to Me, and I will be a father to him. And I will establish his kingdom forever, if he resolutely performs My commandments and My ordinances, as is done now.' So now, in the sight of all Israel, the assembly of the LORD, and in the hearing of our God, observe and seek after all the commandments of the LORD your God in order that you may possess the good land and bequeath it to your sons after you forever."
>
> 1 Chronicles 28:5–8

David was saying, "God did not give me a yes answer. When it came to my own dream, He gave me a no answer. But He did give me other things in place of that dream, and I'm making the very most I can of those other things." We can all glean much from David's wholesome response.

Do you have some cherished desire that you know you are going to have to relinquish? Usually it takes getting up in years to realize that's going to happen, because the younger we are, the greater our dreams, the broader our hopes, and the more determined we are to make them happen. But as we get older, many of us see that some of those great hopes and dreams are never going to be realized. Perhaps it is a dream of some great accomplishment through a unique kind of ministry. Maybe it is a desire for a certain kind of career or recognition. Maybe it is a desire for romance and marriage. Maybe it's a hope for relief from something in your life that you've had to live with for years. Whatever it is, you may now recognize that it is never going to happen, and that's a hard pill to swallow. But, like David, it's an opportunity to find satisfaction in what God has allowed you to do. As he reflects on his life and his own unfulfilled desire, he says, "I want to turn my attention away from what wasn't to be and focus on the things God has done."

This is our challenge, isn't it? We can live the last years of our life swamped by guilt or overwhelmed by failures of the past. We can either "eat our heart out," or we can say, "By the grace of God, I did the best I could with what I had. And I claim His promise that somehow He'll use what I did accomplish for His greater glory." What a wonderful attitude to have at the end of one's life!

SPEAKING TO THE SON: AN UNTRIED RULER

Then David turns and, in an emotional moment, looks at his son Solomon. He must have smiled within himself as he saw in that young man the possibility of his long-awaited dream being fulfilled. David won't experience it, but his son will. And so he passes on advice to his son. These will be his final words during his last days on earth, and he chooses them very carefully. They are measured words, based on his own years as the king . . . full of emotion, rich with meaning. Looking back over forty years as Israel's leader, he must have said this slowly and carefully.

> "As for you, my son Solomon, know the God of your father, and serve Him with a whole heart and a willing mind; for the LORD searches all hearts, and understands every intent of the thoughts. If you seek Him, He will let you find Him; but if you forsake Him, He will reject you forever."
>
> 1 Chronicles 28:9

Not surprisingly, the opening words David said to his son had to do with godliness. "Solomon, know the LORD," David said. "Know the God of your father." That seems almost too obvious to mention, doesn't it? But, you see, David was aware of the tyranny of the urgent. He had been king for four long and tumultuous decades. He knew that on that throne of Israel there was enough to keep a man so busy he would be tempted not to take time to know God. So David said, "Solomon, above all the other things I want to pass on to you, I want you to *know God.*"

If you could pull your child aside before you died and give him or her one piece of advice regarding life, what would that advice be? Or, perhaps more importantly, fathers and mothers, what advice are you passing on right now? What character and lifestyle are you investing in them?

David looked deeply into the eyes of his beloved son, Solomon—the son of grace from his union with Bathsheba. I wonder if he may have seen in him the early markings of waywardness and loose living. Then, looking back on his own life, and knowing what similar patterns might be repeated in his son's life, David said to Solomon, "Know God, my son. Above all else, get to know Him deeply . . . intimately."

The second thing David said had to do with *serving God*. "Solomon, serve the God of your father." He doesn't stop there; he spells that out. Serve him with a whole heart and a willing mind. "Solomon, don't make God force you to worship Him. Do it wholeheartedly. Do it willingly. Hold nothing back."

David could say those things because that's the kind of heart he had. He was the sweet singer of Israel who had composed and sung those great songs of praise to the Lord, and Solomon knew that. Solomon certainly must have witnessed in his father an intense passion for God. His dad's devotion remained an unforgettable legacy in Solomon's mind.

What is your spiritual legacy, dads? Will your children grow up knowing that their father served the Lord God willingly, with a whole heart? Are you modeling that for them in your life? There is no better teaching tool in the life of a child than the model of a parent's life surrendered to the Lord God.

David could admonish Solomon to serve God willingly and wholeheartedly because he did it. Not perfectly, of course. In fact, he adds, "for the Lord searches all hearts, and understands every intent of the thoughts." Perhaps when he said that, David remembered that dark day, years before, when he stayed home from battle and fell into sin. He may have thought, *Solomon, if there's any possible way, don't fall into my shoes there.*

The third thing he says to Solomon is, *"Seek the God of your father."*

> "If you seek Him, He will let you find Him; but if you forsake Him, He will reject you. Consider now, for the Lord has chosen you to build a house for the sanctuary; be courageous and act."
>
> 1 Chronicles 28:9–10

I love this section. In verses 11 through 19 David talks about the construction of the temple, and I love the way it unfolds. I can just see David as he pulled Solomon aside and said, "Now look, Solomon, I've got all these plans laid out." Maybe he even unrolled some rough construction plans, and I can see them get down on their hands and knees together, Solomon on one side and David on the other.

> Then David gave to his son Solomon the plan of the porch of
> the temple, its buildings, its storehouses, its upper rooms, its
> inner rooms, and the room for the mercy seat; and the plan of
> all that he had in mind. . . .
>
> 1 Chronicles 28:11–12

That grand temple was David's dream, remember, but he couldn't
build it. So he said, "Solomon, if you're going to build it, then build it
right. Now look at how it's to be built." And he laid it out room by room
by room. Doesn't that sound like a dad? "Do it right, Solomon." What a
model of diligence, alertness, and keen perception David was. What a
heritage for Solomon to build on.

Next, he addressed the subject of *ruling the people*, because that was to
be Solomon's primary calling and career.

> Then David said to his son Solomon, "Be strong and coura-
> geous, and act; do not fear nor be dismayed, for the LORD
> God, my God, is with you. He will not fail you nor forsake
> you until all the work for the service of the house of the LORD
> is finished."
>
> 1 Chronicles 28:20

David knew only too well the problems Solomon would encounter as
a political ruler. And he said, "Don't be afraid, don't be dismayed. You're
gonna have people on one side and you're gonna have people on another.
You're gonna live in a pressure cooker." But, David says, "You walk with
God. He'll be right there with you all the way."

And then David turns to the people:

> Then King David said to the entire assembly, "My son Solo-
> mon, whom alone God has chosen, is still young and inexpe-
> rienced and the work is great; for the temple is not for man,
> but for the LORD God."
>
> 1 Chronicles 29:1

Can you see Solomon as he stands there? Can you feel his heart pound-
ing in his throat? Inexperienced. Untried. And there stands his battle-
scarred father, after forty record-making years as king, handing over the
scepter of Israel and the plans for the temple of God. His bearded face
was wrinkled with age, but those dark eyes were flashing with excitement.

What a moment! What a father! Solomon would enjoy numerous benefits because of David's accomplishments.

Let me give you a list of the things Solomon received as a result of his father's hand. The nation was now unified under one flag. A royal capital had been established in Jerusalem. The military force of Israel was now respected by all the enemies around them, and every enemy had been subdued, including the Philistines. Israel's boundaries had been extended from 6,000 to 60,000 square miles. Prosperity had been brought in by the extensive trade routes that his father had set up. The people hungered for God and righteousness, and the sounds of his father's song could be heard throughout the land. I'd call all that an enviable legacy, and it was Solomon's to enjoy. If any son ever had reason to be grateful, that one did.

One of the marks of a new generation is ingratitude. How seldom we express our gratitude to our parents for that which they have invested in our lives. And yet we soak up the benefits of their dedicated labors. May God make us more thankful, especially if we have had parents whose lives paved the way for our walk with God . . . and even more so if they invested their time and treasure in us!

PRAYING BEFORE THE LORD: AN UNCHANGING FATHER

Finally, and naturally, David falls on his knees and utters a beautiful prayer, an extemporaneous expression of his worship of the Lord God. The first verses are expressions of praise. Praise leaves humanity out of the picture and focuses fully on the exaltation of the living God. The magnifying glass looks up. Read his prayer with feeling. Take your time.

> "Blessed art Thou, O LORD God of Israel our father, forever and ever. Thine, O LORD, is the greatness and the power and the glory and the victory and the majesty, indeed everything that is in the heavens and the earth; Thine is the dominion, O LORD, and Thou dost exalt Thyself as head over all. Both riches and honor come from Thee and Thou dost rule over all, and in Thy hand is power and might; and it lies in Thy hand to make great, and to strengthen everyone. Now therefore, our God, we thank Thee, and praise Thy glorious name."
>
> 1 Chronicles 29:10–13

Here's David, spontaneously responding to God in gratitude for all that He had done throughout the years of his life. As he thinks of the lavish grace of God that has given the people one good thing after another, his praise turns to thanksgiving.

> "Now therefore, our God, we thank Thee, and praise Thy glorious name.
>
> "But who am I and who are my people that we should be able to offer as generously as this? For all things come from Thee, and from Thy hand we have given Thee.
>
> "For we are sojourners before Thee, and tenants, as all our fathers were; our days on the earth are like a shadow, and there is no hope.
>
> "O LORD our God, all this abundance that we have provided to build Thee a house for Thy holy name, it is from Thy hand, and all is Thine."
>
> 1 Chronicles 29:13–16

Talk about a proper scale of values. David was surrounded by limitless riches. Yet they never captured his heart. He fought other battles within, but never greed. David was not trapped by materialism. He said, "Lord, everything we have is Yours—all these beautiful places where we gather for worship, the place where I live, the throne room—all of it is Yours, everything."

What an important investment it is to pass on to our children a proper scale of values, so that they know how to handle the good things of life, knowing that those good things are just a wisp—here today and gone tomorrow. Such an investment also teaches them how to handle it when things aren't easy. David held everything loosely, another admirable trait.

Then David intercedes for the people he has ruled for forty years.

> "Since I know, O my God, that Thou triest the heart and delightest in uprightness, I, in the integrity of my heart, have willingly offered all these things; so now with joy I have seen Thy people, who are present here, make their offerings willingly to Thee. O LORD, the God of Abraham, Isaac, and Israel, our fathers, preserve this forever in the intentions of the heart of Thy people, and direct their heart to Thee; and give to my son Solomon a perfect heart to keep Thy commandments, Thy testimonies, Thy statutes, and to do them all, and to build the

temple, for which I have made provision." Then David said to the assembly, "Now bless the LORD your God." . . .

1 Chronicles 29:17–20

REJOICING OF THE ASSEMBLY: AN UNDIVIDED PEOPLE

And that's precisely what they did. Spontaneously, in response to David's prayer,

> . . . all the assembly blessed the LORD, the God of their fathers, and bowed low and did homage to the LORD and to the king. . . . So they ate and drank that day before the LORD with great gladness.

1 Chronicles 29:20, 22

Oh, what a moment that was. Though it was the end of an era, it did not end in sadness and mourning and grief, but with gladness and rejoicing before God.

> And they made Solomon the son of David king. . . . Then Solomon sat on the throne of the Lord as king instead of David his father. . . . And all the officials, the mighty men, and also all the sons of King David pledged alliance to King Solomon.
>
> And the LORD highly exalted Solomon in the sight of all Israel, and bestowed on him royal majesty which had not been on any king before him in Israel.

1 Chronicles 29:22–25

And guess who was thrilled by that: David, his father.

> Then he died in a ripe old age, full of days, riches and honor; and his son Solomon reigned in his place.

1 Chronicles 29:28

Now there's an epitaph to be pleased with: "He died in a ripe old age, full of days, riches, and honor." Good for you, David!

When a man of God dies, nothing of God dies. And when a man of

God dies, none of God's principles die. Nowhere is that seen more clearly than in the life of David.

What lessons can we learn from such a man? We learn hope, in spite of his humanity. We learn courage, even in the midst of his own fear. We learn encouragement and praise in the songs that grew out of his hours of despair. We learn forgiveness in his dark moments of sin. And we learn the value of serving the purpose of God in our own generation, even though all our dreams may not be fulfilled.

Thank you, David, for being our model, teaching us by your life such significant truths. And thank you, Father, for being our Master; using us though we are weak, forgiving us when we fail, and loving us through all the Sauls and Goliaths and Jonathans and Abigails and Bathshebas and Absaloms and Joabs and Solomons of our lives. Thank you for showing us that we can be people like David . . . people of passion and destiny.

CONCLUSION

David: A Man of Passion & Destiny

How I love the Bible! How I love reliving the lives of people in the Bible! And how I have loved examining the life of David! This has been my first attempt at writing a book on one of the many Bible characters, but it won't be my last. I have many more biblical biographies in mind that I hope to introduce to today's world during the next few years of my life. All of them are worth our time and attention because they represent such profiles in character . . . the kind of character we need more of in our world that seems to have lost its way. I believe these lives tucked away in the pages of the Scriptures not only give us fresh faith to stay at it but also high hopes to press on.

I appreciate those words in Hebrews 11, where the writer, having just mentioned several specific people by name, suddenly realizes the over-whelming benefits of becoming acquainted with those who have gone on before. It's like he is short on time, so he throws up his hands in exuberant delight and exclaims:

> I could go on and on, but I've run out of time. There are so many more—Gideon, Barak, Samson, Jephthah, David, Samuel, the prophets. . . . Through acts of faith, they toppled king-doms, made justice work, took the promises for themselves. They were protected from lions, fires, and sword thrusts, turned disadvantage to advantage, won battles, routed alien armies.

Women received their loved ones back from the dead. There were those who, under torture, refused to give in and go free, preferring something better; resurrection. Others braved abuse and whips, and, yes, chains and dungeons. We have stories of those who were stoned, sawed in two, murdered in cold blood; stories of vagrants wandering the earth in animal skins, homeless, friendless, powerless—the world didn't deserve them!—making their way as best they could on the cruel edges of the world.[56]

I know how the writer felt. I, too, "could go on and on, but I've run out of time." And because there are "so many more" and because all their lives were so great "the world didn't deserve them," I plan to continue this significant series of great lives from the Bible for quite some time, should our Lord tarry His coming. I am really excited about this new project!

And so, thank you, my friend, for journeying with me through some of the more meaningful moments of David's life. As I expressed all the way through the book, "What a man!" Having completed this study, I am more impressed than ever with his life. Not perfect by any means, but authentic to the core. Hopefully, now that you and I have taken the time to examine him closely, we shall be better equipped to live before our God in humility, dependability, and integrity.

Why? Because that is what our world needs to see in order to find its way back. And, even more importantly, because that is what our Lord expects of those who wish to be men and women after His own heart.

ENDNOTES

INTRODUCTION

1. Boris Pasternak, source unknown.
2. Carl Sandburg, *Abraham Lincoln: The Prairie Years and the War Years*, (New York: Harcourt, Brace, Jovanovich, 1982).

CHAPTER 1

3. G. Frederick Owen, *Abraham to the Middle-East Crisis* (Grand Rapids, Mich.: Eerdmans, 1939, 1957), 45.
4. F. B. Meyer, *David: Shepherd, Psalmist, King* (Fort Washington, Penn.: Christian Literature Crusade, 1977), 14.
5. Alan Redpath, *The Making of a Man of God* (Westwood, N.J.: Fleming H. Revell Co., 1962), 5.

CHAPTER 2

6. Meyer, *David*, 18.

CHAPTER 3

7. C. F. Keil and F. Delitzsch, *Commentary on the Old Testament*, vol. 2 (Grand Rapids, Mich.: Eerdmans, 1960), 170.

8. C. H. Spurgeon, *The Treasury of David*, vol. 1 (McLean, Vir.: Macdonald, nd).
9. G. Campbell Morgan, *The Unfolding Message of the Bible* (Westwood, N.J.: Fleming H. Revell Co., 1961), 232.

CHAPTER 5

10. G. K. Chesterfield, cited in *John Bartlett's Familiar Quotations*, ed. Emily Morison Beck (Boston, Mass.: Little, Brown and Co., 1980), 742.

CHAPTER 6

11. H. G. Wells, *The History of Mr. Polly* (New York: The Press of the Reader's Club, 1941), 5.
12. A. W. Tozer, *The Pursuit of God* (Camp Hill, Penn.: Christian Publications, 1982, 1993), 21–22, 27, 29.
13. Ibid., 30.

CHAPTER 7

14. Bruce Larsen and Keith Miller, *The Edge of Adventure* (Waco, Tex.: Word Books, 1974), 156.
15. Charles R. Swindoll, *Growing Strong in the Seasons of Life*, (Portland, Ore.: Multnomah Press, 1983), 254–55.

CHAPTER 9

16. Wayne Dyer, *Your Erroneous Zones* (New York: Avon Books, 1976), 218–219.
17. Redpath, *The Making of a Man of God*, 107.

CHAPTER 11

18. J. Sidlow Baxter, *Mark These Men* (Grand Rapids, Mich.: Zondervn, 1980), 35.
19. Alfred Edersheim, *The Bible History, Old Testament*, vol. 4 (Grand Rapids, Mich.: Eerdmans, 1959), 149.
20. F. B. Meyer, *Christ in Isaiah* (Fort Washington, Penn.: Christian Literature Crusade, nd), 9.
21. Ruth Harms Calkin, "Take Over," in *Tell Me Again, Lord, I Forget* (Wheaton, Ill.: Tyndale House, 1974), 147.

22. Peter Marshall, *John Doe, Disciple: Sermons for the Young in Spirit*, ed. Catherine Marshall (New York: McGraw-Hill, 1963), 219–20.

CHAPTER 12

23. Thomas Carlyle, cited in *John Bartlett's Familiar Quotations*, 474.
24. Owen, *Abraham to the Middle-East Crisis*, 5.
25. J. Oswald Sanders, *Robust in Faith* (Chicago, Ill.: Moody Press 1965), 121.
26. Christiaan Neethling Barnard, *One Life* (Toronto, Ont.: Macmillan, 1969), 253–254.
27. C. S. Lewis, *Screwtape Letters* (New York: Collier Books, Macmillan, 1959), 132.

CHAPTER 14

28. Carolina Sandell Berg, "Security," *The Speaker's Treasury of 400 Quotable Poems*, compiled by Croft M. Pentz (Grand Rapids, Mich.: Zondervan), 42.
29. Martha Snell Nicholson, "Treasures," *Ivory Palaces* (Wilmington, Calif.: Martha Snell Nicholson, 1946), 67.

CHAPTER 15

30. Karl Menninger, Martin Mayman, and Paul Pruyser, *The Vital Balance* (New York: Viking Press, 1963), 204–5.
31. Ibid., 22.

CHAPTER 16

32. Raymond Brown, *Skilful Hands: A Biography of David* (Fort Washington, Penn.: Christian Literature Crusade, 1972), 99.
33. Dietrich Bonhoeffer, *Temptation* (New York: Macmillan, 1953), 116–117.
34. Meyer, *David*, 195
35. Emily Dickinson, *Laurel Poetry Series* (New York: Dell Publishing, 1960), 97.

CHAPTER 17

36. Paul Tournier, *Guilt and Grace* (San Francisco, Calif.: Harper & Row, 1958), 97.

37. Alexander Whyte, *Bible Characters* (Grand Rapids, Mich.: Zondervan, 1952), 245.

CHAPTER 18

38. John W. Lawrence, *Life's Choices* (Portland, Ore.: Multnomah Press, 1975), 39.
39. Whyte, *Bible Characters*, 309.

CHAPTER 19

40. Eugene Peterson, *The Message, Proverbs* (Colorado Springs, Colo.: NavPress, 1995), 18–19.
41. Hugh Stowell, "From Every Stormy Wind That Blows," *The Hymnal for Worship & Celebration* (Waco, Texas: Word Music, 1986), 432.
42. Thomas Moore, "Come, Ye Disconsolate," *The Hymnal for Worship & Celebration* (Waco, Texas: Word Music, 1986), 416.

CHAPTER 20

43. Samuel Taylor Coleridge, "Youth and Age," *Poems That Live Forever*, selected by Hazel Felleman (New York: Doubleday, 1965), 256.
44. *The NIV Study Bible*, Kenneth Barker, gen. ed. (Grand Rapids, Mich.: Zondervan, 1985), 447.
45. Brown, *Skilful Hands*, 108.
46. Samuel Johnson, cited in *John Bartlett's Familiar Quotations*, ed. Emily Morison Beck (Boston, Mass.: Little Brown, and Co., 1980), 354.

CHAPTER 21

47. Whyte, *Bible Characters*, 297.
48. George Bernard Shaw, cited in *John Bartlett's Familiar Quotations*, 680.
49. Stuart Briscoe, *What Works When Life Doesn't* (Wheaton, Ill.: Victor Books, 1976), 99.
50. Dale E. Galloway, *You Can Win with Love* (Irvine, Calif.: Harvest House, 1976), 129–130.

CHAPTER 22

51. Charles Allen, *You Are Never Alone*, (Old Tappan, New Jersey: Fleming H. Revell, 1978), 88.

52. Mary Bowley Peters, "Whom Have We, Lord, but Thee," *Hymnal of Worship and Remembrance* (Kansas City, Kansas: Gospel Perpetuating Publishers, P. O. Box 2216, nd), 8.

53. J. Oswald Sanders, *Spiritual Leadership* (Chicago, Ill.: Moody Press, 1969), 169.

54. C. Neil Strait, *Quote Unquote*, compiled by Lloyd Cory (Wheaton, Ill.: Victor Books, 1977), 297.

CHAPTER 24

55. Owen, *Abraham to the Middle-East Crisis*, 54.

CONCLUSION

56. Eugene Peterson, *The Message, New Testament* (Colorado Springs, Colo.: NavPress, 1993), 473.